Action Replays

Archie Macpherson was born in
Shettleston, Glasgow, and trained as
a teacher. He was the Headmaster of
Swinton School, Lanarkshire, from
1965 to 1969. The impecunious
nature of the profession, he main-
tains, drove him to write short
stories, some of which were accepted
by the BBC. He began to freelance
for BBC sport in 1961, eventually
joining the Corporation full time in
1969 and going on to present regular
sports programmes and commentate
on major games. He has also covered
three Olympic Games and five World
Cups. He left the BBC in 1990.
Archie Macpherson is the author of
Blue and Green (1989), and is the
winner of the Sony Gold for Sports
Broadcasting.

Action Replays

ARCHIE MACPHERSON

CHAPMANS

Chapmans Publishers Ltd
141–143 Drury Lane
London WC2B 5TB

First published by Chapmans 1991
This paperback edition first published by Chapmans 1992

© Archie Macpherson 1991

The right of Archie Macpherson to be identified as the
author of this work has been asserted by him in accordance
with the Copyright, Designs and Patents Act, 1988.

ISBN 1 85592 632 6

Printed and bound in Great Britain by
Clays Ltd, St Ives plc

To the family, especially for
tolerating the absences

Acknowledgements

I would like to thank John Burrowes, formerly of the Scottish *Daily Record* and author of several fine books, for his early advice on the manuscript. Pat Woods, librarian and researcher, ferreted to excellent effect for me. I am indebted also to Kevin McAra for his editing of the manuscript and his sensible suggestions. I could not have progressed much without the help of countless numbers of people from within BBC Television who were sources of both inspiration and verification for the narrative.

Contents

Introduction

The torch was about a quarter of a mile away when I first saw it. The carrier was completely hidden by an entourage consisting of motor-cyclists, a press and television car and a halo of accompanying runners. So the flame coming from his torch seemed to have an existence of its own. It danced and wavered like a firefly in the mellow Korean evening. The torch burned in a way that reminded me of Leerie the lamplighter piercing the gloom of Edinburgh. It was perhaps an odd thought to have but then the situation was far from ordinary. To be standing in running gear which did nothing to hide the ballast of over-indulgence on a road just outside a Korean city called Chongju was not what I had bargained for even a few days before.

The Olympic flame was heading my way and in my hand I held the oil-filled torch. In a few moments it would be fired into frenzy by the tongue of fire steadily nearing, sending me along the road lined by smiling, disciplined Korean faces. They were taking time out from their slavish commitment to their economic miracle to acknowledge the flame as it made its slow but inevitable progress towards the capital, Seoul, where the 1988 Olympic Games would commence three days later.

The distance I had to run was only one kilometre. I turned and looked ahead and saw a road apparently stretching to infinity and briefly wondered if I would make it. For all the number of times I had appeared in front of a camera I felt that this would leave me more isolated and vulnerable than I had ever been, even though I was not involved in a direct broadcast. Nerves were weakening the legs, like a sudden onset of flu. It wasn't going to be a long run, I kept telling myself. One kilometre was a minute fraction of the global relay which had started on Mount Olympus many weeks before but each section would be shown on television. We had our own BBC unit there to record the moment. I had to speak a piece to camera just before the other runner was to reach me and there would only be one single, solitary chance to get it right. When I turned back the flame now seemed an inferno and was no more than twenty yards away. For the first time I could see the runner. He was a squat Korean with a smile as broad as the 38th parallel. I suddenly realised that after our flames had embraced we would never meet again.

In broadcasting terms it had taken me over two decades to reach Korea. Travelling the world now is relatively easy but the first assignment seemed like a journey to the ends of the earth even though it was only to Hamilton on a red bus. It was on an October day in 1962. The bus wheezed its way through Lanarkshire, halting clumsily at innumerable bus-stops like an elderly asthmatic calling in for sustaining whiffs of oxygen then lurching on its way again with triumphant coughs sending tremors throughout the interior. These buses always suggested the imminence of breakdown and I found myself wondering if it would be no bad thing if it did.

Lumbering towards the first professional engagement in broadcasting was like heading towards a blind date. I was in that early stage of paralysis which, in polite company, is described as stage fright. The mind was wandering. As the bus crossed Bothwell Bridge before crawling up past Hamilton Racecourse I found myself thinking of the battle fought there by the Covenanters of the 18th century and of how incredibly stupid men were to fight each other in the name of religion. These thoughts of a travelling atheist might seem wholly irrelevant now but in the struggle to stay on an even keel it seemed a healthy idea to be contemplating in a superior way the agonies of my ancestors. They put the apprehensions of a baptism in broadcasting into a more acceptable perspective. Only momentarily though. Something like panic intervened again and was not eased by observing the jumbled normality of the bus or the indifference of pedestrians about their business.

Hearts supporters passing in the opposite direction on their way to Hampden for the League Cup Final with Kilmarnock that very same afternoon looked out of the windows of their special buses with undisguised superiority. This merely emphasised the strange feeling of tranquillity inside Douglas Park for I was a follower of fashion and had not seen a football crowd of less than twenty thousand for years. There was a disconcerting air of privacy surrounding the fixture between Hamilton and Stenhousemuir in the Scottish Second Division. I wondered if this is how a foreign correspondent might feel on his first look at an alien setting.

The day was windy, the showers were occasional and heavy. Douglas Park was a stubborn piece of Lanarkshire dreariness that properly reflected the domestic plainness of football within the boundaries of a steel county. I found my seat and was disappointed to discover that the press there were not sectioned off or separated as I thought that exalted species always had a right to be. The homogeneity of the stand was a massive disappointment to me. No press box, indeed! It was like an novice entering his new church and discovering the altar missing.

However, I sat down beside a man bulky in his heavy overcoat and scarf. I was glad I did not have to disturb him to get to my seat for he was sitting at his phone in a manner I was later to recognise as the local correspondent's territorial crouch, like Fagin hoarding his cash. He was in the middle of an unforced drawling discourse which he was addressing to the empty pitch but which was being avidly listened to by other shapes, whose notebooks lay on the ledges in front of them like hymn books.

'What a bastard Kennedy is,' he was saying. 'What right has he to be sending ships out to stop the Russians on the high seas? The Americans have got rockets in Turkey, right on the Russian border.'

Someone mumbled assent; a disciple not quite believing but too scared to take issue. It was not exactly what I had expected. After all I had hoped that in coming to watch Hamilton Academicals play Stenhousemuir it might be easy to put up the shutters against the spine-chilling possibilities of the Cuban crisis. I had anticipated that football, this intensely human game with global appeal, might remind us of the joys of living and of the enduring primacy of the species. But after twenty minutes of a wind-swept anonymous game which left the pages of my notebook pallidly blank I have to admit thoughts of Armageddon began to infiltrate the mind.

I recalled that Pat Arrowsmith of CND had taken off with friends to the western extremity of Ireland to Macgillycuddy's Reeks at the first whiff of the Cuban confrontation claiming that in view of the prevailing winds it would be the safest place in Europe when the buttons were pressed. Not staying to fry with the rest of us had seemed cowardly but on reflection I began to envy Pat in her cabin 'of clay and wattles made' as we sat there at Douglas Park, in the front line.

'Who are you here for?' It was the man with the phone. He had barely turned his head in my direction but the eyes had summed me up. I toyed with the idea of a quick riposte: 'For the mortgage.' But something instinctively told me that the man had been hewn out of a quarry somewhere on Tinto Hill and that he would respect attempts at humour as tolerantly as a Wee Free minister listening to Bernard Manning. I choked back the words. And then I said it.

'For the BBC.' I regretted uttering it with so much emphasis as it implied I was on the pensionable staff and that Lord Reith was my great-uncle. In fact I was merely a trialist who might last only one broadcast. But it had an effect. The man stirred. He looked at my notebook and then back at me. 'The BBC?' There was no doubting the disbelief in the voice. 'Do you intend using a phone?' he asked. It was evident that if I wished to see the end of the game I couldn't exactly say, 'Yes, yours, when you're not looking.' I tried to put his territorial apprehensions at ease. 'I won't need a phone,' I replied. 'They're sending a car for me. I'm doing a live report from the studio . . . in Glasgow.' I knew as soon as I said it that it was a mistake. It sounded hopelessly superior. James the chauffeur coming to pick me up at twenty to five sort of thing.

'A car?' he muttered with a shake of the head and something of a crimped smile around the lips. He made it sound like outrageous decadence. He was the first in a long line of licence-holders who would attempt to induce guilt at the Corporation's extravagant use of public funds. He didn't speak another word to me but every now and again looked down at something I tried to scribble in the notebook. On one occasion I felt like asking him the identity of a player, much as he repeatedly did with his other colleagues, but I sensed I was being left to my own devices. It was a day in which the feeling of impotence increased as the light of a late October afternoon diminished. Elsewhere, the world's fate was being decided.

The match ended in a 1–0 win for Hamilton. The car turned up exactly on time to whisk me back to the Queen Margaret Drive studios in Glasgow. On the way I wrote feverishly in the notebook, preparing to tell the world what Hamilton and Stenhousemuir had contributed to a very important Saturday afternoon indeed for mankind. I infused the match with a life it hadn't possessed. Not distorting, merely embellishing, I thought. Fortunately I didn't myself hear the report. My body went into a sort of trance as I sat down in front of the mike, which reared up at me like a hooded cobra about to strike.

It went tolerably well for they invited me back and continued to do so through five World Cups, three Olympic games, numerous occasions when I left the spittle of ecstasy on the surface of the commentator's lip-microphone, occasional conflicts, blazing arguments, huffs, panics, and triumphs. But the craft first touched upon in Hamilton remains the same. It is about observation and recording and interpreting. It is about trying to balance one's ambitions and inadequacies against the rigorous expectations of one's superiors, amongst whom you have to count the public. It is about selfishness and making a constant mistress of the suitcase. It is about sharing in folly and conceit and the massaging of ego.

Travelling the world from one event to another I have tended to view sport as part of the natural vegetation without which the planet could not survive. This prejudiced standpoint causes me no hardship. The power of access to places and events first conferred on me some considerable time ago has produced images which I can transmit in my mind whenever I choose. It is probably time, though, to offer the schedule to others. The selection is unaffected by what Fred Friendly, the great American producer, called 'the distant drummer of the ratings leading us all on'. These are simply the pictures which stuck and are in deeper focus than others.

That is why it is important to start at the first football field that made any sense to me, for old habits die hard. You would not have called it a stadium, but we thought it was, we from Shettleston in the East End of Glasgow. There I could claim, years before I went into broadcasting, that I had seen the debut of a star, a real live genuine solid-gold football personality. It made its mark.

But I have much to be thankful for from that first assignment to Hamilton. I am grateful, above all, to Mr Nikita Khrushchev for asking his captains on the ships heading for Cuba to please turn round and go home and take their rockets with them. Had he not, Saturdays might never have been the same again.

1

Home Ground

The first stop after getting out of the cradle was Shettleston Juniors. Sometimes I paid to get in. Sometimes I didn't. If you were good at it you could climb in over the back of Greenfield Park from the railway line and if you were caught by the polis (often while onlookers voiced that Glaswegian humanitarian plea, 'Leave the wean alane!') they simply led you round the ground and let you out again. It was not a bad risk to take although I never much fancied a life of delinquency having seen too often the boys from the local remand home. They were paraded in their brown uniforms to the cinema and swimming baths but never to the football park, which suggested that falling into trouble carried harsh penalties.

I paid distinctly more attention to match reports on the 'Town' as they were called, than I did to biblical text. I told adults dutifully that Jesus was central to my life. But in fact he was way down the league. He did not keep me awake at night, or send me to bed holding back tears or make me think that the key to life was a sixpence entry money and ninety minutes of triumph. The imagination was more engaged by the likes of 'Doc' McManus, a Shettleston player who came from that tradition of Scottish inside-forward who owed a great deal to stunted growth, a fondness for the bevvy, a disdain of sprinting any more than six yards and a body swerve in which the heavily endowed backside and torso seemed to part company for a fraction of a second.

I always thought he had been specially obtained for Junior

football from a knacker's yard in the Gallowgate. His lumpiness, reminiscent of a discarded couch, was part of what we liked most about him. He would put his arms out and roll his way towards a defence like a man reluctantly leaving a pub for his work but he occasionally found holes there with deft little touches. Then, he seemed to be defying nature and proving that football's geniuses do not need anatomical symmetry. Greenfield Park was, if not a second home, at the very least an outhouse of the extended family which allowed Shettleston to flourish as a stable, warm and civilised community.

The 'Town' did not own their ground then. It belonged to the adjacent bottle works at a time before plastic containers abominably usurped glass and brought its demise. The works formed a palisade to what might have been called the Kop end of Greenfield Park. It was of course not the only employer in the area. Further to the west for example was the Forge where they had made some of the shells and bombs which, so I was fondly told, helped us to win the war. A huge proportion of the local men worked there. But the football park clung to the bottle works and it helped form for me a strong image of work and play entangled inseparably. Men in dungarees walked to the pub for a drink then straight to the match. It was not an age for much pausing in between. The aroma of honest sweat permeated the queues for football matches. Men went not for gentle relaxation nor to abscond from pressure but simply to take it on in another sphere. Getting away from it all happened at the Glasgow Fair; football was a stimulant not an anaesthetic.

Considering what is on offer now for the working man, life had almost a plodding sameness about it. There was work, football, cinema, the 'dugs' and the pub. For most men, that is. But it had stability and the course of life was linear and true. Or so it seemed. Greenfield Park was right in the middle of Shettleston though boundaries in the East End were ill-defined. Football was certainly the most distinct way in which you could be recognised as belonging to either Parkhead, Tollcross, Bridgeton or Shettleston. Identities were largely blurred until familiarity with a particular football ground was established. I had no problems with the extent of this parish. To me the pull of the 'Town' went as far as the eye could see. North over the nearby railway line was the relatively modern development of Carntyne sloping cleanly to the sky. The eye was also inevitably drawn to the bulky profile of Barlinnie Prison sulking on the horizon.

From the terracings we threatened the jail to many and complained bitterly of the lack of justice involved in their freedom. One man who played for Petershill, a club from a more effete part of the city, was linked almost continually with Barlinnie by our supporters. He had clearly committed some unforgivable misdemeanour in the past and even when he appeared before kick-off the crowd were turned into a baying mob. A child molester could not have been given a less gracious welcome.

I never discovered what his original offence had been. There was nothing else for me to do but to shout and bawl abuse for how could so many of my neighbours be wrong. The swearing was good too since there was nothing quite as emancipating as letting rip with words that you might only have furtively whispered amongst your pals. Coming from a non-swearing family I took boldness to extreme and let vent with such lurid remarks as would have made my mother wish she had committed infanticide. The man, it must be said on reflection, did not seem ever to bother much but kicked everything in sight and played with a leering Bela Lugosi smile on his face.

My father's connection with the club had been one of the main reasons I had such an affection for it. He had gone into baking after school but by that stage of the late Forties had given up professional football. It was still a delight for me to sift through the pile of memorabilia including team sheets, letters from managers, contracts and listen to him recount how he would work night shift in the bakery and then go straight to the match to play. His only training in the week was a one hour rub-down with liniment by my mother. How many men, after all, could play on ash-pitches without having had any sleep, be fast enough to have run at Powderhall and also make perfect doughnuts in a small pot of fat on the kitchen hob? It all seemed noble. Consequently, missing a game at Greenfield Park felt like letting the family down. The addiction I developed for that tiny little patch of ground helped me come to terms with emotions which might have lain dormant and perhaps overwhelmed me at some stage of my life. I had the good fortune to run the whole gamut of them over and over again watching Shettleston Juniors before I moved into my teens.

However, I seem not to have been in an over-wrought state the day Tommy Docherty made his debut there. I cannot claim to have been conscious of the emergence of one of football's all-time stars and colourful personalities. But, as Max Boyce would say, 'I was there!' I do know that whilst most of us were tolerant there was a group who stood just to the east of the pavilion who were not too easily pleased. I swear they would have thought Pele better employed selling bananas in the fruit-market, Beckenbauer a poof and Maradona too wee. They were what critic Frank Rich is to Broadway or General Schwarzkopf to waffling questioners. They could destroy a reputation in a sentence. They enjoyed it. Having disposed of their aggression on the terracings the cat and the wife were probably safe on return from an awful game. Docherty would have known what a critical gallery he faced for he was brought up no more than a couple of hundred yards away from the Park in the 'Bowery', which as its name implies did not feature Palladian architecture.

Decades later when he came to the BBC studios for me to meet him personally for the first time and to interview him he breezed into the building with the cockiness of the man who used to act street saint for the Dead End Kids. For he was always Cagney to me. Nothing could alter that image, not all the years. He had decorated and embellished the quick-witted pugnacious style for it suited the image and it paid off for him in the south.

He had come back to Scotland to manage the national team and had already amassed in England a reputation for speaking his mind in ill-timed circumstances. When he made his point he always managed a decorous little smile but his eyelids flickered nervously, hinting at other meanings. I tried him out with the Shettleston Juniors debut story. He was impressed. He mentioned the Town with a reasonable reverence. His accent of course had undergone various vowel transplants for you cannot reside in England without submitting to some of its ways. Suddenly in almost mid-sentence he broke off his reverie and said, 'Two hundred pounds!'

'I beg your pardon?' I asked politely.

'Two hundred pounds. That'll do.'

'Do for what?' I responded naively.

'The interview,' he said and smiled endearingly at the secretary who had suddenly stopped typing.

'The interview?'

'Two Hundred Pounds,' he added with a little more emphasis, the eyelids blinking irreverently.

'For the Interview?'

'Or I don't do it,' he said mildly and then turned to the secretary to remark, 'Warm for this time of the year, isn't it, dear?'

'But Tommy,' I protested, 'we have set rates for interviews. The BBC tries to be meticulously fair about how it dispenses its money and I am sure you'll understand we are offering you the best platform for your views that you'll get anywhere and given the challenge of the job you face and the need to develop a healthy relationship between you, us, the SFA and the public . . .'

'Two hundred pounds,' he said.

I felt a slight tremor of panic and tried not to show it. We had an entire fully manned studio waiting downstairs for the entrance of the great man and his interview, which was going to be no longer than five minutes. Everything had been set up through me without any money having been mentioned and suddenly I was confronted with a man who clearly was not going to budge. Two hundred pounds even by today's standards still represents something of a handsome bounty but in the early Seventies it was like the gifts of the Magi.

As I left him to find the producer who alone could settle these things I wondered about that slim figure, hair neatly shedded, dapper in movement, sharp in action who had played with such obvious distinction on that Saturday afternoon at Greenfield Park. I had been in on the birth of a marvellous player after all. That in itself had seemed to me to promise kinship. But here I was, held to ransom by this great fellow Shettlestonian.

'The Doc wants two hundred notes or else he won't go on,' I told the producer in the gallery above the studio.

'Jesus H. Christ!' he hissed. (I had recently loaned him *The Catcher in the Rye*.) 'We can't pay two hundred. He won't go on? Look, go back and humour him! I'll have to make a few phone calls. Good God, we've billed him to go on tonight. Go on, humour him!'

Humouring the Doc would have been like trying to raise the level of the North Sea with a garden hose. When I went back to my office I had to restrain myself from laughing. There he was lounging back on a soft chair, whistling, scanning the secretary's *Woman's Own*, the only reading matter available, and putting on such an act of nonchalance as would have made you think he had demanded nothing more outrageous than milk in his coffee. I warmed to that. The healthy East End tradition of dissent was still very much alive. I had visions of BBC apparatchiks scurrying along corridors of power in London shouting, 'Docherty's asked for two hundred' and convening special meetings. I knew, and he knew that I knew, that he was going to get what he wanted. After about half-an-hour the producer phoned me. 'I don't want to create any precedent by this but get him along here and get the bloody thing done!'

As I put the phone down the Doc simply stood up and started walking towards the door. 'Where's the studio?' he asked. 'What was that you were saying about Shettleston? Good wee club the Town. Still got a soft spot for it. Learned a wee bit about the game there you know . . .'

When he sat down opposite me in the studio, two hundred pounds richer, I could see clearly in my mind's eye the youthful figure in the white shirt, as if when the chat were finished he would go to the dressing room, change and run out to play.

That day at Greenfield Park he had quite simply grabbed the eye not just because of his performance, the precise details of which are now lost to memory, but because of the circumstances. A boy sitting beside me dangling his legs over the barrier said with obvious pride, 'Docherty's goin' to the Cellic.' To say as much was to create more than usual interest for if you knew anybody was bound for either Rangers or Celtic you invested him with qualities which more often than not bore little relation to reality. A simple pass from such a lad would be like an exquisite gem. A header would be the perfection of timing, and so on. Potential Old Firm players came and went and most disappeared without trace like the children of Hamelin, never to wear a blue or green and white first-team jersey. But the most important aspect was that they played together, there at Greenfield. The boy, prepared to give Docherty the benefit of the doubt even before he had seen him kick a ball, wore a tiny religious medallion round his neck. We noticed these things. But here tribal identities which could otherwise lead to discomfort were rendered null and void by loyalty to the Town. Here it didn't really matter but just outside on the streets it did, to a greater or lesser degree.

To me religion then was just a way of validating the separation of people. After all we couldn't school together and nobody seemed to mind. Indeed, the policy was extolled on both sides. We couldn't be buried together or go to funerals together or, in most cases, socialise with each other. As we understood it the Catholics did all this according to diktat. The Protestants did it with voluntary exhilaration. But at that time just after the war there were no great examinations of this. Everybody had been concerned with getting rid of the Tories and making the great new socialist society work. Religious divisions were natural, and that was that.

The only feeling of tension probably came when the Orange Walk swung down Shettleston Road; a gloating, raucous, tuneful and resplendent arterial pulse pumping between dark-walled tenements as if it would never come to an end. My grandmother thought it a refined expression of Protestantism to stay indoors and react as if it wasn't happening and to take the progeny with her to play cards, but not for money because she was a Methodist. 'You're not watching the Walk,' my mother would say with the same kind of distaste she used when catching me with a girlie magazine once. I suspect that those reservations about the marchers also contained the feeling that, like the SAS, their methods might not inspire public approval but it was useful nevertheless to have them on one's side.

To me it was a game which adults played which harmed no one and indeed I thought the distaste misplaced. The Walk was colourful and if your elementary freedoms were limited because you could not cross the road in its path at least the marshal did not ask your religion before he broke your bones. The lead cane he carried was quite non-sectarian. If you were the other kind you simply stayed away or watched from afar until it passed. That of course was over-simplifying its effect. Its very existence was at least technically an affront to a large section of the community although, in truth, most Catholics took it with a smile on their faces and treated it as a freakish side-show. They simply dusted themselves down when it was all over and the following day you would not have guessed so much as a single flute had passed along Shettleston Road.

The fact is the bigotry which existed had little to do with the Orange Walk. There was no need for an annual cacophony of Protestant triumphalism to prolong and deepen the feelings of superiority the majority felt for the minority. That Catholics were alien to the basic traditions of Scottish life was simply taken for granted. Friendships did flourish across the barriers but, at the same time, they had an uncanny atmosphere of mutual constraint. Each party gauged just how far they could encroach on the fields of the other. I remember an elderly woman school-teacher of mine being roused by a letter from a priest in the *Glasgow Herald* and telling me solemnly, 'Glasgow was a Whig Presbyterian city. That is its roots and so it shall stay. Do you know that churches rang the bells of triumph and bonfires of celebration were burned in the city when the people heard that Bonnie Prince Charlie and his Jacobites had been defeated at Culloden?'

No, I hadn't known. I had thought he had been on our side. I felt this statement confused all sorts of issues. By comparison, Rangers and Celtic were much easier to understand. There was certainly no merging at their games, which sanctified the apartheid. Mutual hostility and ancient beliefs in religious superiority were considered not only proper and natural but lay like a sacred trust outside the area of any rational explanation. Only the ignorant could not understand that. To be very young and to be there was to be in awe of the sheer magnitude of arrogant conviction which solidified on the terracings. It had a terrible splendour.

The allegiances to Rangers and Celtic permeated the entire city and owed nothing to geography. You might have said the entire East End had a working-class unity which was honourably resistant to religious ghettos. Of course it was understood that by and large the district of Bridgeton was Orange and Garngad was Green, and there were odd little pockets where the identity was clearly aligned one way or the other. For instance, one street just off Shettleston Road was simply and irrevocably tagged 'Little Dublin'. The name was meant to contain insult as well as identity. But the religious spread was largely indiscriminate although people were unfailingly aware of the differences. You would know precisely, and no mistaking, how many Catholics and Protestants lived up a particular close. The Protestants were especially obsessed by the numbers game, fearful of the geometric progression of the Catholic birthrate and used the word 'swamp' with such intensity that it still connotes to me crowded maternity wards.

So, Greenfield Park was exceptional. We could not be educated together. We rarely played in each other's groups. You watched Rangers or Celtic depending on accident of birth. But with not the slightest demur we could rub shoulders together to watch junior football. The white shirt of Shettleston Juniors was the shirt of neutrality. It was that important.

I remember most of all the start of the season and the evening football and the park crowded and the ball bouncing awkwardly on a pitch that for most of the time I went there was largely bare of grass. I recall men of thick unathletic legs and dumpy shin-guards who feared nothing and smote the ball with a vengeance. I recall glowing with triumph after a victory and mixing with the men streaming out of the ground, sharing their contentment and heading for the fish and chip shop where we would queue for an eternity mulling over the game and then walk homewards eating a poke of chips which had been salted and vinegared beyond redemption. I recall the despair of defeat in the Scottish Junior Cup which made a death in the family seem like an endowment.

And if it wasn't Greenfield Park for football it came through the wireless. We would huddle over it listening to a range of voices. Out of them emerged one which gave me a new cause for living: Peter Thomson. Being a commentator seemed like not a bad way of passing one's time.

2

Radio Times

Peter's voice was part of the family. His famous Wembley commentary remains a burnished relic of the great days of radio sports broadcasting. It rang with pleasure and defiance from the depths of the south that Saturday in 1949 as goal followed goal. They were described in detail so clear that when you listen to it again in the archives you can still see Mason's inside of foot passing, Houliston's header, Lawrie Reilly flashing through a defence. He created entire personalities just by mentioning their names. His language was economical, ungarnished besides the likes of the flamboyant Raymond Glendenning, but the more effective for all that. He could strike terror into the heart by incanting, 'And here comes Matthews to Lawton to Finney.' It was a Scots father warning you of the approach of Cumberland's cavalry.

No other game meant quite as much to me in those days as that Wembley international. It came from one of those larynxes which sounded golden and rich in vowel. When the final whistle sounded that day we hugged each other round the backyard and then rushed to the front road to wait for tram-cars. We lifted our hands with the fingers up denoting the score, 3–1, and the first tram-driver to pass us, bereft of such modern devices as transistor radios and ignorant of the dawning of the new age of Scottish supremacy at Wembley, greeted the news with a large beam on his face. His tram went wobbling off into the distance towards Glasgow and he rang the foot bell with relish, the sound carrying the good news to that slender and freakish minority who had not huddled over their

16

wirelesses that afternoon and who had not been intoxicated by the good-natured sonority of Peter's voice.

I met him for the first time in the middle of September 1962. He was gently but deeply spoken, wore very heavy glasses and was quite Magooish in a way for when he took them off there was a blinking naivety to the eyes that suggested he would walk straight into the nearest wall. It is awkward to make contact with a man who is a public figure and whose familiarity as such simply increases his strangeness. All the tiny mental calculations I had made about him in preparation for the meeting didn't seem quite right. Smaller, quieter, more nervous, hesitant. I think he was actually proud that he had excited such public interest in his day. It wasn't vanity for he was as modest as anyone I have ever met in television or radio although, in common with everybody else, he liked to be recognised publicly. I think he never escaped from the need for public recognition to help counter his deep feeling of insecurity which I believe constantly plagued him. He was almost the definitive example of how a lad with hardly any academic credentials could join the Corporation and get to the top of his own area. But I always felt he suffered an inferiority complex amongst other broadcasting luminaries, some of whom rather looked down on him while at the same time envying Peter's popularity.

He was making the transition from radio to television but clearly he was more at home in the claustrophobic ambience of the groundfloor radio studios at Queen Margaret Drive in Glasgow which housed his cronies. That is a word which might have a certain pejorative sense but Peter had to like the broadcasters he gathered around him. They were, firstly and foremost, friends. They did have to have a certain ability at the microphone but essentially I do not imagine that anyone who could not get on with Peter socially could have lasted. This led to outrageous sycophancy to which he was deliberately myopic but the Saturday get-together in that sound radio studio to broadcast everything from top class football all the way through the Highland League via shinty and road races round Mull and other parts had a Pickwickian, clubbable feel to it and I suspect Peter enjoyed that aspect as much as the broadcasting itself.

There was not a real journalist among them and I found this

strange. There would be the occasional use of John Blair, who wrote for the *Sunday People*, Percy Huggins of the *Evening Times* and athletics writer Dunky Wright, but no more than that. In his use of part-timers like myself, from a wide variety of professions, he had created a gulf between broadcasting and journalism which led to outright hostility between the two areas. He did not seem to mind this in the least but it bothered me grievously for there was little doubt in my mind when I entered the portals of Queen Margaret Drive that I would attempt to embark on a career and not simply supplement my teaching income. I found little evidence of such burning ambition in any of the others I came across weekly and the cosiness of it all made me uncomfortable at times.

I wanted to know how to get on in this business. Some of the advice was breathtakingly frank. They sent me to Firhill to do a report for radio in one of my first outings. I learned early on that Firhill was something of a free-speech zone. You could say virtually anything you liked about Partick Thistle, there was hardly any come-back. People could safely give public support to them without being hounded for it. Others of course had to harbour private allegiances to the two major Glasgow Clubs, like the love that dare not speak its name. I sat beside Jameson Clark the actor, who did a lot of freelance work in both radio and television then. That day hunched within his overcoat and with his soft hat pulled to the back of his head he might have been playing the part of the hardened hack wearily mulling over in his mind the threadworn clichés of his craft before the game started. But in fact he was never other than the couthy approachable man who made you feel completely at ease even if you were a newcomer. So began a conversation that was to last on and off for about fifteen years. That day he lectured me and the words stuck.

'Listen,' he said. 'Keep as many interests going as you can. Don't get too ambitious just for television. Let me admit something to you. I sometimes waken up in the middle of the night in a cold sweat. Drenched. Just thinking about what's to come next for me when I can't guarantee that I'll get another piece of work in my life again. I've no guarantees. Nothing. In the news room I've just to wait and see what happens every day. Whiles I draw a blank. And someday they'll turn their back on me. Maybe next week for all I know. You never can tell. Cinema comes along once in a while but even there, sooner or later, they'll cast somebody else in the part you think you should have got and that'll be that. You've got to have guarantees. Whatever you do, get guarantees. If you're freelance like me you can be very vulnerable. Be warned.'

I tried hard not to take that to heart for I wanted to believe that once I had got my foot in the door nothing could stop me. Surely Jameson Clark, who at one time in the films played every kind of Scot short of the lead in *Greyfriars Bobby*, didn't have cold sweats?

However, having written short stories for the BBC before approaching Peter to get into sport I had obviously convinced him I was a cross between Guy de Maupassant and Jim Baxter. Such is the brimming confidence when opportunity stares you in the face early on. I was off and running. Every week I was at some ground to report a game. Normally it would be a match of no great significance and I would come to recognise that stratum of journalists who worked painstakingly in the middle regions of the game. Some were older and resolutely beyond any change. Others, younger like myself, were bursting with ambition and biding their time for the day when the Old Firm clamour would not merely be a distant sound of battle but the real thing, with the political shrapnel of the occasion making them the hardened correspondents they all wished to be.

Peter took great comfort from having these people around him but underneath his usually phlegmatic appearance he was a profoundly uneasy man. 'It is difficult to recall some games,' he told me not long after I started to work for him. 'I got so uptight about them sometimes I didn't know whether I was at Hampden Park or Wembley when I was working. All I could do was concentrate on the match. It just got so I wanted the game finished, over and done with. I just wanted out of it, away from it all.'

This feeling of desperation never really surfaced in his commentaries which were models of sure, simple statement. He certainly treated the 'phoney' commentator with disdain. He vividly recalled for me the occasions he observed the Canadian commentator Stewart MacPherson, who attained a formidable reputation in the UK just after the war, arriving at the Outside Broadcast position with pre-arranged phrases written out on cards. These were slipped in at 'appropriate' moments during a broadcast. 'If you're going to do this,' he said wryly, 'don't write them out on cards for people to see. Memorise them. Or better still, try and be spontaneous. That, I suppose, is what we are here for.'

According to Peter, Glendenning described one of the famous goals at Hampden Park, Billy Steel's thirty-yarder for Britain against the Rest of Europe in 1947 as they were centring the ball to restart the game. He was expressing both criticism and admiration for the famous English commentator who could both be so behind the play yet salvage himself with a seamless verbal patch-up. He was in effect warning me, without expressing it in a deliberately censorious way, of the ethics of sound radio broadcasting, of the awesome power of the commentator. That person had a duty to be accurate and honest and yet he might also have the ability to create images and events of his own, as his tongue and ego got the better of him. It was a Scottish puritanical observation, much too concerned with guilt, and for me seemed to make the possibility of the twinning of inspired rhapsodising and objectivity an impossible ideal. But the more I got to know Peter the more I realised that broadcasting had become a bed of nails for him. At times he looked and sounded a tortured man. The pressures which grew through his sound radio experiences intensified cruelly when he had to make the transition to television.

Whilst I gained the impression that everybody in broadcasting had rubbed their hands in anticipation of this new challenge I sensed, even though I entered the scene some years after the revolution had started, that the deeper feelings were of regret. This was a period of transition from the medium which had forged the BBC's reputation to something which was as yet untamed and volatile, and clearly at times beyond the discreet and careful control of the sound radio programme. After all, Peter Thomson had been a pioneer of radio and here he was like a wagon master having reached the coast with his charges being asked to head for the unknown again with barely a rest. Few of his contemporaries were equipped for such a dramatic change. In many ways they suffered the same sort of fate, in inverted form, bequeathed Hollywood by the *Jazz Singer*. Voices became handicaps in the movies. So, on TV, faces and presentation very often did not suit the new medium.

Nothing was hidden. Looking straight at the television camera either in a studio or out of doors without the aid of script, which one could crouch over in a radio studio, was like facing a firing squad. The transition produced victims.

One man who coped well was George Davidson. He was the ex-sea captain whose almost imperious voice had virtually shoved Peter's off the air in commentating on football. George looked authoritative in the studio and sounded almost professorial behind the mike. He was of enormous value to me, not so much in strict broadcasting terms but in the way he seemed to be able to ride above crisis like the veritable mariner in the storm. I have been with him when he was harangued by supporters and he treated it with the verbal disdain of a headmaster quelling a rebellious class of kids. In his days at sea, he had been in the first boat to land in Yokohama after the great earthquake of 1923. He used that experience to try and enlighten me as to the demands of broadcasting.

'You know,' he said to me once, 'I have been virtually assaulted by supporters, insulted by the occasional manager, made mistakes in front of camera, been criticised by the public for all kinds of things and yet it is nothing. I am surrounded by people who worry about the slightest thing, they are obsessed with broadcasting and don't know what the real world is. After seeing the bodies piled up in heaps in that city that day and the maimed and the barely surviving crawling in the streets it does give you a kind of perspective on life. We can become too self-obsessed. Broadcasting is not easy. But it's only as difficult as you make it yourself. Keep a sense of perspective and don't put up the shutters around you in here. There are other things in life more important.'

The most important thing for me then and there though was to make it. To where in broadcasting I was not sure, but I had now got it into my system. Even after only a few weeks a new impetus had been added to life. I was afflicted by Saturday afternoon fever.

It is about five-fifteen. We have returned from the games we have been reporting. Papers are strewn about the table, on the middle of which is the microphone, the object of all our desires. On the immediate outside of the studio, through the glass in the production suite, Peter Thomson paces up and down, his hand interminably in his pocket worming away nervously at his balls. A voice is linking the items, ponderously but with great sense of diction. It belongs to the small Toulouse Lautrec figure of Andy Cowan Martin, whose physique does not immediately suggest the power of voice or the capacity to lower tumblers of the gold stuff after programmes. He was once about to make an announcement when he handed the piece of paper hurriedly to his co-presenter who had one look then shoved it to the reporter who after a hurried glance passed it back to Andy who simply threw it to the floor without a word. He had vowed never to try to announce the result of the dreaded Buchan Firkin Trophy which was to him 2–1 on for a spoonerism.

We are relaxed. These are friends together. In the insulated studio the impression is that nobody is listening anyway. We have our notes in front of us. They have been changed several times. Adjectives have been strewn around, metaphors normally revolving round strength, endurance and character are curlicues on our pages. We launch into it and are finished after about ninety seconds but hungering for more.

Only a few yards away is the television studio. We arrive breathless seeking to know how the game finished because invariably we have to leave half-way through the second half to get back in time. Someone wearing headphones greets you without a smile for this is grim business bringing the news in. The door is squeezed open noiselessly. Dark shapes are silhouetted against the crescent of light which dominates the back of the studio where sits Peter Thomson tense and so smothered in make-up an audition for a Japanese Noh play seems imminent. There is no evidence of camaraderie. In the artificial division of harsh light and bulky darkness the impression gathers that you are about to be cross-examined by a public prosecutor. You are ushered to the set beside Peter. He is too involved to acknowledge your presence and when you hear his words of introduction, slow and deliberate, the feeling deepens that you have had no preparation and that sentences are cruel obstacles in the way of your ultimate escape. A red light goes on, a hand waves under a camera and you are on.

Those almost off-the-cuff reports in the early days still represent to me the hardest of all the television challenges. When the lights flooded on after the programme the sense of relief would gush through the studio. Whereas the radio experience suggested travelling in a well-upholstered limousine in some considerable comfort, television was like shooting the rapids in a leaky canoe.

About a month or so after I had started regular reporting Peter sat in his office assessing me. 'People will start recognising you in the streets,' he said. It was a sort of coded way of saying he thought I would be around for a while. 'You get used to it.' I didn't really believe that sentiment then and still don't now. One way or the other that sort of distant recognition produces a self-consciousness that is as comfortable as a hair-shirt.

'Just smile a bit more and you'll be all right,' he went on. Smile? It was an effort of mind merely to breathe in front of a camera let alone get brain and muscle co-ordination for a smile.

'Not too many big words,' he said, smiling. It was the gentlest of reprimands. I had used the phrase 'peripheral vision' about one player. My phrase had come straight from the coaching manual of one Walter Winterbottom of the FA and I thought I was being clever. I was being told very nicely I was being a smart arse. 'What are your ambitions?' he suddenly asked. Well, I couldn't resist. 'To do a commentary at Wembley,' I replied. He looked away and tilted his head as he had a habit of doing then looked back straight at me, with a wry smile bending his mouth. 'You never know,' he said.

Not long after that I was invited to London by the sports editor there, Angus Mackay, who on the strength of a few radio broadcasts offered me a job at the time Eamonn Andrews was leaving *Sports Report* to go to ITV. My head was greatly turned by this but I recall most of all from that whirlwind visit Brian Moore, who was still involved with radio broadcasting, turning to me out of earshot of Mackay and saying with great deliberation, 'You'd be mad to come here. If you don't suit you could be back to Scotland in a few weeks' time, right out of a job. This can be a very cruel place.'

It can be and probably was and I didn't accept. I did not need to agonise all that much for another seed had been sown, television commentary. Peter had used the offer of this to keep me in Scotland. More than that though, I had gone with George Davidson to Celtic Park just before the London visit to watch as he commentated on film. This was a close observation of a new technique and a new power. I certainly wanted a bit of this. I especially liked the way he had developed a rapport with the crowd, some of whom detested him, whilst others loved him. I saw him then not just as a commentator but a catalyst. I marvelled at this. I felt myself becoming infected with this new possibility of becoming a figure of some controversy. The lure was infinitely stronger than the distant attraction of Portland Place, W1.

3

Camera Capers

It was the year Nelson Mandela was put in prison. It was the year Baxter broke his leg in Vienna and was never quite the same player again. I prefer to think of 1964 though as the start of the Mack Sennett period of television for me. It was still the age of black and white film even for the coverage of a football match and most times we were able to get images on a screen which looked as if they had been sent to the Shettleston 'steamie', put through a wringer and hung out to dry before being seen by the viewer. In those days technology was still dependent on the Good Fairy of the North to get us on the programme in time and in one piece.

We worked off tiny little platforms mostly tucked unobtrusively against grandstands at the back of enclosures. The vantage points were roughly equivalent to that of a worm emerging from subterranean safety before being plucked out by the early bird. Even Eisenstein or Cecil B De Mille would have found it hard to make anything of a film camera down there. Nor did they have to deliver the goods every week to a Saturday night audience. It clearly possessed a tolerance level then which makes your urbane viewer now seem like a cynical shark.

I was introduced to my first film unit one Saturday in August of that year on the little postage stamp platform at Fir Park, Motherwell. We were strangers. All five of us. As it was the cameraman just happened to be Eddie McConnel, one of the most respected documentary film-makers in the country. I remembered an award-winning film he had made about a drunk coming to terms with wakening up in the centre of Glasgow. His actor had been Phil McCall and one of the shots had stuck in my mind; a low angle view along the steps of the Commercial Library just off Queen Street, with a bottle in the foreground. His ability to handle the camera at that low angle, I thought, would stand him in good stead at Fir Park where there was a fair chance of some exciting shots of the players' studs, from below. But of course that had been a perfectly framed static shot. What was a respected documentary maker doing here?

'Earning a living,' Eddie told me before the camera rolled. I could tell he was also a philosopher. Apart from being there to do my first commentary for television I was coming face to face with the realities of surviving in the film industry in Scotland. Football would help finance Eddie for other projects. With that end in mind he kept his eye glued to the viewfinder for ninety minutes trying to spot the ball. Four years later he was to make *The Celtic Story*.

Although it was always referred to as the 'unit' the main feature of the coverage of football then was how disjointed everything was. We were all separated from the studios for the whole afternoon so they had no idea what was coming back to them. We employed drivers to speed canisters of film back to Queen Margaret Drive so that they could be developed as quickly as possible. Some had the intrepid spirit of the Pony Express in their bones. Others would dally along the taverns or bookies of Great Western Road, thus sending the film-processors apoplectic. On one occasion, coming all the way back from Easter Road with a can which contained the only goal of the first half, the driver absconded altogether. He was never seen again and since he was known for humming 'The Sash' as he traipsed the highways and byways of the land we could only assume he was carrying a goal for Hibs against Rangers. He had sacrificed himself and the can of film for the cause. Another became a friend of goalkeepers. He didn't wait for us in the car-park but instead boldly watched the game from behind the net along with the photographers. Unlike them, he had nothing much else to do and would regularly confer with goalkeepers. A goal-keeper once asked him to put a bet on for him during a game. Walking round the track, out into the street through the tunnel, up the street to the bookies and back again, he duly did so as play raged on.

But as we sat there together on those Saturdays on these platforms each of us would never know for certain what was actually going on to film let alone how or when it would get back to the studios. I lifted up the mike just before kick-off that first day hoping that somebody would say something in the way of guidance of when to start and stop. All Peter had said that morning was, 'Remember it's not radio. Don't overdo it!' I no longer had the supreme advantage of radio's immediacy. Here we would have to cover the equivalent of the Grand National before reaching the public, if at all.

I launched into it though. Ten minutes of the Motherwell–Hibs game had elapsed when suddenly there was a violent tap on the shoulder. It was the sound man. 'Stop,' he said abruptly. I also saw Eddie pull back from his camera and a flurry of activity exploding round the camera as his assistant pulled frantically at the hump of the magazine of film. 'Fault?' I asked with a sudden, falling heart. 'No. Change,' the sound man said. 'Changing the film.'

It is here I have to admit to a technical blindness which has afflicted me all my broadcasting life. Somehow I have always wanted to remain quite distant from anything to do with television's innards. I want the large intestine to function with regularity but I do not necessarily want a working knowledge of the process. Perhaps I ought to put it down to that day when I felt it was better not to get involved, not to fret, but just to let skill, expertise and sheer fate take over. As the unit only had one camera and as the film only lasted ten minutes they had to take out the old magazine and put in the new and do it pretty bloody quick, for the rules of association football did not allow for stoppage whilst cameramen changed reels.

Nobody had prepared me for this. It did occur to me to ask, 'Yes, but what happens if a goal is scored while you're changing mags?' I didn't, though, for it would have betrayed ignorance of the whole process and in any case a cameraman or his assistant involved in this is as easily lured into idle conversation as a man grappling with a lion. I simply put down the mike and watched this feverish activity as Motherwell and Hibs quite inconsiderately tried to score goals against each other.

They seemed to take an eternity, the unit that is. As they fumbled to get the casing snapped shut a Motherwell player took a ball in that inimitable stride of his and from ten yards struck for goal. It soared towards Motherwell Bridge Works well over the bar. A Motherwell supporter just in front of us shouted, 'Ya mug.' I felt like shouting, 'Stay there, ya beauty.'

I struggled with this new medium, all the time thinking, 'What's going to happen after another ten minutes?' That in itself was discomfiting but the essential unrest came from the practice of restraint. On radio you treat your larynx and the listener to a veritable avalanche of words. Here, I knew I had to practise, although was not at all sure that I was managing, the art of verbal contraception, of shielding myself and the listener from the possible birth of irritation. Alas, no foolproof method of control has yet been devised for this.

The gods were kind to us that day, or so we thought. The studio had already started the editing of the film before the first half had ended so by the time we returned they were well into shaping the game for the evening transmission. I stood for the first time at the back of the BBC building overlooking the Kelvin, examining the first examples of our work. The film was edited in negative which I found most disconcerting. Faces were black, jerseys were white. The sound track was separate, so the editor was working with two ribbons of celluloid which he had to keep in 'sync'. Juggling these different elements made it difficult to concentrate especially as he was working from a hand-cranked machine with a viewing screen not much bigger than a credit card. This would be about the same 'window' as the cameraman had at the actual game except he had to keep his eye fixed on it and pull a camera-head around at the same time to follow the ball. Even standing there peering at the tiny screen I could barely make out any spherical object at all. My admiration for Eddie increased as I realised he missed little and I also began to appreciate that only one tiny slip, an eye watering, a hair in the works, a slip of the hand, a sneeze and the programme could be made to look ridiculous. He was far and away the most important element in our coverage.

Then the sound came. Peter Thomson had come down to the cutting room desperately anxious for me to have succeeded. When a producer picks out a potential broadcaster and puts him up front he is, to a great extent, staking his reputation on him. He certainly doesn't want to be let down and made a fool of. Conversely, if he has found a star, his stock rises. Sometimes, because of that, he is not entirely objective in appraising the early results. He is invariably optimistic. The film editor took the sound reel off the small hand-cranked machine, put it on some other contraption and we listened.

My voice sounded as if it were coming from a catacomb. It had more of the timbre of the basso profundo of grand opera than league football commentary. It didn't relate. There was a long, horrible moment when we all stood around listening without any-body wishing to volunteer a comment. After a while Peter said, 'Could you stop it for a moment?' and then added, 'Who was the sound man?' Right away I could see he was being defensive of me. It was somebody else's fault. But it wasn't of course and I think he knew it. I suddenly realised that the voice was a pure mimicking of his own, that I was trying to do a 'Peter Thomson'. Imitation might be the sincerest form of flattery but in this instance it soun-ded like pure pantomime and I could see that Peter was disturbed.

Worried or not he put it out that night and frankly in a succeed-ing television generation it would never have seen the light of day, so droning was the voice. I didn't watch the programme: I had seen and heard enough in the film-cutting room. A friend said to me the following week, 'I thought at one stage you sounded like Paul Robeson.' He was, I think, trying to be kind.

As the weeks went by and I got over the trauma of hearing my voice on film for the first time I got slightly cuter about it all and tried to save any eloquence for those moments when I knew it was more likely to be used; for example immediately after a goal had been scored or at kick-off. What I had to take into account, though, was that the film would pass through many tests before it would reach the screen. It would have to be processed firstly. This was either handled by an outside company or within the BBC itself. Wherever it went there was absolutely no guarantee that it would come out unscathed or indeed come out at all. Much of our film looked like chopped liver. This had nothing to do with lack of professionalism within the system but much to do with the hazards of rushing it on to the screen.

But collectively we knew there were constraints we had to work within, some of which existed during the actual commentary. You had never to talk over a goal-kick. You had never to breathe a word during a throw-in. You had not to open your mouth as a player was being treated for an injury. You had to shut up instantly whenever you had identified a free-kick. You had not to ramble on after kick-off unless there was a quick goal. All these were clearly recognisable edit points through which the editor could slice the razor and make neat joins. If you were not talking over the goalkeeper kicking the ball upfield the editor, if he so wished, could make the ball land ten minutes later by inserting a cutaway shot of a player simply looking vacantly into space. Crowd shots were the best means of editing though. They simply filmed the crowd standing on the terracing and could use them over and over again. Sometimes they didn't match. You would see a ball rolling over the touchline for one team to claim a throw-in and the next shot would be of the crowd hugging and kissing each other. Only at Firhill was that edit not thought unusual. When we had problems with sound we would simply lay on some other stuff from the library stock. One night we showed Hibs scoring at Easter Road, followed by cheering and a distinct choir in the background singing 'We'll Guard Old Derry's Walls'. As you can imagine, the culture shock in Auld Reekie was immense.

With all of this in mind it was an accomplishment merely to get through a commentary and see the end product on the air at all let alone being concerned with the niceties of style. Frequently, Peter had to go on and face the public to make apologies for some sort of breakdown and the man must have been near to tears on some occasions although he put a brave face on it. One night I was lending some support in the background when the film came in from Celtic Park after an Old Firm game. Celtic had won 1–0.

'Jesus Christ,' Peter said just as he was going on for a rehearsal of the opening. 'We've not got the Celtic goal. It's lost.'
'Lost? Where?' I said as I saw his features dissolve into those of a man getting his first taste of the thumb-screw. 'God knows. God

knows,' he repeated in a demented way. Technical mishaps were far from unique but this was somewhat different. An Old Firm game? A Celtic goal? The only goal of the game? Not going to be shown? As we would say in the trade, 'Batten down the hatches.'

Celtic did not trust the BBC then. In a way, you could hardly blame them for their circumspection. In the famous 7–1 victory over Rangers in the 1957 League Cup Final a technician in London, tele-recording the match all the way down the line from Hampden, put a dust cover over the lens at half-time when the score was 2–1 and forgot to take it off at the re-start of the second half so Celtic's other five goals and the cavalry charge of white horses into the riotous Rangers end could not be shown. Try telling that to a Celtic supporter. Then think of what it must have been like for Peter Thomson to have had to explain it away to Bob Kelly, the Celtic chairman. The game in its entirety has never been seen publicly although a private amateur film was subsequently uncovered and I am surprised Celtic did not commission Carl Davis to put it to music.

That night, after a po-faced Peter Thomson had calmly announced that Celtic had won but, sorry, their goal could not be shown for technical reasons, I experienced the violent reaction of the public for the first time. Each call I took either started, concluded or was interspersed with the soubriquet 'Orange bastard'. It is the characteristic of these calls that they do not really expect a rational explanation. It is the letting-off of steam that is the most important issue. I was reminded that man does not live by bread alone but thrives also on the imagined plottings of the establishment.

As it happened, we discovered much later that that particular piece of film had been chewed up in processing. But it has to be said that there was a liberality to the 'buggeration factor', which then was as virulent as Asian flu. When we went to Hampden Park on an October evening in 1965 to cover the Rangers–Kilmarnock League Cup semi-final it seemed like any other night. It was not to be though. Going into Hampden Park then was considerably worse than it is now which means it was horrendous. I believe the lights have since been upgraded but then the luminosity was that of a ghost-train tunnel at the carnival. To pass through the underbelly of the stand to get to the back of the enclosure required the courage of a pot-holer and the directional sense of a Bedouin finding the last water hole in Arabia. You had to grope your way alongside the men's toilet, which was dark and sinister enough to make Joe Orton water at the mouth. Once out in the open with a decided sense of relief you were pinned up against the bottom of the stand just behind where the players' dug-out is now.

What followed was the apotheosis of the age of technical blunderdom. Firstly, Eddie was not there and that caused anxiety since in his place was a young fresh-faced kid who looked as if he had only photographed his sister's wedding or Masonic harmony. I was aware early on of a jerkiness to the lad's movement that suggested he might have been finding the ball elusive. What unnerved me slightly was that while he was pointing the camera on one occasion at the Rangers' goal the ball was still in the Kilmarnock penalty area. Still, even at a football match one ought to expect some poetic licence. But the game did not require an aspiring Ingmar Bergman. We just needed the ball. At all times the ball. Alas we were not to get it as often as we would have liked.

The camera suddenly jammed. He rushed to the other one. It jammed as well. Rangers scored, then almost immediately added another as two cameras hung in a kind of post-coital droop incapable, it appeared, of any more. The 53,900 crowd, who were perhaps amusing themselves with the thought that they could hurry home and see the highlights later that night, were blissfully unaware that the filming of the game had been entrusted to Dad's Army. We managed to get one camera going. Then Rangers got a penalty just before half-time. This was surely it. Our first capture of the night. George McLean took it and scored. The cameraman looked relieved enough and when half-time came we sent the film winging back to the studio. The game ended 6–4 to Rangers with Tommy McLean getting a hat-trick for Kilmarnock in the last twenty minutes.

But when we got back to the studios we were met by a doleful Peter Thomson. 'How could they have missed a penalty? How could they?' he moaned. For when the film was transmitted the penalty looked as if it had been shot from the wrong end of a telescope and when the camera jerked towards goal the ball was already being kicked back up the field for the centre. Peter admirably and coolly used up his whole year's quotas of apologies as he tried to explain to the viewers why, when the score was 6–4, we had made it look something like 3–1 or, for those who didn't have twenty-twenty vision, 0–0. A young trainee cameraman helped us that night, not, I hasten to say, that he filmed any of the fiasco. His name was Bill Forsyth. In later years I was to remind him of that as he went on to win laurels for his wry film-making. 'At least we could see the ball in *Gregory's Girl*,' I ventured. Like me he could see the funny side of it but, then, neither of us had had to face the public directly.

We were slaughtered mostly by Rangers' supporters after that. For the first, and certainly not the last, time in my life in answering a call I was called an 'Effing Tim'. A newspaper, I think the *Sunday Mail*, published a letter from a viewer comparing our coverage to 'filming with a Brownie whilst jumping on a Trampoline'. It was time to hide but it was difficult to do so. Certainly not from one particular member of the public who did not let much pass him.

It was a couple or so weeks after that I heard his voice directed towards me for the first time. 'Heh, you,' it rasped. 'They say you're a teacher. You couldn't count at the Rangers game, could you? You'll have to get your arithmetic right before you watch us. What about that fiasco? Where did you get your cameras? The Barras?'

He was standing on the steps of the entrance to the Central Hotel in Glasgow. He was wearing a black woollen coat which emphasised the breadth of his shoulders. And his name was Stein.

4

Please Can I Go to Lisbon?

He was off out of sight into the interior of the hotel even before I could open my mouth in reply. It was a classic Jock Stein manoeuvre. Hit, destroy, depart. I was to experience and witness it for another couple of decades as he towered above every other influence on my career. It was 1965, the year Churchill had died, and I now recall the words Harold Wilson used in tribute of the great man:

> For now the noises of hooves thundering over the veldt, the clamour of hustings in a score of contests, the urgent warnings of the Nazis . . . all are silent.

I think of that first meeting with Stein and of the crowded, turbulent, magnificent, depressing, tumultuous, incandescent years that followed; and of the day in 1985 when I sat down in a deserted BBC studio in Cardiff trying to think of words which were adequate to his passing; and of how, preposterous though it may seem to those who are strangers to football or who simply did not like Stein, Churchillian analogies kept offering themselves.

The brand new Celtic manager of 1965, who had been with the club only a few months and had led them to a Scottish Cup win, was then bristling with vitality and bore the impression of a man for whom the immediate future couldn't come quickly enough. At that stage his relationship with the BBC and myself was foul. Within the sports corridors of the Beeb in Scotland he was regarded as almost being the Great Satan. It took years before he ceased to be my nemesis. Later, though, he would give invaluable advice at critical junctures in my professional life and work with relish with me on several outstanding broadcasting occasions. There was never any intimate relationship for he was both man and citadel and resisted with ease almost everybody I know who attempted to slip into his private fief. Few managed it and many who claimed that achievement were really deluding themselves. But at least I shared a great deal of his public life. The transition from outright animosity to a tolerable level of personal friendship took me on a long and exacting course, mostly over rocky terrain but at least ending in a pleasant amble that quite literally carried us round the world together.

It's difficult to convey the impact of that first meeting, however brief. It got into the bones and stayed there. The sudden onslaught, very often delivered, as it had been then, with a smile on his face, became renowned throughout the media. It left you feeling as if you had just developed a very bad hangover without the preceding pleasures. He had dismissed me contemptuously, although he did not know me personally. He did so because I came from the Peter Thomson stable and in Stein's eyes that automatically made you an Ibrox lackey. 'If the man at the top of the house is like that then you're all the same,' he once barked at me in the early days. Then, of course, he knew I was a teacher. I wasn't really part of the game. He hardly thought much of some of the most experienced journalists who were barnacularly attached to him then so what chance of credibility did I have? But I certainly was not part of the media who danced attendance on managers daily or weekly so there was little opportunity of developing any kind of bond with anybody in football, let alone this man I had never met before. But he was the first to make me acutely aware that I was, in football's province, an 'outsider'. I was still very much in that category by the time Celtic had qualified for the final of the European Cup in 1967.

I flew to Lisbon with a suitcase the size of a garden shed, a plastic bag with two litres of duty free whisky, the *Michelin Guide* to Portugal, the BBC medical officer's tips on hygiene and communicable diseases in the Iberian Peninsula, a good-luck card from a couple of pupils in the school I was headmaster of at the time, Kenneth Wolstenholme and a small bottle of phenobarbitone. It was difficult to say as we lifted off from Heathrow which was going to be the most helpful.

Certainly the suitcase contained enough gear for a fortnight's stay when it was only going to be a couple of nights. The whisky I had vowed not to touch until I got back home. The Michelin was a typical 'I-have-never-been-abroad-before-on-an-assignment-like-this' sort of gesture and tilted me more towards the tourist category rather than that of broadcasting journalist. The medical officer's strictures neither terrified nor elucidated.

The card from the children really told me that when I got back home I would have to come down to earth very quickly. Kenneth Wolstenholme I had never met before, but he was polite if distant when we met in the lounge at Heathrow where he took me to the VIP lounge ('Please come in, Mr Wolstenholme. How nice to see you. Champagne I suppose? Where are we going to this time? Lisbon? What's on? Oh, Celtic! In the European Cup final? Are they really? Now what can I get *you* to drink, sir?') and I felt more like a batman trailing in the wake of his public recognition. The feeling of inferiority was accentuated when we boarded the plane and separated, he to first-class, myself to the back.

Perhaps I could have done without all of them bar the phenobarbitone. Only armed assault would have taken that small bottle away from me and even then I would have gone down fighting. It was a lifeline, or so it seemed to me. With much apparently prospering for me – a headmastership in my twenties, a constant commentating role, more writing of educational scripts for schools broadcasting and now a trip to commentate on the European Cup final – it might have seemed that life had taken on a lustrous pink glow. The world, in fact, had developed a dingy monochrome appearance as gloom followed me like a swarm of harvest flies.

It's difficult to know when or how this started but that I suppose is the nature of depression; you disappear up your own backside if you try to work it out logically. Events were happening around me which I barely recognised, even though I was supposed to be part of them. I recalled Peter Thomson telling me about his mental disorientation under pressure and sometimes in a broadcast not being able to identify at a particular moment in time where he actually was. I wondered if all this was some kind of occupational disease: that obsession with broadcasting brought an emotional torture which the body wasn't too willing to put up with and caused it to send less than amorous messages up the spinal cord to the cerebellum. Or perhaps it had nothing to do with that. There was confusion.

I was living a private life of lacerating self-doubt, instinctive mistrust of people and the sure certainty that I was terminally ill. Apart from that everything was fine. I had suddenly become a devotee of *Black's Medical Dictionary*, sneaking into the public library at Baillieston ostensibly to meander through the fiction section but in reality to flick through the pages of the dictionary with a deep sense of foreboding and guilt to determine whether the headache I had was the beginning of migraine or an inoperable brain tumour. I believed the odds heavily stacked on the latter. In a period of a year I assumed I had every disease from leukaemia to Parkinson's. Even a stitch in the side running for a bus conveyed the idea of a colostomy to follow. A tiny little blemish on the skin meant melanoma was nigh. I had taken on hypochondria with the dedication of a religious zealot.

'You are doing far too much,' the doctor said when I went to see him about the amputation which I believed would be the inevitable outcome of a nasty corn on my right toe. 'Here,' he said. 'Take these! They'll be a help.' He gave me those tiny little white pills which, then if not now, doctors tended to hand out like Smarties at a children's birthday party.

There seemed to be thousands of them in the bottle but, to any hypochondriac worth his salt, that only indicated that they had given me up for lost and were trying to tranquillise me against the inevitable outcome. He might as well have been handing me strychnine. The pills had the effect of drying the mouth up completely. He hadn't warned me about that so after stuffing myself with them one fine day I set off for Ibrox to do a sound report for Glasgow and London and, when I came to speak, discovered to my horror that my mouth felt as if it had just been stuffed with an old sock. Lips, tongue, cheeks and even teeth seemed afflicted with the drought of Death Valley. The words were dying before any sound got past the epiglottis and the report sounded like a man whose teeth had snared the tongue like a gin-trap.

A commiserating voice from London enquired up the line, 'Are you pissed, Arch?' Afterwards the doctor did say in the most non-chalant way, 'Oh, yes! You did notice that effect. I wondered!' I was about to ask him if, realising what I actually did for a living, he would recommend a blindfold for shortsightedness. However, I was too much in debt to medical science during this period to mock its practitioners. Pure faith in medical solutions, as I had, only led to this ambivalent mistrust of anybody putting his pen to a prescription. I would be more careful in the future. It took me about a year to get through this and in retrospect 'hypochondria' is but a term I use to make light of something deep-rooted and infinitely more like a nightmare.

So Lisbon might have seemed the perfect antidote, better than anything dreamed up by the lads in the Swiss labs. The sun didn't let us down but shone with a clarity that took us out of our north-European stiffness as soon as we left the airport. We had arrived in a ruthless dictatorship but we were not disposed to look for evidence of it although I distinctly remember the heavy-set, dark-jowled, solemn, corpulent police with their fat holsters. It occurred to me that authoritarianism bred indolence amongst the security men. The system might have become so rigid, and habitual to its citizens, that the police just stood around and got fat with nothing more to do than look threatening. The air of menace they exuded contrasted sharply with the freshness of the coastline between Lisbon and Cascais, the plush holiday resort which lies about three miles outside the city.

At least the dictatorship had the advantage of an immediate coastline which easily drugged the visitor into indifference to Dr Salazar's peculiar notion of civilised behaviour. We relished the invading blueness of the Atlantic and a marbled hotel, polished and gleaming with pride, humming with greatly practised and highly efficient subservience. It was only a mile from Celtic's base. All of this made it easy for me, however fleetingly, to dissolve into background and camouflage myself from the problems continually dogging me. The mood did not last all that long for things were not going to work out during this forthcoming broadcast. The whole atmosphere changed after my first chat with Wolstenholme that evening.

It had been agreed that a Scottish commentator was required for such an occasion. Since George Davidson was unavailable Peter Thomson asked me if I would travel. 'You will assist Ken on commentary,' Peter assured me. 'You will split up each half between you. Straight down the middle. Can you be released to do it?'

I said yes without really knowing whether it would be possible or not. This sudden turn of events only compounded the tension I felt trying to occupy two roles. There was no way I was going to turn this opportunity down and I immediately began concocting contingency plans for the possibility of the Director of Education saying no. I could hardly claim time off for my grandmother's funeral when the whole of the UK was going to be listening to me in Lisbon. Nor could I simply resign. There wasn't enough time. The final was only a couple of weeks away. It was not that two to three days away from Swinton was going to disrupt the education service. It was just the awareness that I was cheating on myself, that despite having thrown myself into my teaching job I was really looking in another direction. Nor could I bear the thought of the Education authorities turning a request down. I decided to play my political card.

I knew that a straightforward letter to the Education offices in Hamilton might get short shrift. But I also knew that a large number of the ruling Labour group in Lanarkshire were Celtic supporters. I let it be known to our local councillor that I had been asked to go to Lisbon and, quite correctly, that if I didn't Scotland would not have a commentator at the greatest club match in the history of Scottish football. I knew the call had taken the trick when Jimmy Hamilton, my MP, called to say he would do all he could for me. Jimmy, one of the most likeable of men, sat every week in the directors' box at Celtic Park. I was told simply to write for formal permission for release and it looked plain sailing. But they did ask me why the BBC thought it so necessary that I attend this match. I duly passed on Peter Thomson's explanation, little realising the difficulty I was eventually to face as a result. It was accepted. I was granted three days' leave.

So that first night in a little fish restaurant in Cascais I sat with Wolstenholme and had lobster and champagne as if it were part of my daily diet. Being abroad for the first time with the BBC, and not knowing what might be accepted on expenses, I was a trifle tentative to start with but I had vowed after watching Wolstenholme being escorted into first-class on the flight that I would not act the country bumpkin. 'Another bottle, Ken?' I heard myself saying, fists clenched apprehensively under the table. No need to record the reply. But he waited until near the end of the meal before he broke the news.

'Has anybody explained what is happening tomorrow?' he asked.

'In what sense?' I replied.

'Well, you see, I was on the phone to London this afternoon and they thought they'd let you know what they wanted you to do. I had to pass it on to you.'

'I'm doing half of each half.'

'Well, not exactly,' he went on after a sip. 'What they want you to do is summarise.'

'Summarise?'

'Yes, I'll bring you in for a minute before kick-off, then a minute after the half-time whistle and a minute at the end of the game. Perhaps a little more if it goes to extra-time.'

Christ! Was I hearing right?

'What? Are you sure?'

'Absolutely sure. That's been agreed.'

'By whom?'

'London,' he said tersely.

'And Scotland?'

'I don't know about Scotland. I know that's what Ginger has agreed.'

'Ginger' was a coded message. Brian 'Ginger' Cowgill was the dominant force in BBC sports broadcasting then and a man not to be taken lightly. In full spate in a television gallery Cowgill was an awesome sight, with his blunt north of England, stentorian delivery sending underlings jumping through any hoop the master indicated. He had, in fact, created a nervous tension within sports output that greatly added to its professionalism. Only a department continually on its toes would suffice. It was reflected in the sharp, brilliantly-honed voices of Coleman and Wolstenholme and lent BBC network output a distinction and authority which has never been surpassed. Cowgill helped establish the foundations of that before leaving to join ITV some years later. He scared the hell out of most of us. It wasn't likely that I would be phoning him from Cascais to complain.

Nevertheless, I felt shattered. To get to Lisbon I had just done a deal with my MP, had the backing of councillors, and the under-standing of the local education authority. The explanation had been that I was to be the indispensable Scottish voice sharing commentary. Now I had come all this way, through that process, to be told I was to do about four minutes' work. It was like a brickie arriving with the tools only to be told he was now the tea-boy.

I had a sleepless night, especially as the sea-front at Cascais also attracts rasping motor-cyclists as much as it does seagulls. I was beginning to panic. I put in a call to Peter Thomson in Glasgow. Phoning from Portugal in that era was an operation involving the mangling of the English language and rising doubt about the sanity of the human race. After four hours I got through to him and gave him the whole 'cri de coeur' bit.

'How am I going to face up to my employers and my colleagues in Lanarkshire after travelling all this way just to do a couple of minutes or so. That was not the agreement. It is very embarrassing. Do you understand that?' I shouted down the line, not angrily but just so he could hear me. 'I will be crucified!'

His normal depth of voice seemed to disappear around the Bay of Biscay and the tinny reply sounded like, 'I'll see what I can do. They are bastards, you should know that! I will try and get in touch before kick-off!'

I believed him. I went to the pre-match lunch in one of the most beautiful restaurants in the world just outside Cascais. The Amoexes is set on a rocky promontory beside a horseshoe curve of golden beach and the surf pounded all around us. I watched Wolstenholme mix with the other European commentators and envied him his cosmopolitan confidence but felt rather smug in the knowledge that political wheels were turning within the BBC and I would gain full restitution of rights. It was then he strolled up to me with a glass of wine in one hand and a canapé in the other and almost nonchalantly declared, 'Oh, by the way, I meant to say, London passed on a message this morning. If there is a replay, which would be on Thursday, could you stay on and do it for them by yourself as I have another commitment? Think you could manage that?'

Was I the only man who arrived in the stadium that afternoon hoping inwardly, in the most selfish way, for a draw? Probably. I had no idea how I was going to cope but not even the threat of a sacking, which might even then have been imminent, would hold me back.

The Portuguese television people had built tiny cubicles which were both to shelter us from the sun and to section us off from the many other commentators sharing that area. They had also installed huge television monitors on the bench in front of us. Neither of us was tiny and we could barely squeeze into the space allotted. I had found Wolstenholme very pleasant company but I did not fancy our bodies being virtually intertwined for almost two hours. What is more, we could not budge the monitor from in front of us and the only view I could get of the pitch was by half-rising out of my seat in a sort of constipated lavatorial pose. Then, a slot of about letter-box size was opened to me. By adjusting my head I could view certain selected areas but at no time that afternoon was I able to see the entire playing area. What is more the sun was changing its angle and by kick-off I realised that it would be shining straight at the screen of the monitor making it almost impossible to make out the play on it. Thus it was under the worst possible broadcasting circumstances we prepared for this historic game.

About twenty minutes or so before the teams came out I put it straight to Wolstenholme.

'I take it that everything has been worked out and I'll be sharing commentary?' I asked in a matter of fact tone.

He shrugged.

'What I told you last night stands,' he replied innocently. 'I've been instructed only to bring you in as I said. Sorry. Nothing I can do about it. London's instructions.'

'Four minutes' worth in total?' I stressed in an almost contemptuous tone.

He shrugged again.

'Perhaps you could talk over the line to London,' he said. 'They might listen to you.'

I knew this was the last thing they would do and I realised that Peter Thomson and BBC Scotland had been put in their place. Yet now I find it difficult to find fault in this, other than in the second-hand manner by which I was informed. Professionally speaking, Wolstenholme was a network football commentator of the highest calibre, perhaps the best they ever had. I had never been involved in a live commentary before and I could well imagine 'Ginger' Cowgill's reaction to news that 'his' audience was being entrusted to a Scottish voice he had never heard within the BBC. After my original enthusiasm to do well, though, I was now quite inconsolable. Right up till then I had been reciting my broadcasting catechism with fond remembrance of the rule of verbal contraception, my head saturated with facts which I had passed on the night before to Wolstenholme, my voice like a greyhound in the trap ready to be let loose for a sprint to glory. I am sure great poets have had words for that particular agony of denial, of unconsummated desire. I simply felt knackered.

The game worked wonders. I forgot my own selfish introspection. Even when they were one down you could feel a Celtic victory in the air like the tangy aroma of a woodfire, unseen, but somewhere in the vicinity. I got cramp trying to see the game through this tiny space in front of me. At the same time I was listening to Wolstenholme steer his expert way through one of the great games of all time. How I envied him! So near yet so far. When the final whistle went he made his own buoyant comments and then turned, handed over the mike to me and shrugged his shoulders in a heavy, sleepy sort of movement, almost as if to say, 'What more can one add?'

I had only spoken twice so far during the game. One minute's worth of less than sparkling wisdom. Now with the ecstasy of victory in its first throes I tried to match the occasion. I was determined to make this sound like an oratorical masterpiece. Now when I listen to it, it sounds like a schoolboy shouting at his mates across the playground: slightly hysterical, the style and substance of little merit. I had added nothing to this momentous day other than a soprano-like postscript. There are few fates worse than falling into the role of token Scot.

What did not occur to me then is that the Celtic supporting councillors back home, my MP, and whole swathes of the population couldn't have cared less at that particular moment if Humpty Dumpty had done the commentary. Celtic had won.

The engineer who had helped us throughout the broadcast told me in a matter of fact way that London had been in touch and that they would now like to interview Jock Stein. I was to go down and bring him to the commentary position. I looked from our position half-way up the terracing onto the seething mass of invading supporters who now covered the pitch below. My God, I recall thinking. Where is he? I knew for a start that at that stage in our relationship Stein would not have given me an interview if we had been alone on a desert island together, but I had to make the effort. Down I went and joined the swirling mass of supporters who had engulfed players and management and the pitch resembled a Corryvreckan of jubilation with Stein in the middle trying to control the tide.

I got within about ten yards of him but there was no hope of getting nearer. On his face was not the slightest indication of triumph or satisfaction. Indeed he looked angry. He was trying to push supporters away with a ferocity that would have been the envy of a night-club bouncer. At one stage he attempted to prise Tommy Gemmell free from a group who looked as if they would suffocate the player. Gemmell looked on the point of exhaustion and even in the circumstances of spontaneous and understandable jubilation it seemed the Celtic supporters' enthusiasm was about to get out of hand. Stein continued to fight and push and struggle and get angrier. I recall him throwing one supporter off his feet with a mighty sweep of his arm.

The shirt was almost torn off my back and I knew as he managed to help his players fight free of the throng that my task was hopeless. I went back and reported this to London who did not take too kindly to failing to get the first British manager to win the European Cup for live interview. But as I tried to collect my senses in this curious mix of personal disillusionment and infectious celebration an English-speaking Portuguese liaison officer asked me if I wouldn't mind coming to the public address microphone to ask the crowd if they would please get off the pitch so the presentation of the trophy could proceed. It would help if the plea came from a Scottish voice. Why not?

It wasn't until I actually got to the cubicle I realised that I had as much chance of success with this as going into the 'Sarry Heid' of a Saturday evening to ask the clientele if they would mind giving up the bevvy and join the AA. I spoke. I shouted. I pleaded. And I enjoyed it I suppose because it was the longest period I had spent with a microphone all afternoon. But it was just another of my lost causes that day, for the Celtic supporters were now beatifying the pitch. It was theirs and would be for eternity. They were oblivious to all except the texture of Portuguese grass, which they embraced and dug up, pausing only momentarily to watch an exhausted Billy McNeill climb up to the presidential box to receive the European Cup.

Later, that same trophy, full of champagne, was presented to the teetotal Jock Stein in the dressing room and he raised it to his lips to drink, then decided against it. 'Why should I?' he said in a display of self-control that reminded everyone that a superb afternoon in Lisbon and his own acquisition of 'immortality' would be less important to him if he were to step out of character. This was emphasised later that night in the heart of Lisbon.

We went there to the UEFA banquet. Up the narrow winding hill in the centre of the city and into a restaurant that was packed and noisy and uncomfortable. It had been liberally gate-crashed by about half the Portuguese nation and the scene was chaotic as people fought for seats. Stein sat at the top table, not at all comfortably. He looked dour. There is little doubt he could be the life and soul of the party if he wanted to be. Nobody had a sharper wit. But he was essentially a man of anti-climax. On numerous occasions I was to see the incongruity of this almost sad demeanour in the middle of euphoria; tense, unable to unburden himself, smouldering, as if he could create victory yet not understand the language of it. That night, if you were to have come upon the scene and compared him to Helenio Herrera, the Inter manager, you might not have been able to discern who had triumphed that afternoon. The only difference was that whilst Herrera sat in deep contemplation and looked thoroughly morose (and no wonder) Stein was tense, fidgety and fit to burst.

I was sitting some distance from the top table in the middle of a raucous debate between Bill Shankly and some Dutch journalists who had never forgiven the 'Shanks' for some of the insulting things he had said about Ajax prior to a European game. 'You are nothing but a very big loud-mouth,' was one of the kinder comments being made to the Scot. As the UEFA officials tried to get some order to make speeches so the hubbub grew. The Inter players were sitting in abject dejection at a table just behind me, their sullenness as thick as the smoky atmosphere. But I thought I might get some sort of comment from Herrera so I got up and squeezed my way towards their table. I never reached it. As I passed by the table where most of the Celtic players were sitting I paused to congratulate Ronnie Simpson. I had only managed to say a few words when the massive figure descended and a hand gripped my shoulder. The very large hand indeed of Jock Stein.

'Don't talk to my players,' he barked at me, almost incoherent with rage.'You are only a guest here. You never talk to my players at the best of times so you're not talking to them now. Sit on your arse!'

Even at the height of this unique triumph he could not relax his vigilance towards the 'enemy'. Victory was no antidote to the old suspicions lingering constantly in his mind. Indeed, it seemed to have heightened them. The look of contempt on his face would have turned a bull-mastiff to jelly. He pushed his way back to the top table and in the general rowdiness of the restaurant I hoped that the confrontation hadn't been noticed. I now felt bitterly angry and realised that if I were to be much longer in broadcasting this would have to be resolved.

On that glorious day I felt like a complete alien within a celebrating family. They with their cup, me with my phenobarbitone.

5

Taking on Mr Stein

In 1969 Neil Armstrong bounced on to the moon with his well-rehearsed tribute to mankind's ability to look further than its navel. A new age of pushing back frontiers seemed to have dawned but the relationship between Celtic Football Club and BBC Scotland had, conversely, sunk into a primeval swamp. It was based on ignorance. We didn't really know each other and not an effort was being made to rectify this.

Peter Thomson, frankly, was terrified of Stein. I did not look upon him as an avuncular figure myself at that time and when I was in his presence I always put myself on red alert for sudden swoops. But the issue was avoided. In all the time I worked with him during the Stein era I cannot once recall Peter Thomson setting foot inside Celtic Park. I had always believed that this bizarre situation had to be sorted out at the top but I knew it would not be. Then, things changed. And it started with a man who wouldn't have known Celtic from Inverness Clachnacuddin if they had run on to a field together. He was Alasdair Milne, who had become Controller of BBC Scotland and was later to be Director General.

He offered me a job. I was now Peter's first substitute to introduce 'Sportsreel' on occasional Saturday evenings. I preferred this to commentary simply because it seemed so much easier and I was carrying the banner for the entire output. I was also still teaching and the accumulation of pressures to keep both ends up was taking its steady toll. Something had to give. Milne's offer of a full-time

job came as a relief therefore. It was when I stepped into the BBC
for my first full-time contractual position that I vowed, whatever
the cost inside the BBC, I would strike up new relationships with
the press and with the man who held us in almost continual
contempt.

When I commentated on my first Scottish Cup Final in 1969 I
realised that that task was not going to be simple and straightforward. It would have been an exacting commitment at the best
of times but I went to Hampden that day knowing that a major
row had broken with Celtic and, according to one of my colleagues
who had spoken to me the previous evening, Stein was 'looking
for blood!' At Hampden, when the teams arrived the procedure
was to go through the enclosure out on to the track and then up
the stairs to the dressing room area where you could approach
the managers for the team numbers. Without them, most of our
cameramen would have been shooting in the dark. For at an outside broadcast the quickest way for commentator, director and
cameraman to keep up with each other is for the director's secretary, if required, to shout numbers rather than names through the
headphones. 'Rangers 6. On to Celtic 8' and so on. The procedure
of 'getting the teams' was no academic exercise but of the utmost
importance. The quicker we had that information the better.

I had just missed Stein. He had had his brisk walk out on the
pitch as usual with the players and had gone inside to the dressing
room. A message was then passed out to us that we would not
receive any help from anybody with his club that day. No teams,
no numbers. In fact we did get them from another source in
time for kick-off which made the apparent petulance all the more
irrelevant. All managers, and that includes perhaps the greatest of
them, have the propensity both to enter a stadium like a gladiator
and also to behave, at the same time, like a spoiled child demanding
more pocket money. Stein's message was clear. He wanted nothing
to do with us.

What had incensed him was a review of that league season which
we had broadcast prior to the Cup final. Celtic had won the league
all right but in so doing they had also been beaten twice by Rangers
in the process. We had shown these games properly as part of the
summary of the season. Stein had been so enraged by seeing them

included that he had phoned immediately after the programme
from Seamill, unknown to me, claiming we had distorted events
and that some English people watching the programme in his
company at the hotel had concluded that Rangers, not Celtic, had
won the championship.

So he shunned us.

Celtic won that day in the very first couple of minutes when
Billy McNeill headed in a Bobby Lennox corner when he should
have been marked by Alex Ferguson. They won in a canter 4–0.
He told our stage manager, who tried to grab him on the track
immediately after the final whistle, where to stick an interview.
What he did do though was accept an invitation to talk straight
down the television line to *Grandstand*'s David Coleman. As he
waited to go on I was sitting in the television area in the enclosure
watching the television monitor replaying the first Celtic goal. I
saw a broad smile cross Stein's face and he said wryly to Coleman,
before the actual transmission, 'Macpherson sounded sick there.'
There were, it has to be said, people working with me in the BBC
who couldn't have cared less about this situation.

The wishful thinkers or the divine-right-of-Rangers-to-rule
brigade believed Stein was nothing more than a temporary
phenomenon anyway and that he would be put in his place before
long. I instinctively felt he was as temporary as a Californian Red-
wood. But here was Stein cultivating BBC London and by-passing
his own patch. He was rubbing it in to us. Sam Leitch, ex-*Daily
Mirror* and once Sportswriter of the Year, who was then working
for BBC London, warned me not long after that, 'I don't care
what your own views on the big man are. He goes over the top,
all right. But you know he came from the other side. He knows
what it's been like to look down on people. I come from King's
Park so I know what it's all about. He knows what goes on in some
Protestant minds up there. He's trying to change that whole scene.
But how can you get anywhere in this business if we know down
here in London he won't even talk to you! I know it's not your
particular responsibility but if nobody else is going to sort it out
then you'll have to do it yourself!'

Leitch was right to point up the practicalities. Celtic were going
over the barricades. Rangers were merely digging in behind them.

Celtic clearly had a man who embraced the future with clarity of vision, great self-confidence and ruthless ambition. Rangers were bogged down by their past and simply did not know how to react to this. Celtic had a manager whose personality would have emerged distinctly in a throng of celebrities. Rangers had Davie White, a decent little man of honest intent shrouded in anonymity. For BBC Scotland not to have access to Celtic in these circumstances would have been like a trader setting up in the market place with an empty stall. The objective was not to prove our altruism to Celtic. We were simply being thoroughly unprofessional in not trying to cope, even though there was a danger of some of my colleagues interpreting any move on our part as succumbing to naked intimidation.

Rangers themselves were aware that Stein was beginning to sway opinion within the media. But there was little they could do about it. Their efforts at reaching the minds of those communicators in the business were puerile by comparison. It was like comparing a faded hoarding on a derelict building to a sparkling television advert.

I had publicly supported the Davie White appointment when Rangers, albeit crudely, got rid of Scot Symon. At least they realised that Symon, even with Rangers at the top of the league at the time, did not fit the future. In retrospect it was the footballing equivalent of the dispatch of Margaret Thatcher to the back benches. When I interviewed that honourable little man Ian McMillan, of the deft touch, about this matter he launched a totally uncharacteristic attack on Symon, claiming he was not fit to lead a team in the modern game. He cited the lack of pre-match tactics in the European Cup semi-final against Eintracht in 1960, where Rangers lost twelve goals over the two ties, as the prime example. I bumped into Symon by accident three days later in a restaurant in Perth and he advanced on me ominously. 'If my wife had got hold of you on Saturday night,' he said, 'she would have torn the eyes out of your head.' And then he added, 'However, you are entitled to your opinion.'

He uttered the last statement with such dignity I thought I was going to weep. The mix of sudden guilt, justified or not, and the sight of the retreating, greying figure walking out of the restaurant reminded me suddenly of the essential transience of figures in the game, even those of the stature of a great Rangers manager whose time was so clearly up.

Davie White was swamped by circumstance. Against any other opponent he might have survived. I saw him with Stein once at a function at the BBC and you could see he was in awe of the other man. Perhaps he wasn't aware of it himself but he moved circumspectly in his presence. Stein, in a fit of sudden ecumenism that night but calculated, I believe, to be heard by some of the press, claimed that he would never go out of his way to 'savage' White if they were to appear in a television interview together. He wouldn't have, of course, but in that more public setting of television he nevertheless possessed the ability to put people away with a subtle wit that was quieter but more lethal than any overt display of aggression. There was never any doubt that White would not last long. He didn't. By the autumn of 1969 the press was obsessed with the question of who would lead Rangers' revival against Stein. This was something which both greatly amused and irked the Celtic manager. When we travelled to Hamburg for the West Germany–Scotland World Cup qualifying game around that time he was in the official Scottish party.

In the magnificently chandeliered Reichshof Hotel, with the heavily carpeted staircase down which the fräuleins of the Third Reich must have made grand entries, the speculation was not just about how Scotland could qualify for the World Cup finals in Mexico but also of how much longer White would last and of whether Stein was domestically unstoppable. Other questions were asked, like, 'What did your bill cost you last night?' In the company I was keeping, and to which I subscribed with little protest, passing an evening in the art galleries and museums of this Hanseatic League city was not a preferred nocturnal activity. We found ourselves pleasantly enough diverted by the proliferation of entertainment which flourished around the Reeperbahn and which can easily take the mind off such compelling subjects as whether Willi Schultz would be fit enough to play for West Germany or the likelihood of Scotland using the sweeper system. There were certain machismo obligations to attend to which lent one the proper credentials over and above the holding of a union card. I undertook then and there to be indented into the custom of ensuring that the evening before a game did not entail you turning into a hotel-room-bound Trappist monk, cramming yourself with largely irrelevant statistics.

On the other hand, lest some misinterpret this as an irrelevance or indeed irresponsibility, some of the best discussions I have had on football have taken place in rather dingy and bizarre settings in the middle of the night when the tongues have loosened and the jackets are off, metaphorically speaking. We got involved in such a one that night.

We had trawled, my senior companion and I, through some lurid places and had ended up wiser but poorer in a bierkeller of some relative respectability. In other words, the waitresses in this one wore clothes. It was there a kind of 'Stop Stein' conversation began at the centre of which was a journalist from the *Daily Express* called Willie Waddell. Two other prominent journalists, the SFA doctor and myself suddenly became embroiled in an argument about the decline of Rangers. The doctor, revealing an impassioned interest in Rangers, took it upon himself to turn the tide of the increasingly turbulent argument into a plea to Waddell to demand the Ibrox job. This was taken up with some surprising eagerness by the other journalists who looked at any moment as if they would go down on bended knee. Waddell himself was not only unmoved by all of this but quite vehement in his denial of any interest in the post. At the same time he heaped scorn on Rangers, almost as if they were beyond redemption.

This was hardly surprising since the club looked as if they were moving into a fantasy world in which things would work out well for them by natural law. What they needed of course was not only a new footballing brain but strength of character. That became clear to me in a personal way when Waddell, despite his protestations that night, became manager a few weeks later. I interviewed the Rangers chairman John Lawrence, who sat in the studio with me and pleasantly forgot the name of the manager he had just sacked.

'He was a very nice fellow, David . . . eh David . . . eh!'

'White!' I had to remind him.

Now they were going to get a spokesman of some considerable

strength. But that evening in Germany demonstrated to me that Old Firm politics preoccupied minds in a way which made Scottish international football pale into insignificance. We had hardly talked about Scotland's very important game. One way or the other it was Stein who was dominating everybody's mind, either negatively or positively.

The following morning there he was sitting in the lobby, the familiar black coat on, bristling with confidence. As I walked up to him he put on that by now familiar smile which told you something was about to come forth. 'I hear you were all trying to get *the job* for Waddell last night,' he said. In later years he was to use that same sarcasm when he admitted to me that Willie Allison, Rangers' PRO, had unofficially tapped him for *the job* when he was still with Celtic. It may even have happened around the time we were in Hamburg.

What surprised me was that between the wee sma' hours discussion and breakfast time he had learned about it. Had he been hiding in the shadows, furtively taking notes? No, he had not. He was demonstrating, as he would so often do, that he had a network of informants which the CIA would have envied. He seemed not at all perturbed though, just highly amused.

'You're all worried men,' he added, the smile becoming more taunting. 'And you're all trying to get the other wee man the sack. What kind of people are you, eh?'

His defence of White was not all that surprising for he had been angered by Waddell himself after he had written an attack on the Rangers' manager under the heading 'The Boy David' which had amounted to a journalistic slaughter. Stein had expressed his views to the press in no uncertain manner. He no doubt did have a certain amount of genuine sympathy for White. But this display of displeasure was also an indication of Stein's burgeoning self-confidence and of an ability to command an audience on issues which did not have a direct bearing on Celtic Football Club. It was also, of course, true that White's remaining at Ibrox was unlikely to give him an ulcer.

The conversation didn't last long although I tried to engage him on the subject of his apparent paranoia about the BBC in Scotland. He exercised his apparent prerogative, ending a conversation whenever he wanted and rising to walk off as if it had never started in the first place.

That night in the vast openness of the stadium in Hamburg I broadcast live on TV for the first time from abroad. Scotland, drawing 2–2 with under half-an-hour to go, lost 3–2; 'Stan' Libuda ripping Scotland apart, Tommy Gemmell almost ripping Helmut Haller apart and being sent off. I felt more like a member of the travellers' club after that trip. I was anxious to be seen as a member of the travelling corps now that I had joined the BBC, for there was decided hostility directed towards the broadcaster from at least certain members of the press.

Television was still feeling its way forward in football coverage. If football clubs were suspicious, newspapers persistently clobbered us for having the potential to kill off football. So, some of the older members of the Fourth Estate were delighted by the war of attrition taking place between Stein and myself. On that trip, and others, I learned to identify the professional gloater, someone smirking in the background or nodding assent as Stein waded in and I tried to counter. Sycophancy in the reign of terror was rife. It was imperative to come to terms with Stein without being seen to be enslaved, as some clearly were. I knew that he would virtually dictate the copy that certain writers put out. In a way it was a tribute to the man's immensely powerful presence that in such a relatively short space of time he had almost all of the media by the short and curlies. If you wanted your share of the goodies from him you had to play ball. He, of course, had a lot to offer. If you missed out you were obviously in trouble.

When I returned from Hamburg I told Peter Thomson that I was going to Celtic Park to have it out with the manager. 'No way!' he said. 'I wouldn't approve of that. We'll bide our time. He'll need us before we need him.'

That was all very well to state within the confines of a BBC office but for the outrider like myself, who was being ambushed every now and again, it was scant comfort. I had got on well with Peter initially but I realised I couldn't accept this philosophy. He was my mentor and on this issue, which he regarded as vital, I could hardly be seen to be out of step. At the same time, I knew this wouldn't last.

Stein actually tried to stop me from travelling on the official team plane to the quarter-final of the European Cup against Fiorentina in 1970 but was over-ruled by the chairman, Bob Kelly. He was, however, far too contented to bother about any particular individual joining the party to Milan for the final itself in the merry month of May. In truth, I believe he, and the rest of the Celtic players for that matter, thought they had actually won the Cup by beating Leeds in the famous game at Hampden Park in the semi-final.

We stayed in Varese in a hotel on top of a hill and hardly ever during our stay there would you have thought that Celtic were approaching a European Cup final. In Lisbon I saw the manager pounce on a player sitting in the Palacio Hotel in Estoril simply because he had his head exposed to the sun coming through the window. And that was his reserve goalkeeper! In this sumptuous hotel north of Milan there were times when you might have deduced the players were on an end of season jaunt. Nobody at the time queried Celtic's approach to any great degree. It certainly raised some eyebrows to see the manager allowing the players' representative to hold meetings with them and strike deals there and then in the hotel. Stein himself seemed to have unburdened a great deal of the tension he normally stored up on these occasions. The exception was the night before the game when he strode into the large foyer, saw me sitting with Hugh McIlvanney of the *Observer* and thought he would have some banter.

'How are Feyenoord going to play in midfield?' he asked me abruptly. I had been caught cold.

'If you tell me how you're going to play it, I'll tell you their plan,' I said, trying feebly to appeal to his sense of humour.

I might as well have kicked him in the groin.

'You mean to say that you've come all this way and you don't know Feyenoord's midfield . . .'

'I know their names,' I pled. 'But how they'll play it . . .'

'You should be up all night thinking about this game,' he barked and looked around for sympathy which, of course, he got. 'I'll kick every ball tonight. I'll go through it over and over again. I can see everybody's face, I can see their build, I can see the way they run. You should be the same, thinking it out, all the possibilities.'

This was more like him – impassioned and part brutal with a languishing audience. It was as if he had come out of a dream. Perhaps the sight of the men who were going to be writing or commenting on him on the morrow had summoned up his Lisbon self. In that identity he spent every second immersed in trying to arrange the future, and anguished by the fact that not even he could guarantee that.

They lost. People have become very clever about this game and have laid the blame largely on Stein for misreading Feyenoord. He certainly underrated them and every player I have talked to from that team would admit it. On the other hand hardly anybody says that Feyenoord were quite simply the better side. They were technically far superior and in Ove Kindvall they had one of the most exciting traditional centre-forwards in the game, the sort of player Jock Stein loved. Of all the famous Argentinians in their World Cup winning team in 1978 the attacker, Luque, appealed to him most of all. Kindvall scored the winner a few minutes from the end of extra-time.

Perhaps Lisbon had been burning far too brightly in people's minds. This setting under floodlights in a gaunt bowl of a place seemed inappropriate to Celtic. They had procured an identity of triumph associated uniquely with blue skies, sweat, brilliantly green grass, trees and the sun gleaming off a trophy. This wet, drab night in northern, industrial Italy, however reminiscent of Glasgow, felt quite alien to me. I am sure it was for everyone associated with the club. Perhaps their memories helped beat them even before they started.

I got back to the hotel before the rest of the media by chance in picking up a convenient taxi. Frankly the last man I wanted to see that night was Stein. And yet there he was sitting in the foyer in his favourite position, in a large chair in the corner so that he could see everything that moved. Jim Steele, the physiotherapist, was with him. The players had vanished. The hotel was like a morgue. I went straight up to him.

'I'm sorry about that,' I said. What, after all, do you say in these circumstances?

'They were a better team than us,' he said softly, his face drawn and tired. 'Look at their support too. They outnumbered us. The

Dutch have got more money than us. They can afford to travel to a place like this. How did the broadcast go, by the way? Would you like a drink of champagne? There are bottles of the stuff over there. Help yourself.'

From defeat came the first sympathetic conversation I had had with him. It was not the occasion to exploit it or expand it any further. I would have been very wrong to read too much into it in any case.

In the following season Celtic played Rangers in the Scottish Cup final. In the game on the Saturday Derek Johnstone scored the equaliser for Rangers to make it 1–1 with only seconds remaining. It went to a replay where Jimmy Johnstone was outstanding and Celtic won 2–1. I was there to do the interviews. Weeks earlier Celtic had played Aberdeen in an important league game at Pittodrie. I had invited in some people to watch it in the studios at Queen Margaret Drive. That match ended in a 1–1 draw. The audience watching with me that afternoon were of mixed persuasion. Inevitably, when Aberdeen scored there was a positive reaction from those present who did not go to Celtic Park regularly. By the time the Cup final had come around I had forgotten about that game and that audience. Others hadn't.

When I approached the Celtic dressing room door at Hampden not long after the final whistle on the Wednesday night I could hear the natural sounds of jubilation from within. I had to bang on it for anybody to hear. The door was opened and there, just inside, was Stein, naked but for a towel wrapped round him. He wasn't smiling.

'Could you come out for interview?' I asked.

'Well, well, well. Look who it is,' he said cheerily enough. Then added, withdrawing the smile quickly, 'You know what you lot are? A bunch of bigots! I heard about it all. All of you standing up there at the studios cheering when Aberdeen scored against us at Pittodrie. You're nothin' but a bloody bunch of bigots!'

The door was slammed in my face. He had just won the Cup but he had stored up this wrath and not even in the moment of triumph was he going to stifle it. It fair took the breath away, largely because, as I was walking away from the dressing room, I was still trying to work out what he was talking about. It wasn't until I had got back on to the running track beside the camera that I remembered the occasion and realised that the spy network had been in operation. He had accepted a highly selective interpretation of events, probably because it accorded with the general anti-Celtic conspiracy theory. I knew this state of affairs could go on no longer.

Two days later I went to Parkhead. I didn't tell Peter Thomson nor did I tell Stein in advance but presented myself at the front door and asked to see him. He was out with some of the younger players and came back in and was surprised to see me sitting waiting for him in the hall when he came back. We went into the boardroom and he stood in his mud-caked black tracksuit with his back to the main road, a photograph of John F Kennedy just over his right shoulder. I can't remember exactly what I was doing when Kennedy was assassinated, as many can, but I will always remember the day he looked down on two Protestants about to confront one another about the running sore of sectarianism.

It's not that I rushed at him, for frankly, to use W C Fields' phrase, I would rather have been in Philadelphia. The conversation wasn't a long one. I kicked it off by saying that he had got us wrong and that we were no worse or better than anybody else he had to deal with and that, in any case, he listened to too much gossip about us. I put it to him that he would be as well speaking his mind about me and the BBC here and now, so that I could answer any allegations or criticisms.

'Where's your boss?' he asked.

'I've taken it on myself to talk to you,' I answered.

'He's the man who employs you all,' he said. 'He doesn't employ many Celtic supporters, does he?'

'You mean Catholics, don't you?'

'All right, Catholics? How many have you got up there?'

It's not that he wanted numbers. It was a point he was making. I gave him the stock answer.

'I don't know anybody's religion,' I said. That was a mistake.

He laughed in disbelief and I remember he turned away and waved at me dismissively.

'All right,' I added. 'I suppose none. At a guess!'

'It would be a good guess,' he said, laughing now, and I felt a thawing. 'Look,' he said and straightened up and put both hands out like a man about to accept a hank of wool for unfolding. It was a posture I saw him adopt on countless occasions. It always prefaced a fit of real candour and not some of the feigned and controlled outbursts of which, I believe, he was the master.

'You know as well as I do how this club has been treated in the past. Are you really going to tell me it has had a square deal in the press compared to the other lot? Some of them come in here and butter me up and I just have to take it, but all they're doing is patronising Celtic. How many of you really genuinely mean it when you wish us good luck?'

He didn't wait for an answer.

'Very few. What you do is your own business but you want to get away from some of the old-fashioned habits.'

What followed I can recall so well I can virtually hear the little puffs of breath in between.

'You're starting out. If you've got any sense you'll see this is where the real action is going to be. We're going to be in Europe for a long time to come. You've got to get your feet in this club and not treat it like it was inferior or else you're going to be left behind. We've all got to forget the old boyhood stuff. That's for your own sake I say that. Times have changed. If you want to come to any training session at Celtic Park at any time give me a ring in advance. Now, I'm away to have a shower.'

And with that he pushed himself away from the wall and made for the door with a slight limp, breaking into song as he did so. I heard him singing Sinatra's 'Strangers in the Night' at the top of his voice in the dressing room as I made my way out.

It was hardly a great leap forward for mankind but at least he and I now seem to have recognised that we dwelt on the same planet.

6

One Disaster after Another

Those of us who experienced the times of Stein, and particularly the early years, must have come as near as anyone could to experiencing the power of the absolutist reign of the Sun King, Louis XIV at Versailles in the 17th century. To become a courtier at Parkhead and enjoy Stein's patronage bestowed on you the sort of privileges enjoyed by the fawning aristocracy of those distant times and with it the feeling of attributed power. Rejection by him also carried the distant fear that your very professional life would not be worth a damn.

Rangers were painfully aware of his dominance but could do nothing about it. They had re-introduced Waddell to Ibrox but that entailed not just some flag-flying and the installation of a spiritual leader but also having to beat Stein on the park. That was proving to be the hard bit. There was still this stubborn assumption amongst the Ibrox loyalists that the deity would see the Protestants through to a rightful ascendancy in the end. To listen to the average Rangers supporter then, when Stein seemed invincible, was like hearing the forlorn plea of a Palestinian for his rights to a homeland.

By this time I had begun to feel a growing adherence to the BBC and often found the company at Queen Margaret Drive sophisticated and stimulating. I should record, though, that all of us in our different ways were driven daily by harshly practical considerations. In my case, I was advised to concentrate my energies on Rangers and Celtic. As the newcomer I tried to resist this and to broaden our focus. Peter riposted that a Saturday night audience wanted the Old Firm as the staple diet and get them they would. The audience figures were his legions in support of his view and anybody who disagreed was a smart arse who really ought to be off doing documentaries on 'Weaving Traditions in the Borders' and subjects like that. Peter, of course, was entirely right. I was too callow to realise that a programme enjoying popularity was also fulfilling a public service.

It was an imbalanced scene I was surveying at the beginning of the Seventies. Celtic were far out in front of Rangers. Stein was looking back contemptuously over his shoulder at them. But then came a period of eighteen months which changed the course of the Ibrox club's history and into which I was sucked willy-nilly as a broadcaster. It produced traumas that are beyond repair. The events began on a chilly winter's afternoon when, presciently, Glasgow was wearing a sombre mask.

We were in the ground floor studio listening to the sound commentary when we heard the news that Celtic had scored in the last minute against Rangers at Ibrox, to go one up. At the height of the Stein era there was nothing terribly surprising in that except that on this occasion they had left it later than we had assumed they would. I walked out of the studio to prepare my script for the late afternoon television programme which was Scotland's fifteen minute contribution to *Grandstand*. I was mentally composing a headline of sorts as I paced slowly out of the ground floor with a piece of paper and a pen in my hand. I had barely got to the end of the corridor, literally a few yards, when I heard a yell which, within the natural calm of a quiet BBC building partially deserted on this public holiday, almost stopped the heart. Peter Thomson came racing out of the studio, bouncing up and down.

'You're never going to believe it,' he shouted. 'Rangers have equalised! Colin Stein!' and rushed past me. I tore up my thoughts and immediately imagined that in the press box at Ibrox there would have been a massive journalistic double-take like mine. Copy would now be in the process of a total re-write.

We had a late afternoon programme to do and we had to go about it as if the pulses were unaffected, hoping we could appear to be calm and self-possessed. We went through our programme and thought we had smoothed out the news crisply and unsensationally, although two goals in the last minute of an Old Firm game is what you dream about for headlines. You gloat over it as if you yourself had created the news in the first place. We felt quite pleased with ourselves. Indeed, we thought that it was going to be a smooth day and we looked forward to later that night when we would celebrate the New Year with a few drams.

But the year was 1971 and the day was 2 January.

I can't precisely recall at what particular time we heard about deaths. It was about five fifteen. Frank Bough, with a slight look of puzzlement on his face, near the end of *Grandstand*, simply said, 'I believe that twenty-two people have died in an incident at Ibrox.' We stopped talking and writing and could not take this in. First came the inaction of bewilderment, the walking around bumping into people who were also unwilling to accept this as fact. Then came the rush to phones to call God-knows-who. It was the pretence of purpose. The information we were getting was sketchy but before Bough went off the air he did chillingly allude to the fact that the casualty figure might be much worse.

It was decided the best thing to do was for me to take a taxi and get to Ibrox to find out at first hand. We were unable to make contact with our radio or television people for reasons which became clearer later on. The stadium loomed up, a spectral hulk in the chilling mist. There was an eerie calm near the front entrance. Stein was just stepping out when I got there and I recall a journalist asking him if he had any comment to make about the game.

'In the name of God,' he said. 'This is no time to be talking about football. There are far more important things to think about now.'

Inside I had a glimpse of Willie Waddell hurtling up the marble staircase, his face tight and mute with incomprehension. The scene under the stand was one of bizarre tidiness with a neat linear arrangement of dead bodies where one had, I suppose, expected to find chaos. A man asked me if I had a fag. I don't know who he was. Relative, supporter, first-aid man?

'It's no' real, is it?' he said in bewilderment.

In truth, it wasn't. I knew I was refusing to accept this and that

I was actually making an effort to be solemn and grave at the same time, like an interloper on a family tragedy. The reality came more easily from the mouths of others.

'Sixty-six confirmed dead' the police inspector told me.

I returned to Queen Margaret Drive with these appalling statistics to be confronted by a Corporation which didn't quite know what to do. Risk at a football match consisted perhaps of getting a toe trod on, or pneumonia in bad weather, or somebody peeing down your leg. But sixty-six dead seemed to belong in the environment of the airport, or the mine, or the tanker at sea. And therein lay the reason for our confusion in the sports area. We could not duck out and simply leave it to our news colleagues, who by now had set their professional ball rolling.

News departments, both in London and Glasgow, were incensed that there were no pictures available. This might seem ludicrous when you consider that the BBC had a full outside broadcast unit in the stadium which had covered the game that afternoon. This was the festive season, though, and they had packed up and gone with more than the usual speed, not knowing of a single death. Indeed some members of the crew who were only a couple of hundred yards away from where it happened knew nothing about it until much later that night. The accident occurred on the terracing steps in the north-east corner right at the end of the game and it took many minutes for the news of what was happening to filter back across to the other side of the stadium. By the time that had happened the cameras had departed. It was understandable.

But to the disaster experts in television news departments nothing is understandable if there is no access to pictures when cameras are in the vicinity. So, the fur was flying without there being any legitimate reason for it. 'You bloody people can't do anything right, can you?' a broad anonymous London voice said on the phone to me from their news department. 'We're sending people up right away!'

I little cared about that information. But I did care about our response. Senior BBC executives together with the News Editor and Peter Thomson met with me three hours before we were due to go on the air. I kicked off the discussion by suggesting that we drop the programme altogether and put on something in its stead. This, admittedly, was going to prove difficult. There was no immediate package to replace it and we did not want simply to put on an English sports programme. We were stricken by uncertainty. I stuck to my line, though, that we could not put out the programme. The opposition to that view was beginning to grow and it was noticeable that Peter, my editor, was taking no part in the discussion at all, but leaving me to make the running. I knew I was heading for trouble.

The senior BBC executives were among the most charming men I ever met within the Corporation but there was a decided edge to our conversation that night. They were in effect telling me that I was too closely bound up with the tragedy to make any objective judgement and that we had to remain dispassionate. For my part, I was beginning to think that this distancing from the event was producing not good judgement, but insensitivity.

'How many people were at the match?' I was asked.

'Eighty thousand or thereabouts,' I replied.

'Sixty-six dead out of eighty thousand isn't all that many really!' came the retort.

To this day I have preferred to allow that remark to be shrouded in anonymity for I do think that we owed it to each other to admit afterwards that we had become, by different routes, emotionally unstable. I was livid.

'If they had been miners, or people come down with an airliner, you would have been moving heaven and earth to have the whole schedules altered and outside-broadcasts brought in. But because they are just football supporters sixty-six out of eighty thousand isn't all that many!'

The argument then descended into a slanging match for a few moments until Bob Coulter, the Controller of BBC Scotland, admonished us with a patrician, 'Come, come! From now on I'll do the talking. We'll put a programme on the air. But what's going to be in it?'

They compromised. The Old Firm game of January 1971 has, to this day, never been seen on television. We broadcast highlights of the English 'Match of the Day' and I interviewed the Lord Provost, Sir Donald Liddell and Sir James Robertson, the Chief

Superintendent of Police. It is the only programme I have ever wanted to avoid. We were weeping before we went on and during the programme Donald Liddell's tears flowed constantly. This made it difficult for me to control myself. I had to keep nipping my thigh hard to keep some semblance of order in what I was doing, and doing with the deepest reluctance. Nobody else in the BBC had seen the bodies. That had made its deep impact on me. I had, after all, been too affected by that sight for me to make objective judgements.

But of course in the final analysis that did not matter. They were right to put on a programme of sorts. They were right to reflect something of the grief. They were right to remain, in their own context, as clinical as the surgeons who at that very moment were operating on some of the survivors. Later that night, though, while trying to ward off nightmares, I recognised that I had probably done myself no good by speaking up so vigorously. I also knew that it was the end for Peter Thomson, who had contributed nothing to the debate in the office but had been quite overwhelmed by the event.

Waddell wasn't. On the Monday we doorstepped him. Journalists from around the world had arrived to put Ibrox under siege, waiting for the first statements. BBC London had indeed sent their own men. John Simpson, who has more recently distinguished himself with his war reports from Baghdad, was on one of his first broadcasting assignments. He asked me if I would point out Willie Waddell when the time came. There has been repeated criticism through the years of BBC London muscling in on events which occur in Scotland which could be covered by local correspondents. This seemed a perfect instance of this.

However, experience has taught me that one of the most important corner stones of creating even news programmes is building up identity and authority. You establish your own men or women and you persist with them on the basis of their own expertise. Being English and not knowing who Waddell was by sight was much less important than knowing what to ask and how. In the scramble to get hold of Waddell, as he came out to face the world for the first time that freezing cold morning, Simpson was to the forefront, barking his questions well above the cacophony of noise that erupted on the front steps of the main entrance at Ibrox Stadium.

Throughout the entire year to come Waddell was to face up to horrendous problems and managed to maintain a rugged indomitable dignity which held the club together. There was nobody on the Ibrox board to match him as the world seemed to fall in upon the club. Its board consisted of very successful Glasgow businessmen from the 'Wee Arra Peepul' school of thought and suffered the consequent myopia and inarticulacy which rendered them quite unsuitable to face up to all of this. Joe Beattie, the police superintendent put in charge of the original investigation, went straight to Ibrox on the night of the disaster and recalled to me how one Rangers director had greeted him in the boardroom like a long lost friend. The man then regaled the company, to some merriment, with amusing stories of how they had played football together at Ashfield and of how they weren't really up to scratch and what a great time was had by all in the good old days. Beattie remembers thinking immediately that the reality of sixty-six bodies lying just under their feet on the running track had still not seeped into the boardroom. On the other hand, it might have been said that it was a night when many rational people trying to come to terms with the disaster were turned into headless chickens.

Waddell, however, faced the world full square and the directors lined up eagerly behind him. From his obsessive drive to create order out of what, at least initially, appeared to be chaos emerged the character who was eventually to rule Ibrox with a rod of iron. Cometh the hour, as they say. His every interview carried strength and understanding. It was extremely difficult to try to make anything of football for a long, long time. The first commentary I did at Ibrox afterwards was like watching a silent movie.

Life had to go on, however, and Waddell could not shake off Stein. The Celtic manager was at the height of his powers, coaxing, cajoling, bullying, exhorting and able to give his club the momentum of a runaway train. Derailments occasionally happened but he was good at repairs. He was also seeing Rangers off, despite Waddell moving to Ibrox. We must never underrate Stein's passionate desire to do so. He would, from time to time, say that the Old Firm needed each other. But that particular sentiment rings of sanctimony. It implies that the football parish for them is extremely limited.

In reality, Stein's vision was limitless. He could not have survived without his excursions to Europe. It meant freedom to him. It meant throwing off the shackles of traditional values and joining a commune of the élite to which he felt he rightly belonged. For, although he had the gently expressed touch of the common man at crucial times, he most certainly enjoyed being part of the aristocracy of achievers. He didn't need Rangers for that.

About then he gave an interview to Arthur Montford of STV in which he expressed the view that footballing success came in cycles and that 'Rangers' turn will come again'. This implied that nature took a hand in these things. Stein would have allowed nature no such wanton liberty. He was to Rangers' existence what an avalanche would be to a Swiss hamlet. He wanted to bury them.

Waddell led the club out of the despair which followed the accident on Stairway 13 simply to face the comparatively trivial, but nonetheless endemic depression felt by the large community of Rangers supporters. They were beginning to suffer Celtic's success as a chronic ailment, akin to colitis. Any cure offered only temporary remission before the agony returned all over again. The effect was especially severe for those who had grown up with Struth and Symon, believing that bloodstock would lend the species supremacy.

Accordingly, it was not simply a European Cup Winner's Cup final they all sallied forth to in Barcelona the following year but an occasion in which they might rid themselves of this pervasive influence back in Glasgow. To many Rangers supporters the final in Spain could be seen as an exorcism.

We made our plans to cover this game thinking that, having now taken on board two European finals, everything would fall into place easily. Of course it didn't. To our utter astonishment we could not work out an agreement to broadcast the match live. It was to be shown as a 'deferred relay'. That is, transmitted in its entirety but only immediately after the final whistle. It seems odd now that such a situation could have been tolerated but we travelled to Barcelona with a sense of anti-climax, for as broadcasters our natural habitat for such an event is in the 'live' zone.

We went in advance of the official Rangers party to make a film for showing immediately prior to the broadcast. Anybody listening to radio would have found it odd for us to be previewing the match on television whilst it was actually being played. It was the first time I had been involved in filming in any depth, although it was eventually to become my stock-in-trade. I took a liking to it there and then and I suppose I have to thank Barcelona for that.

Film-makers could set up permanent base around the grand harbour, where there is an atmosphere of constant wheeling and dealing between sea and land. You fear that moving away from the fat, squatting ships and the constant hubbub around the ferries might provide an anti-climax. But it does not. Just across the road from the Med is the Ramblas. This broad avenue mixes the tranquillity of its tree-covered spine with the sheer fanaticism of its traffic and invites comparison with the stark contrast set at the corrida where genteel ladies sit courteously and watch the gorings in the ring. It runs to the heart of the city but, most importantly, its congested and narrow side streets are filled with enough attractions and temptations. There is a constant sense of menace and impropriety. Which is why we took the camera in.

The night we moved off the beaten track, the American navy had done the same. An aircraft carrier had berthed in the harbour and the entire strike force of the Fourth fleet, or whatever, seemed to be on shore leave. They were pointing their missiles in other directions that evening with the consequence that their truculent dealings with the ladies in the doorways would not have endeared them to the Daughters of the American Revolution. They certainly were not behaving as Gene Kelly did in *Anchors Aweigh*. Two sailors who got completely out of hand were brusquely separated from the others by a couple of burly Guardia Civil. Arms up their backs, they were bundled down a tiny little alley and the last I saw of them batons were striking them about the head. I had always understood that the American Shore Patrol was the only body allowed to handle these guardians of democracy but the Spanish police that night were not waiting for diplomatic notes to be interchanged before meting out summary justice.

In all of this we should have seen something, a portent, a clue. The booze, the haphazard nature of the city, the atavistic nature of the police, the somnolent heat; all of these ought to have hinted at a possible confrontation for the lads from Larkhall, Dunipace and other parts who might not make the right kind of cultural adjustments. It's easy enough to say that now, yet even in hindsight our innocence of the potential for disaster looks unhealthily close to stupidity. We went into Los Caracoles restaurant for a filming conference. A good restaurant is one of the most effective settings for beating down differences of opinion amongst a film crew. If you can get the cameramen drunk, all the better, for the following day they cannot remember what it is they have agreed to do for you. 'But I swear you did say you would go on the top of the crane and swing down to the water level on the harness and get a close up of the propeller of the ferry going out! Didn't he, lads?' Sometimes it worked.

This restaurant is now a kind of tourist trap but then it was a genuine cathedral of Catalan cooking. You walk through the kitchen to get to your table in one of the tiny alcoves which honeycomb this magnificent old building. The famous original owner Boffuril, now deceased, was sitting there in all his resplendent corpulence, breathing heavily and also shouting out the orders to the chefs through his microphone. It was as noisy inside as it was out. It was while sitting there, wolfing down the sucking-pig, that my producer John Coleman said to me of the city, 'The Rangers supporters will have a ball here.' That must now go down as one of the finest examples of dramatic irony since the about to be assassinated King Duncan in Macbeth uttered, 'This castle hath a pleasant seat'.

A few days later Rangers arrived. They were staying in the Don Jaime hotel, half an hour's drive from the stadium, on a hilltop in Castelldefels. The receptionist proudly told us that the film actor, George Sanders, had committed suicide in one of their rooms a few weeks before. She made it sound as if the Spanish Tourist Board had sponsored it. Still, everything was promising. The hotel looked directly into the eyes of the sea, the players had that right mix of taut expectancy and almost insolent disregard for the perilous situation they were in. They had won nothing that season and were now following in the European footsteps of Celtic. The weather was idyllic, the mosquitoes seemed only to bite the bad guys in the media and we also heard that the Russians had injuries and were worried. No European tie would be legitimate without such rumours but we set off anyway, two days before the game, to watch Moscow Dynamo train.

We weren't allowed in. Not at first anyway, for it is the prime rule of filming never to give up. The tiny Spaniards manning the gate explained that it was under instructions from 'them'. They pointed at two large figures in tracksuits standing on the edge of the track. These were the days when no Russian side left their country without a heavy escort from the KGB. They bulged with heavily-armoured arrogance. If a smile ever broke over their faces when they were on duty you could only think they were looking over your shoulder at something which amused them, like a lorry running down a blind child. We bribed one of the Spaniards with enough pesetas to buy him a smallholding in Majorca and he let us slip through another gate on the understanding that we would not take in the camera.

In fact the cameraman slipped an overcoat over his arm, covering the camera which he jammed under his armpit and held tightly with his right hand. Since we were not requiring sound the idea was to start rolling it mute with the lens poked through one of the sleeves. Overcoats in Barcelona in May are usually food for moths in attics so I felt we might just as well have put up a placard reading 'We have a camera hidden under here!' Nonetheless, we filmed the Russians for posterity employing the method James Bond would have used to reveal a Scud missile site outside Omsk. The fact of the matter is that there was nothing of any importance to record. Training sessions are normally of unremitting boredom and all of them bear a sameness that can be very deceiving, as I was later to find out more dramatically in Argentina. What I did notice was that the players were downbeat. Russian sportsmen and women can look inordinately dour at times but I detected something more than that, a lack of sympathy with this setting they now found themselves in. They knew they would be playing with hardly any support in the stadium in front of an antagonistic crowd who simply refused to think that Rangers could be beaten. Moscow Dynamo looked as if their souls had refused to come west with them.

One Disaster after Another

We arrived for the game early on a pleasant summer's evening and, to our astonishment, discovered the pitch was already covered by Rangers supporters. They were still trying to get used to the strange fact that one of the greatest stadiums in the whole of Europe scarcely had a security system. Getting onto the pitch was probably easier here than on Glasgow Green.

That might well have preoccupied us if we had not discovered that our commentary position in this huge bowl which towered above us was in fact only three rows away from the pitch side and amongst the supporters. They were already drinking. This was not a surprising fact given that a bottle of the hard stuff cost them no more than a postage stamp would back home. Those on the pitch were slowly ushered back by the police in a manner which now bears some special consideration for it was going to turn out to be a key element in the events which followed.

The police were all tiny men by comparison with the Glasgow 'polis'. If you can imagine your average Spanish welterweight and put a uniform on him you might get the picture. But they were sturdy and dapper with gun-holsters blistering their hips and truncheons rigidly appended to them like spare walking-sticks. But at that moment they struck a false posture of geniality which utterly deceived everybody including the Rangers supporters, who must have been convinced that they were a soft touch. It was at this extremely early hour, before the floodlights were required and the players walked onto the pitch, things went seriously wrong. We had not allowed, none of us, for the fact that Franco's police had one method for all circumstances, suppression. At that stage, though, they looked no more than park wardens ushering children from a flower-bed.

The game went well for Rangers. The Russians played, not surprisingly, as if the whole occasion was too much for them. They had come emotionally neutral to a setting which required passion. It was a case of surly technicians versus a tribe on the warpath. The tribe was three up before their legs began to wobble. Then, the Russians' greater fitness and athleticism took its toll on a Rangers defence which seemed about to draw its last breath and conceded two goals.

With twenty minutes to go and the crowd around us in turmoil

71

a Rangers supporter with a bottle of Fundador came and sat on my knee. My producer tried to extricate him but it was no easy matter. He was trying to pour me a drink, which was decent of him, but I was still chuntering on. The drink was slopping out of the bottle all over the pair of us and soon I was beginning to reek like a distillery. Colleague Bill Malcolm, who was attempting to do his own job, was now standing and had the man round the neck to drag him away.

He never fully left us for the rest of the game and the tumbler of brandy was still occasionally pushed under my face. From then until full-time events were interpreted by me with one eye on the field and another on the invitation to oblivion. The Rangers supporters, particularly those on the opposite side of the stadium from us, had invaded the field after the second and third goals and just before the end of the game, when they mistook a referee's decision for the final whistle. The police stood by and ignored all. This, coming on top of their casual initial approach to the night, seemed now to have completed their offer of *carte blanche* to the Scots. The fans were determined to out-Lisbon Celtic with their pitch celebrations. When the game ended 3–2, with Rangers near total exhaustion, the character of the evening suddenly changed.

The following events are not at all blurred by the passing of time. What occurred was so out of kilter with the benign preamble to the evening and the impassivity of the police, which made their presence almost superfluous, that it stamped itself clearly on the mind. Nor did it take you by surprise with its speed. The character of the Barcelona riot, as it then became tagged, unfolded itself in a slow, avoidable, almost choreographed way. From the ringside seat we had, you could not make too many mistakes about what you saw and heard.

A few minutes after the end of the match, the crowd, in a considerable frenzy, had advanced right across the pitch to the main stand where they waited for the Cup presentation. At that stage it was not much different from Lisbon. But the ceremony which in fact was supposed to be at pitch level couldn't take place because of the congestion around the touchline. The police had by then merely retreated until they were standing, their backs to us in the stand, within touching distance. It would not have taken too much re-organising to have brought the Rangers captain to the middle of the stand and presented the cup there. Instead, they waited for some time for calm and order, which they were not going to get, and then ushered him down the steep steps of the tunnel which led to the dressing rooms for the first ever subterranean presentation of a football trophy.

The crowd, having come all this way, still felt entitled to public acclamation of the triumph. The authorities tried to cap the gusher. If the supporters had simply been allowed then to protest vocally, or carouse on the pitch, Barcelona would have been forgotten by the following week. Disastrously, the police decided to act.

It started slowly with the thin line of light brown uniforms pressing against the crowd, their batons held with both hands in front of them, like drum majors in a slow march. The crowd ebbed and flowed a little under this pressure without retreating any considerable distance. It was stale-mate. So it should have remained. We were still actively recording and I was involved in commentating on this although viewers back home had not yet seen even the start of the game. I was becoming conscious of an agitation right in front of us. There, a martinet of a Spanish policeman, of some rank, was barking at his men. I remember him raising his arm and giving a signal that was a bit like one-handed tic-tac, a magician's sleight of wrist wiggle.

It was not as if it all happened then in unison. The action was on cue but some were faster than others. It was ragged to start with and I saw a baton flailing just to my right. It seemed to strike a supporter on the shoulder and I have this image of him dropping to his knee and suddenly cowering. Then it became like a threshing machine as the whirl of batons advanced on a crowd whose front rank could not escape this onslaught because of the pressure of those at the back. They couldn't see the touchline, did not know what was happening and weren't budging.

In this jam a terrible price was being paid by those at the front. The batons were slashing recklessly and supporters who had stumbled just in front of me were being openly kicked. I saw two of the police taking turns hitting a man on the ground. I recall how one of them was using the backhand technique in an almost nonchalant way like a Wimbledon player in a casual warm-up.

By this time, the Rangers supporters were in full flight back across the pitch, some stumbling and being hacked mercilessly, the rest getting to the safety of the enclosure on the other side. Then, my attention was diverted by something which still seems to me of some significance. As soon as the first real assault had taken place the Spanish television director turned his main camera away from the high shot of the pitch in a very quick pan to a view of the brightly-lit streets outside the stadium. It remained there. Not a single television picture was taken of the police in action. The reason for this was to fall into place later on.

From being a reckless, but nevertheless jovial crowd, the Rangers support had been turned into a wounded beast, licking its sores, insulted, angered and seeking revenge. We thought it was all over but, to our astonishment, we then saw supporters going into the seating area and smashing the wooden seats with their feet until they had some fragment from which they could improvise a missile or a spear. Having regrouped in a remarkably spontaneous way, which might have drawn praise from a Field Marshal if moral judgement on all of this was suspended, they mounted a counter-attack.

The police broke ranks and retreated at more than a jog trot as a flood of red, white and blue swept back across the field carrying fragments of the Nou Camp with them. The fans were a ragged army, stupidly caught up in their own hurt pride, venting their frustration suicidally on the malicious puppets in uniform who had caused it all. First they drove the police back to our side of the stadium. Then they would retreat under another onslaught of batons and boots. Objectively speaking, the supporters were giving as good as they got. Hand-to-hand combat was going on all over the pitch, bits of seats flew through the air, supporters wielded pieces of wood like machetes, while the police swung madly away with their batons in an increased tempo. By this time, on the principle that war correspondents do not actually need to report from the trenches themselves, Bill and I had climbed from the pitch-side and sought safety high up in the stand.

'Any moment now the guns could come out, for God's sake,' a man said gently beside me. He turned out to be Reuter's correspondent in the area. I recall his words vividly.

'What you're seeing down there is the Fascist police in action,' he went on. 'That is the only way they can handle any disturbance. They are the experts in ruthless suppression. They are not even local police. They are not Catalans. That is why they are so hated in this city. They are Franco's men. They are recruited from Castile or Murcia. Anywhere but from Catalonia. They are principally in this area to maintain a dictatorship. They have regarded these supporters from their very first invasion like an assault on the Caudillo, Franco himself. That is how they are conditioned to act. Respond to command, don't think. These supporters simply do not understand that their lives could now be at risk.'

The height that we had gained had miniaturised the battle. It now looked like the Munchkins versus the Subbuteo Invaders. Unbridled violence now appeared no more threatening than a *son et lumière* spectacle. I wondered if this really was the sort of detachment achieved by the war correspondent. I also thought of how much odder it was to be spectating on a full-scale battle from the high safety of the top tier of the stand and being lectured at the same time on the iniquities which had befallen the Catalonians since the revolution. But it made much more sense than some of the thoughts expressed immediately afterwards.

It occurred to me then that the television director had turned his cameras away not by command but through the general convention of obliging the autocracy. The media, as part of the system, knew how to handle insurrection – by turning a blind eye. Of course, the Rangers supporters hadn't picked a fight with Franco. Theirs had been conflict on a different level. They had been turned into a street gang. It has been suggested that this was their own intrinsic response to provocation; that only they would have responded in such a way. It is a theory that dangles irresistibly in front of you, awaiting confirmation from outside the prejudiced Old Firm context.

All the same, those of us who have subsequently seen much trouble around Europe originating from gratuitous violence, and taking place in all manner of environments, can now look back on Barcelona and at least appreciate more clearly the logic of events. It was police batons which started the battle, the supporters finished it. Perhaps they should have gone meekly to the exits and made off home. But somehow I do not think it is in the nature of the Scot to take a battering without some aggressive reaction. So, the battle had been lamentably predictable from the moment the first supporter was felled.

We watched it come to an end, running out of steam as even the angriest lost the taste for more. People were bundled away and downstairs I saw a supporter receiving a mauling from two small men in uniform who, as they pummelled him with their batons, digging him in the ribs and twisting his arms even though he was as lethal as a rag doll by now, looked as impassive as two ledger clerks rubber-stamping a series of documents. I was actually no longer horrified by this and that is a sure sign you have had enough.

We hailed a taxi and returned to the Don Jaime hotel where, by now, the team were well advanced in their celebrations. They simply were not aware of the scale of the disaster and it would have been churlish to intervene with the bad news. Waddell only intermittently looked like a man who had won a European trophy. He knew full well the implications of what had gone on. The following day the Scottish morning newspapers had arrived at Barcelona airport and the team sat stunned in the aircraft just before take-off, looking at front pages which resembled reports from Vietnam rather than summaries of sporting achievements. Alex Miller, one of the reserves, picked his head up from reading the news and said to me with a distinct expression of disbelief, 'Will they take the cup off us?' It had sunk in.

But perhaps 'sunk' is too mild an expression. No detailed inquest could possibly have taken place into the causes of the riot in the time available. The emphasis was being placed naturally enough on the conduct of the Rangers supporters. In other words, on the aftermath of the assault by the police. The riot was not fully described. Scandalously, it never officially was. When we made efforts to try to rationalise and apportion blame fairly we were condemned by the public. There was one special reason for that. We had not shown the riot. Letters and phone calls poured in on us. We were accused of hiding the truth, of toadying to 'that' club, of being cowardly. In fact, we were discovering that trying to tell the truth was not enough.

We could not back up anything I said later, in introducing

programmes and discussing the matter with a variety of people, because we simply did not have the pictures. The Spanish director had seen to that. Any effort on my part to try to drive this point home was greeted with aggressive scepticism.

A prominent Celtic director told me solemnly, 'If it had been our supporters you would have shown the scenes, more than likely.' I was stunned by this, although I was to hear equally stupid remarks being made to me from the other camp in my time. In other words, we hadn't given at least some of the public what they desperately wanted to see: the Rangers supporters in disgrace. I knew, of course, that had it been Celtic in identical circumstances, the same adverse reaction would have come from the other side.

We had come back from Spain, with a reputation deformed by a riot, to a society still disfigured by its own introspection. Only eighteen months or so after having experienced a suspension of suspicion within the city's two footballing communities, through the cruel means of a disaster, fighting on a foreign field had restored the normal service of recrimination. Perhaps we ought to have expected nothing less.

What we then hoped was that some lessons would have been learned from the scale and nature of those two sad episodes, not just for Rangers but for others too. Waddell's dour dedication to rebuilding the club in all ways, and particularly in a straightforward business sense, was successful, given that its reputation had been reduced almost to rubble. Although their traditions made them vulnerable to universal condemnation and sometimes led them to a bunker mentality, they did learn vital lessons about their economic well-being. They also at least veered towards a tentative ending to their social myopia. Ironically their great rivals, replete with every success at that time, saw fit to close their eyes to the future.

We now know which of the two great Glasgow clubs gradually acquired the closer resemblance to that ancien régime of the French which 'learned nothing and forgot nothing'.

7

1974 *Weltmeisterschaft*

As the Germans had once tried to kill me I had taken a long time to agree with the idea of rapprochement. My notion of vengeance does not extend to setting fire to their towels and deck chairs in Majorca, but even yet I bridle slightly at the sound of the thick accent suddenly rasping its way into my presence. This awful prejudice was slightly diluted by the coming of Hildegard Neff to the silver screen in the Sixties. Her voice and presence temporarily eased my squeamishness at the sound of the 'Horst Wessel Song' or the sight of the scars that nation had left on others.

This irrational distaste sprang from the night they came to bomb Clydebank and I was taken out as a child in arms to a half-completed bomb shelter which actually had no roof. Looking upwards, I heard adult voices trying to distinguish amongst the stars, the lights of any German planes, the flares, and the search-lights. On its way westward one bastard dropped a bomb in the garden of a house only a hundred yards away but it failed to explode. I also, therefore, do not go along with the notion of German infallibility. I am thankful for the slovenliness in the Ruhr factories but think the near miss was too close to comfort and I cannot accord their race an accolade simply because they also produced Wagner and Beckenbauer.

To carry these old thoughts around with you in the Seventies, when the Germans were enjoying a resurgence of their supremacy in almost all sports, was like harbouring a heresy. So, what then was I to do about this Dr Wilfrid Gerhardt, who was standing in front of me in his office smiling and extending a genuine hand of friendship?

'Welcome to Frankfurt,' he said. It was 1974 and, by now, they were richer than us anyway and Wilfrid Gerhardt was no Dr Strangelove. He was an extremely pleasant and urbane gentleman who spoke the kind of superb English which rather humbles you, the more so since he was able to switch to fluent Spanish and French on the phone during interruptions to our conversation. He was also Secretary to the West German Football Association. The following night the draw was to be made for the World Cup Finals and Scotland were there for the first time since Sweden in 1958.

He was politely explaining to me the method of the draw which, in turn, I would need to explain to viewers. World Cup draws, you must understand, are not all that simple. What I admired about this man, whom I was to meet repeatedly over the years, was not just his command of language but of himself. He was extremely calm and relaxed, in rather hectic circumstances, and personified the great sophistication of the German footballing system. He was briefing me not just on the draw but about the stadia which would be used that summer. I was now a member of the Scottish Sports Council and with plans being mooted for a new Hampden (yes, even then!) I had a notion of bringing a study of them to a council meeting.

'You must go to Dortmund,' he said. 'You never know, perhaps Scotland will be drawn to play there. It is the sort of stadium which represents the best way forward for our game because it has been built principally for football. There is an intimacy to the ground as a result. No running track to distance you from the play, just a place to watch closely in comfort with the emphasis on good facilities for the customer.'

It was on the tip of my tongue to tell him it sounded like Cappielow but, even with his mastery of our tongue, the allusion might have been lost on him. The following night, in the main broadcasting hall of the Hessicher Rundfunk Television Company, the draw was made and, sure enough, our first game turned out to be in Dortmund, against Zaire. This neat coincidence seemed to augur well for the coming summer, with an apparently easy first game in a stadium I wanted to examine closely and with the Germans assuring us that this would be the best organised tournament of them all. This is a claim made dutifully before every World Cup finals and, as then, the actuality is invariably rather different from the boast.

That night we toasted our good luck with Willie Ormond, the Scottish team manager. If the meek really were to inherit the earth then Willie could have laid claim to most of the northern hemisphere. He was quite the nicest man I have ever met in football, apart from Celtic's Jimmy McGrory and Willie Thornton of Rangers. These three men seemed remarkably unadapted to football management. They didn't wear humanity like a suit which could be hung on a peg and forgotten when the brute necessity of commanding men arose. It was in their veins. It is possible that they did lose their temper and became aggressive at some stage or other. After all, I can hardly lay claim to knowing every detail of their personal or professional lives. To conceive of them doing so, however, is like trying to imagine the minister telling blue jokes in the middle of a Sunday sermon. They were all driven to management because they had been successful players but they did not have the armament to ward off 'the slings and arrows of outrageous fortune'.

I had first met Ormond up in Perth, when he was manager of St Johnstone. We sat one night in a hotel where a burn rushes madly underneath you in the lounge. He liked sitting chatting with a drink in his hand and, although some would have it that his favourite pastime ultimately became his obsession, I only had experience of mutually pleasant conviviality, with his gentle nature fired up into anecdote. He recounted to me that night his real fear of flying which originated in a horrendous attempt at a take off in Yugoslavia in winter when he had St Johnstone on a European trip.

'I could see we weren't making it,' he said. 'The branches of the trees were brushing against the wings and the whole plane was shuddering. I thought this was going to be it. I don't think I even prayed. I was too terrified to think of anything. Then, somehow or other, the pilot swung the plane round and I kept my eyes shut. But we landed. We got off the plane and I remember they told us they were going to have another go at taking off in about an hour.

"Not on your bloody life," I thought. But I knew I had to get back somehow so I went into the lounge and drank it dry. I was paralytic when I went back on and I remember bugger-all about anything else until we landed back in Edinburgh.'

There was a self-deprecatory flavour to much of what Ormond said about himself, which in itself was endearing, but in the run-up to the summer of that year you constantly wondered how this homely little man could possibly measure up to the stature of his rivals. Men like Rinus Michels of Holland, Miljan Miljanic of Yugoslavia, Helmut Schoen of West Germany, and Mario Zagalo of Brazil all had impressive international pedigrees. But at least he was there. The night Scotland qualified he brought back thirty-three-year-old Denis Law to play against Czechoslovakia and although the Czechs scored first it was a night of voluptuary appreciation of the Scottish 2–1 victory. Scottish Television were covering the game and as a Czech bore down on Bremner, commentator Arthur Montford cried out 'Watch your legs, Billy.' In that now famous declamation one sensed the communal nature of that evening at Hampden. We all wanted to lay on hands and help eleven men levitate to a level we had originally thought beyond them.

Naturally, the thought of going to a World Cup for the first time turned us into virtual kids although, compared to the hysteria which was to follow the next time, en route to Argentina, we were almost gripped by inertia. Television broadcasting had now established itself in colour and only snobs declared they would retain black and white. When we made the change I am sure the first sight of us, revealed in full Pre-Raphaelite hues must have shocked many to the core.

I did receive a call from a rather sardonic member of the public who complained that the colour could not possibly be accurate as it did not show up my 'blue' nose. I wondered at the time if it had been Jock Stein, with false voice, again sending me up and to this day I have never been quite sure. Make-up girls would spend a long time pondering my face before deciding that perhaps it ought to retain its natural vampirish sallowness. Thus, I was consigned to a pat or two with powder-puff and left looking for years after as if I suffered from pernicious anaemia.

Peter Thomson was on the way out so the World Cup was to be his major swan-song. It was to be the last time I was to work under anybody, in the rest of my career with BBC Scotland, who had not only an innate love of football but who, despite his unbending distaste for Stein, possessed an instinctive understanding of the political undercurrents. Lamentably, they were to be too often disregarded as unimportant in succeeding years. My only regret was that after I had arranged for Stein to be part of a studio panel for the first time, so confirming his change of relationship with BBC Scotland, Peter did not show up on the night. I considered it something of a personal triumph that I had persuaded Stein to identify himself with us. In the same year he had answered, '*Sports-reel*' when the Aberdeen match programme asked him for his favourite comedy show. Peter was allowing me leeway in helping to prepare programmes and make decisions about our contributors but he nevertheless felt that having Stein in the studio was nothing more than grovelling sycophancy. I found the necessity of having him seen with us to be infinitely more important than tittle-tattle about subservience to the Celtic manager. I discovered its true value, in the most practical way, when we eventually got to Germany for the Finals themselves that summer.

We did not go direct but, momentously, via Belgium and Norway. Relationships between the media and the entire SFA party, including officials, Ormond and the players, ranged from ragged to rancid. The Jimmy Johnstone rowing boat incident, which occurred prior to the England match, before Scotland left for the Finals, was much played up in the newspapers. It had been a good story after all: Jimmy out on a boat without oars heading in the general direction of Manhattan, the players in stitches on the shore and the Celtic star trying with difficulty to see the funny side of it. It is not your 'We have a player with a slight thigh strain' stuff which is sometimes all there is to deal in before a major game. This was *Drop the Dead Donkey* material and was greedily mawed by everybody in the press bar the *War Cry*, who were not accredited for the World Cup anyway. Ormond and the players did not like this. It smacked of disloyalty, not to say downright treachery. At the end of the England match at Hampden, won 2–0 by Scotland, the players looked skywards, not to acknowledge divine support but to catch the eye of the busily-working media. Their body language on the pitch below then sent the blatant message, 'You are a bunch of wankers.' Water off a duck's back though. We all loved this stuff.

So off we set to Belgium that morning from Glasgow Airport, the heroes at the front of the plane, the vampires and vultures at the back. I've often wondered if the carriers British Airways sensed the division. They certainly brought the mediation to end all mediation. Out came the bottles. By the time the plane had nosed its way to the first layer of cirro-cumulus, and was still apparently at an angle, we each had a bottle of champagne. The players were not excluded. It might seem hypocritical to criticise the amount of booze downed on that relatively short flight since none of the media on board were actually championing the cause of abstention. Yet, it has to be taken as a real factor in the entire World Cup trip which was to last another four weeks in total.

It seemed to consecrate the drifting, meandering and generally undisciplined nature of the tour. Apart from the abstemious secretary of the SFA, Willie Allan, there were few who left the plane who did not now see dull Belgium as Judy suddenly saw Technicolor Oz after the monochrome of Kansas. We were, in fact, heading for the World Cup like bus trippers bound for Blackpool and the September weekend.

Needless to say when the players lined up against Belgium in the warm-up game two days later they hardly looked like frisking lambs. Now, athletes, footballers in particular, have wonderful recuperative powers after a night on the tiles. Stein used to recall receiving a phone call from a sneak accusing Jimmy Johnstone of having stayed up all night and saying he had just been decanted from some pub in Glasgow. Stein prepared a welcome party for him that morning consisting of Willie Wallace and Bobby Lennox, the two fastest men at the club. He told them to put a pallid looking Johnstone through the hoop. The outcome? The manager simply shrugged his shoulders and said, 'The wee man was brilliant. He did everything asked of him and came back for more. What could I say to him?'

We could say, however, that on the performance that day in the little stadium in Bruges Scotland looked like a pub team playing in borrowed boots on Glasgow Green. They looked hungover. We had a sharp, sudden intake of breath to rouse us from our slumbers. This rabble to play Brazil in a couple of weeks' time? Never! It was then we began to give serious thought to the leadership of the party both on and off the field. By the time we travelled to Oslo, for the last game before heading for Frankfurt, the trip was disintegrating into something which Feydeau or Brian Rix would have adored.

The setting was a students' hostel. We had been told in advance that it was a hotel but in fact it was part of the university whose students' quarters were used during the summer for tourist accommodation. The rooms were like tiny cells into which you could manage a suitcase and yourself plus, perhaps, the odd termite. Everything, bar the soap in the bathroom, was made of wood. I do not exclude the mattress from this description. The sophisticates within the Scottish party, accustomed to five-star comfort, thought they had landed up in an Outward Bound school and were not amused. Footballers normally live in the lap of luxury when they travel abroad; the best hotels, the best food. It is a boring cycle admittedly of hanging around, training and hanging around once more. At least, however, they have beds where they can lie without having to hang their feet out of the window, as a rule. Here, the claustrophobia of rooms obviously built for masochistic wood fetishists only compounded the misery that had originated with the appalling display in Belgium. Austerity was in. Surliness was blossoming. Anarchy was spreading. And some of us began to contemplate the unthinkable, that perhaps the players should turn round and go back home while the going was good, before Rivelino and his mates could get at them.

The ensuing days I sub-divide into two distinct categories:
1 The Great Bremner-Johnstone Affair.
2 The Bans.

The Great Bremner–Johnstone Affair

There were certain consolations living in this student area. The beer was good and cheaper than elsewhere, although still expensive enough. The atmosphere of the howfs, with their student life, was relaxed. We all spent some time in them, including the players. But a curfew of sorts had been set by Willie Ormond, although thankfully this did not extend to the media. We sat there one night, looking dispassionately at the leggy, languid Norwegian blondes and yearning for nothing but our own student days, when we spied Billy Bremner and Jimmy Johnstone. They were in fine fettle. It was past midnight.

I had been joined on the trip by John Motson, from London, with a film crew who were now to make some preview programmes with me. We were sipping our way through those apparently bottomless glasses of beer when the two players spotted us and made straight for our group. They were singing. There was nothing wrong with that and indeed I have never been much in favour of treating footballers like schoolboys. They turned out to be good company and in a few minutes we discovered nothing more startling than that Jimmy Johnstone could sing better than Billy Bremner, although knowing the little Leeds man's conviction about himself I was not going to be awarding him 'null pwann'.

Of course, there was more to it. This was a gesture of outright rebellion. It was an act by a captain, Bremner, who obviously didn't give a damn for the manager and who knew that Ormond wasn't the kind of personality who would shed blood. That assumption was proved correct. They regaled us with more songs, to the great delight of the Norwegian students. If they were studying anthropology it must have been a highly educational half-hour. Then, Willie Ormond suddenly appeared at the top of the steps leading down to the cellar. He took one long look at his two players, turned on his heel and left. If it had been Stein or Waddell or Wallace the two of them would have been picked up by the neck like a couple of dachshunds and not released until they were in their rooms.

As it was, the SFA and Celtic doctor, Dr Fitzsimmons appeared on the scene five minutes later, whispered in the players' ears, put his arm round their shoulders and ushered them out of the room. They went peacefully. He had been sent down to perform the fireman's act. It was a scene which, in fact, symbolised the reversal of power roles. Willie Ormond was not an insignificant figure in

Germany, of course, but he was certainly subordinate to Bremner in terms of influence amongst the players and that, as it turned out, was no bad thing.

By the morning the place was rife with rumours of the incident in the night. So began the debate, even before any official SFA statement was made, as to whether it would be right to send the two players home as an act of support for the manager. The manager might have been crudely challenged by the pair but in essence this stemmed from his own liberal attitude towards behaviour. In the days before a game in the home internationals he had allowed players to visit pubs, so long as they were back by a certain time. As he had also avoided a confrontation with the pair this time but had sent somebody to do it for him, I didn't think he deserved much support.

On the other hand, coming after the farce on the Clyde, the debacle in Belgium and the constant press criticism of the general indiscipline some kind of purge seemed a sensible idea. We were bewildered largely because of our own naivety. Apart from a journalist or two and perhaps a couple of officials, none of us had prepared for a World Cup before. We assumed that players would approach this task like men studying for the priesthood, or soldiers doing bayonet drill before going over the top. We believed it was the time for asceticism. I think most of us would have thought a player seen licking a stamp was acting like a footloose libertine.

In this nervy atmosphere, bullets were fired off willingly by the press. After all, there was nothing else to write about except sunsets on boring old fiords. To a journalist this incident was like finding caviar in a bacon sandwich. Bremner and Johnstone were pulverised on the front pages back home. The tension in the entire squad of players, officials and media was growing. The notorious pair themselves were actually preparing to fly home. The SFA cloistered themselves to determine their response. We believed the whole fate of the World Cup campaign hinged on this fateful decision. Bickering started amongst those whose duty it was to report the whole affair as conflicting views were offered. They ranged from banning them *sine die* to, in one specific and caustic suggestion, awarding the twosome the Willie Ormond Award for Late Night Drinking. These divisions were hardly healed when the announcement was made that the players would remain with the party.

The general view was that the SFA had blundered again and that they should have sacrificed the players in the interests of morale and the establishment of some code of inflexible conduct. Bremner and Johnstone, not unaware of what had been written and said about them, looked sullen and embittered. Care was taken about walking along corridors in case you found yourself alone with either of them. In that circumstance Norway might have experienced its first incidence of mugging.

The television people like myself were slightly withdrawn from all of this. It was not our prior obligation to ferret out news or banner headlines. We were merely filming largely innocuous interviews for use in previews just before the tournament started. Consequently, we were perceived for a time to be as harmless as inter-round card carriers during a title fight. This was the wrong assumption to make about us for there is little doubt anything newsworthy would have been passed on in the usual commercial way to my colleagues. You suffered sharp little intakes of breath when a Scottish player beside you called a pressman in the vicinity 'vermin', as if we on TV were above it all. However, this could have been called the honeymoon period. There was to be an aftermath to the Johnstone–Bremner affair which continued the conflict and drew us in as well.

The Bans

The director with the film unit was a pugnacious little Londoner called Bob Abrahams. His true television idiom was film-making, particularly those short films which encapsulated so much information about people and places. Give him four minutes and he could link Peer Gynt, the trolls and cod with the newly designed World Cup trophy. He carried a street-fighter's instinct with him to the corridors of the BBC which helped him to endure so long. He was probably one of the few men in London who would dare tell Ronnie Kray to his face he was a poof and not rush to exile. He was very much the man's man and was popular with the Scottish players, with whom he had struck up an affinity that was also professionally useful. With no England in Germany the BBC were expending all their energies on people who, at the start, were quite foreign to them.

We had been given free rein to move amongst the squad in their rooms, much to the disgust of some pressmen who perhaps did not appreciate that we were paying through the nose to the players' pool for the privilege. One evening a roomful of players besieged by events, and not wishing to arouse any more hostility by breaking curfew, sent Bob for a carry-out of lager. He duly did this out of sympathy for footballers who were looking, by the day, more and more bedraggled. He slipped off to the howf, gathered the nectar, took the lift back upstairs and walked straight into Willie Ormond, about to head in the opposite direction. Bob said, 'Good evening' and walked on.

That deft attempt at normality did not work. Wrath descended upon us and despite the access money which television had liberally paid we were now tarred. We had become part of the fraternity of wolves snapping at the heels of innocent victims. We were detrimental to Scottish chances in Germany. We were banned. We were no longer given the access to the players' area of the campus. We were looked at suspiciously by everyone, except by those who had asked for the lager and others who, no doubt, would ask a favour again. The ban also gave us a curious kinship with the press who, in a show of solidarity, revealed themselves to be tickled pink by our shared plight.

The late John Mackenzie, the 'Voice of Football' of the *Daily Express*, in full view of the others in the reception area as we waited for a morning press-conference, was taken aside by Willie Allan. After a short, mumbled conference John returned and said with a wry smile, 'I've been banned.' He had been told that, because of his communiqués, he was no longer welcome in the official SFA party and that, perforce, he could not travel on the flight to Germany with the rest of us.

Willie Allan, dapper and officious, carried out his duties with a sanguine unconcern about folks' opinion of him. He could be a soft-spoken hatchet man when he wanted to be and his instinct for the administration of SFA business was acute. Errors of judgement by the SFA were borne with an equanimity which sometimes gave him the appearance of a man wearing a blindfold and heading straight for the precipice.

John Mackenzie was not in the slightest perturbed. Indeed you could see he was suffused with the glow of anticipation at what his editor might do about this back in Glasgow. Vibrations of envy were coming from other journalists who thought they fully deserved to be banned every bit as much as Mackenzie. They were probably now thinking that being allowed to travel with Scotland to Germany might be interpreted by their editors as a dereliction of duty. Banning can raise one from either mediocrity or anonymity overnight to that highly-treasured level of notoriety. So, Willie Allan had done nothing more than confer on John Mackenzie the impromptu Norwegian Order of Merit for efforts above and beyond the call of duty.

However, the others were not to be disappointed. It became more democratic after that. We sallied forth dutifully to a training session at the tiny little national stadium in Oslo, arriving just ahead of the team bus, and ascertained where the players were to alight and enter. What then followed might have been scripted by Chaplin, Keaton or Mack Sennett.

The media trudged after the players into the pavilion and made for the passageway to the pitch only to be confronted by a large Norwegian who announced ponderously, 'You are not allowed into training. Mr Ormunn has instructed!'

As we had anticipated an evening of unremitting tedium these words fell on our ears like caresses. The late James Sanderson of the *Daily Mirror* – snappily dressed as always, hair slicked down to perfection, shirt sleeves well in advance of jacket sleeve, tinkling slightly with gold about his person, cigar simmering in right hand – was in the first stages of pink, incandescent rage. But he, like others, had come alive. They could not have asked for more. We waited eagerly for 'Mr Ormunn'.

After about an hour, someone spotted the team bus rolling down the street to a different exit at the other end of the stadium. We rushed out of the pavilion and ran, cameras, pencils, notebooks clanking along, to cram round a small door. Just as the group of about twenty of us had drawn breath in relief, the bus suddenly reversed quickly back up the street to the entrance we had just left. We turned and scurried after it but just as we reached it again it changed direction and started off back down to the other entrance. Expletives rent the air. We scrambled down the street again thinking that scoops might yet have some connection with basic physical fitness.

Ormond was eaten alive when he emerged. He had eventually realised he would have to dig his way out of the stadium to avoid us. Now, he was shaking either with rage or nerves and spat out a great deal of uncharacteristic venom towards us, explaining that he would no longer put up with unfair and inaccurate reporting of the trip. The ban would continue until further notice. An ordinary evening had been turned into a treasure trove for those eager to have their credentials withdrawn like Mackenzie. They dutifully sent the wires humming back to Scotland, the reports replete with scorn and abuse. It was about then Hugh Taylor of the *Daily Record* wrote above his copy the superbly descriptive, succinct heading, 'The Tour de Farce'. This alone would have warranted him being thrown off the Lorelei into the Rhine by the SFA International Committee when we got to Germany.

We slunk into Frankfurt feeling as if the whole journey was quite unnecessary and that we would be back home pretty quickly. Travelling from the airport to the hotel, the television stage manager, who organised outside broadcasts, pointed out the former headquarters of the Gestapo in the Sachsenring.

'That's where they took all the major political prisoners,' he declared. 'Every diabolical torture known to man went on there.'

Not quite, I thought. The Gestapo's victims, so far as I know, had never been on a football trip to Norway. I felt it was going to take us a while to recover from all these traumas and time was in short supply. The players headed for the Taunus Mountains and all the television personnel entered a glass and concrete edifice on the outskirts of the city called the Arabella Hotel. It was besieged by perpendicular columns of glass and concrete office blocks, so giving the illusion that you were looking out of your room into a gigantic mirror. The whole area was devoted to the architecture of commerce, harsh, rectangular, teutonically tall and soulless. By about six o'clock of an evening when all the surrounding buildings decanted their staff it was like coming across some eerie Druidic meeting place. After a few days the hotel itself seemed as congenial as Colditz.

Sam Leitch, the World Cup editor back in London, had advised us not to fraternise with the enemy in the hotel. Not the remnants of the SS, of course, but ITV who, led by Sir Alf Ramsey and Billy Wright, were staging a considerable challenge to the BBC's expected supremacy of coverage. Nothing was to be given away indiscreetly. Careless talk in the bar could cost professional lives. Sam was serious. Don't mix! The bar being about the size of a lounge in a doll's house, this became impractical. After we had been plied with drinks we discovered all that the lads in ITV really wanted to know was where the action was in town. We did, however, send them on some wild goose chases.

Stein was there. He had travelled to Germany to work with the BBC as a match analyst. He had his closest friend, Tony Queen, the Glasgow bookmaker, with him. Stein gobbled up the information we gave him about the trip thus far. Privately, he could hardly disguise his contempt for the manner in which things had been handled up till then. Publicly, throughout the tournament, he remained respectful of Ormond. We travelled together the following day, after arriving in Frankfurt, to Erbismuhle, the quaint little village in the mountains in which sat the ski-lodge housing the Scottish team. Security was intense. Following the Black September attack on the Israeli athletes during the Munich Olympics two years earlier the Germans were taking no chances and had spent a considerable amount on protecting the teams. The security force were all plain-clothes men who smiled a lot but were meticulous in their policing.

They refused to believe that Jock Stein, David Coleman, myself and a film crew were not Palestinian terrorists at first and frisked us as rigorously. The team looked slightly more relaxed in a setting that reminded one of the lodge in which the film *The Lady Vanishes* starts. It was all Bavarian hunting-style, although far from Bavaria and redolent of 'lederhosen' and matronly waitresses carrying brimming-over tankards. They, however, had been replaced by a rather more chic cast. We had to travel an hour-and-a-half every day after that to this charming spot just to keep in touch with the news. There was still a gulf separating manager from media but the main concern was whether morale had been shattered beyond repair. This, of course, was not put to the test until the night we all went to Dortmund for the Zaire match.

It had been stingingly hot during the day. When we arrived I went with Stein and Tony Queen to the Scottish team hotel in the city, not far from the stadium. It is my contention that Jock Stein's influence in Germany went well beyond that of temporary BBC broadcaster. I was made aware of the fact forcibly that late afternoon. We sat in the lounge tolerating that agonising no-man's land of time when nothing much else can be done in preparation for the match and you resort to eating salted peanuts as your only mental exercise.

Even in the cool of the air-conditioned hotel the nerves were still preparing for shock. It was our first World Cup in a considerable time and although we were playing a team from a continent still undistinguished in football, people were still casting up Belfast Celtic in New York, and Paraguay in Switzerland to us as examples of the Scottish tendency to self-destruct. Just as we were ruminating on that Billy Bremner joined us. He flopped down on a leather sofa, looking pale and tired. He launched into an account of all that had gone on in Norway and Belgium although, not surprisingly, in a selective manner. He made it plain that he was happy neither with the general reporting nor the managerial style thus far. He did not specify too much but it was abundantly clear he was baring his soul.

Stein listened to this patiently for some time, then, suddenly, he heaved himself up from the seat he was on until his back was erect and I could see the flush developing on his face, the sure sign of anger. The big fist suddenly stretched across the table towards Bremner until it was only inches from his face.

'Don't bloody well lie down to all of this,' he snapped. 'The answer is in your own hands. You're experienced enough to get things going on the park. You get your players geed up. Never mind about anybody else. Use your own influence. Don't be moaning about everything, just get on with it and stick it right up the press. Just tell the players to remember everything that has been said about them and get them to go out and stuff it right up them.

Bloody well right up them. Get out there tonight and show us you're in a different league from these pygmies you're playing. Go on, stick it right up all your critics. Think of their faces just before kick-off, think, "We're going to stuff everybody tonight." Get out there and show us.'

He sat back after this rapid tirade. Bremner, who might well have been expecting tea and sympathy, had received a psychological kick in the pants. Its suddenness had struck forcibly home for he probably hadn't been talked to like that on the entire tour so far. The vacuum of authority had been filled, if only for a fleeting moment. There was no doubt that I had experienced a proxy team talk which would find its way back to the dressing room. Stein acted with great restraint thereafter during the tournament but it is also clear he became the father-confessor figure to certain prominent players who went to him with their worries. We should not, therefore, underestimate what he did for Scottish morale in Germany, even if he was being paid by the BBC.

At 2–0 that night Scotland put on the brake and, ever after, Bremner has been blamed for it. I regard this criticism as glibly simplistic. The Zaire team would have been content to run like stags all night in this, their first World Cup match. It cannot be proven by those who seem to know better what the score would have been had Scotland played flat out for the ninety minutes in extreme humidity. It might not have been many more. It is easy to quote the Yugoslavian 9–0 victory over them as an indication of a misreading of the situation that night. Zaire, I think, had given all they could in their first game.

On top of that, the Scottish team had just finished the most disastrous trip they had ever undertaken. The desire to grasp two points and leave it at that is not too surprising. Dortmund, far from being the disaster it has been interpreted as in retrospect, was the foundation for taking as much as we could from the rest of the tournament. Scotland had reclaimed some of their pride. And, as the Brazil match was to prove conclusively, they had rediscovered how to fire themselves up at the right time.

That was back in Frankfurt in the Waldstadion. Prior to the match, I interviewed Ormond at the hotel before we journeyed down from the hills to the city. He was nervous but pleasant and slightly detached, as if he was unaware everybody expected an annihilation. I somehow could not picture him taking on the Brazilians. What we eventually produced that night was not down principally to him but to the proper application by the senior professionals in the side, led by Bremner.

We had been told by the German television authorities that BBC Scotland could not have a television commentary position at this match because one had already been allocated to London for David Coleman. A political battle ensued which was won in Glasgow and when we got there that night we discovered that there were at least ten empty commentary positions in the stand. This duplication of BBC effort was to dog our footsteps in every major event involving a Scottish team and I suppose will never be satisfactorily resolved.

It was, debatably, the best performance by a Scottish team against class opposition in any World Cup. I recall the Davie Hay twenty-five-yarder which just went over the bar. I still remain stunned thinking of Bremner, acting on reflex, jabbing the ball past the post from right in front of goal. I admire the way they refused to succumb to reputations like Rivelino's and largely tamed the 'Europeanised' Brazilians, who had come to the Continent thinking, mistakenly, they had to change character to gain success. Brazilian international football has never recovered from that metamorphosis.

We simply were not good enough to beat Yugoslavia. We had now forgotten the Nordic mess and thought we were on the verge of greatness. I was built up for it as I have never been before. When Yugoslavia scored with two minutes to go I felt they had destroyed me personally. The equaliser had a cruel futility to it. I was to become more experienced in coping with disappointment but desolation is what I experienced then. I know my colleague in STV, Arthur Montford, in disgust, sped back to the hotel without talking to anybody, jumped in his car and headed for the North Sea Ferry. Unfortunately, I didn't have my car with me.

We returned by air. Glasgow Airport was thronged by thousands who treated the players like conquering heroes. After all, they hadn't lost a game. Willie Ormond, shedding tears, cut exactly the figure the nation wanted to see. Strube's little man in Scottish guise. The amiable little guy who had cheated fate and come through a test of character was back amongst his ain folk. He has been given great credit for the performances in Germany. His principal asset was his eye for a player. He was not the driving force you need to be at that level. Frankly, despite the initial disciplinary problems he provoked, Bremner's assertion of his own idiosyncratic personality on the Scottish squad had been vital. Without it, Ormond would have been seen as a disaster and the airport would have been deserted on our return.

In any case, this euphoria owed much to a decided sense of relief. After the traumas which preceded Germany and which prompted thoughts of imminent national disgrace, we had been resurrected. But as I look back, I appreciate now that the scenes at the airport were unhealthy. For that day the seeds of self-delusion were being sown. The bitter harvest was to be reaped in Argentina four years later.

8

Bitter Lessons

Scene: The television production gallery somewhere about five o'clock of a Saturday evening.

'Who comes next? . . . Bill McLaren? . . . Is he there yet? Edinburgh Studio! . . . Is Bill there yet? . . . What do you mean you don't bloody know? . . . Go out and bloody look for him or else drag Alistair Dewar back . . . We'll have to go on to Aberdeen, Archie . . . Aberdeen are you receiving us? . . . Whose tea cup is that . . . Get it out of there . . . Three minutes left . . . We'll never get to the Highland League results . . . What a damn pity, hee, hee, hee! . . . Go on to your second last page . . . No! No! Don't! . . . Ad lib the English results . . . and we have Bill McLaren . . . No we don't have Bill McLaren . . . He must be stuck in Princes Street . . . Ad Lib, Archie . . . Ad lib . . . Listen to the countdown . . . Ten-nine-eight-seven . . . Remember we're back tonight don't forget the trail . . . the trail, say it . . . Sportscene 10.30 . . . say the trail for Christ sake . . . four-three-two-one . . . We're off the air. Jesus!'

Something like that. It was the crammed, jumpy kind of programme, like being on the dodgems and not knowing how it was going to work out apart from the inevitable bumps. It was a repeating tale of the unexpected which led inevitably to a flirtation with mishap. Particularly that late afternoon programme. But broadcasting sometimes is less frenetic. Sitting much later on a Saturday evening in the studio after a more than adequate script preparation and with the auto-cue, your umbilical cord to coherence, clearly and distinctly in front of you, the red-light suddenly going on stimulates rather than unnerves you. You simply say the words with a smile. That is broadcasting by auto-pilot. Whereas, the scramble to get news and views on the air in our late afternoon slot was as tidy as the Calgary Stampede.

As you talked to the public so a constant barrage of instructions could be passed on to you by means of the 'deaf-aid', a little plastic pod inserted in your ear. They could communicate directly and consequently dangle you like an electronic puppet. In the earlier days, though, when that technology was still being developed, they simply rang you up on the phone on the desk. I sometimes took more calls than the Samaritan service on a bad night.

So, we live on edge as broadcasters, fearing all the while the unknown, and the mistakes occur more often than not when you adopt, as is so easy to do, the 'look-no-hands' approach. The thought of the slip of the lip is never very far from our minds. I once introduced a programme by coolly announcing, 'The two games tonight are from Hambley and Wemden.' With our adrena-line bubbling over, we really ought to expect the mishap.

Errors are inerasable. They stick with you like reputation. In a live broadcast near one New Year's Eve I discussed sporting values with Hugh McIlvanney, Ian McLauchlan and Peter Alliss. The latter was waxing lyrical about how values, in general, had descended so low that an old woman of eighty couldn't walk down the street for fear of rape nowadays. McIlvanney, wishing to lighten the subject somewhat, said, *sotto voce*, 'Depends what she looks like.' Humour of that sort is sometimes not quickly appreciated and fearing a rush of protest from the switchboard I rushed in where angels fear to tread. I found myself interrupting to get quickly and diplomatically on to the next subject by saying, 'Don't knock it till you've tried it!'

As I moved heedlessly on, the heavens opened and the switch-board lady in Broadcasting House was bombarded by a nation indignant at what I had taken to be a flippant remark of no conse-quence. We had been invited, as a family, to Kilconquhar in Fife for the first few days of January, immediately after the programme. It is a beautiful spot but I felt inundated with resentment. My anguish had turned the East Neuk of Fife into Siberia. Blunders like the one I had committed clung to me much more tenaciously than I would care to admit in public. I suffered the pangs of hell as I saw people looking at me at the functions I attended. I could almost hear them saying to one another, 'Dreadful fellow that. Speaking like that about old ladies.'

I wanted to rush up and explain that it wasn't like that at all. I really didn't want old ladies raped no matter how seductive they looked. Why didn't anybody understand me? Ah, the public! If only we could do without them, I thought. No one should imagine that such classic broadcasting non sequiturs are confined to those in front of the cameras whose egos have been bruised. I always comforted myself that others in the business could exceed that. Hugh Moran, who was the Industrial Correspondent at one stage, was once asked indignantly by a BBC admin type, 'Do you think we're here to help you make programmes?'

In the mid and latter part of the Seventies there was hardly a sports programme produced in Scotland that I wasn't part of. In the dual role of presenter and commentator there was not much pause for reflection, especially as my links with London were becoming stronger as well. It was about then I began a long and happy association with *Grandstand*. In the final analysis, though, it was, ironically, to prove a handicap to me in BBC Scotland. Perhaps the most challenging type of broadcast I have ever done was standing at the edge of a Scottish football pitch speaking live to London.

This happened virtually every week on *Football Focus*. The editors of *Grandstand* have come and gone – Alan Hart, Sam Leitch, Mike Murphy, John Philips – but the voice that guided me along the tightrope over the abyss of the live report was the producer Martin Hopkins. He was the voice in the ear telling me when they were about to come to me and above all giving me the crucial countdowns as I spoke to camera. I never had a script. I worked off memory and would give London the cue words earlier in the morning so they knew when to run the pictures that I would be leading into. As soon as I hit the right word, Martin would very coolly start the count until the pictures came up and I would shut up. If there was some problem and the pictures were not there at the last second, then this soothing voice would merely put you back on course for a bit of ad libbing, which you always had to be prepared to do. It didn't matter what the weather was like, the show never closed.

At Easter Road one day I launched into my first piece, which Martin cottoned on to when the cue word was mentioned, and right on the dot the pictures came up. As they did so, the weather changed in the most dramatic way. Suddenly a gale-like monsoon blew up from over Calton Hill and an umbrella was thrust at me by one of our assistants. I grabbed at it but it twisted in my hand and I wrestled with it the way a deep-sea diver might fight with a giant octopus, the spokes going in all directions. In the space of a minute the weather had gone from bright sunshine to blizzard. It was one of the few times that Hopkins was beside himself. He struggled to fight against the mirth which had taken over the production gallery in London.

When eventually they came back to me for my introduction to the next item the viewers must have thought I had been transplanted, in about that space of sixty seconds, to Reykjavik. I had to try to recall what I was supposed to say and still prevent myself from blowing away and as I did so I knew I had forgotten the cue words. I meandered into waffle whilst at the same time trying to rack my brains for what they might be. Of course I had given them to London but they didn't know that I had forgotten them. Down there at Television Centre they waited and waited as I waded verbally on, trying to keep myself on my feet and the umbrella from blowing into the North Sea. For the first time I could remember on the programme I was panicking. I still didn't want to admit in public that I was lost although I suppose I should have.

Then, Martin twigged. If he hadn't I might still have been speaking through *Dr Who* at tea-time. 'Ah!' he said softly, without a hint of flurry, 'I think the words you are searching for are, "inevitably Easter Road . . ."' and then chuckled slightly. Saved! I took breath and garbled them into a sentence and as the umbrella was about to win the fight the pictures came up. It was the only occasion in about fifteen years' connection with *Football Focus* that we didn't get it quite right. I credit Hopkins with being able to sit inside the performer's head, realising that there is sometimes agony being experienced. Not everybody in his area has that inclination or ability.

I had decided that the main style of presentation on that programme would not be pontification but would allow a little whimsy. This suited the style of both Mike Murphy and especially his successor as editor of *Grandstand*, my fellow Scot John Philips. Philips eschews the obvious. His idiosyncratic approach to devising the programme has produced some of the most individual interpretations of sporting events in an area where much is routine. Since the eye is used to more predictable accounts not everybody appreciates the way he diverges. He is a kind of Edward de Bono of sports broadcasting. One kaleidoscopic lunch-time survey of sport previewed what we were to see on the afternoon of the Grand National. It moved in and out of Aintree, to other venues, to other sports, with no linking script, allowing the pictures to explain why each leap had been made. The sequence was underpinned by a musical motif. The venerable old flagship of BBC sports presentation was pushed towards a kind of television pointillism.

If it jarred with some, it stimulated others. Sports coverage has been blessed by great technological advance, to the extent that we can all be privy to the worm's eye view at the foot of the stumps in a Test match. In too many cases, there has, however, been no comparable leap in its aesthetic. The conservatism of the emphasis on plain good coverage of events has led too often to a disregard for the imaginative exploration of the sporting character. In that sense, you might regard Philips as a redoubtable maverick.

My input fitted his philosophy and vice versa. We always tried to venture outside the boundaries of conventional presentation. One lunch time I turned up as usual to deliver the piece from Tannadice and discovered that the North Pole had spread to Dundee. The pitch was buried in snow with no chance of the game being played. Bill Malcolm, my producer, reading the situation brilliantly both in terms of the weather and the flavour we wanted, had got his men to build a snowman. They put my distinctive sheepskin coat and bonnet with scarf on it and when London came over to us they saw it rather than me. Just off camera, I ventriloquised my words for the snowman. It was a risky thing to attempt. This was before trivia was institutionalised by the Saint and Greavsie. It perhaps ran counter to the solid, authoritative nature of *Football Focus* then. It seemed to work all the same. London solemnly thanked me for the services I had rendered through several seasons and bade me adieu. They were now putting the snowman on contract.

The public were increasingly taking a hand in my life though. Criticism did not pass through me quickly but persisted like an unidentified virus which even a good overnight sweat won't budge. I discovered this earlier, in 1969, when the home internationals went into an end of season package and I was asked to do all three matches 'live'. It was not a happy experience. In the first game at Wrexham I arrived to discover that BBC network and ITV had actually constructed their television platforms on top of scaffolding which stretched right along the track in front of the centre stand. The ticket holders paying handsomely for the privilege were going to have to watch the game through a fretwork. This was an outrageous piece of arrogance by both channels who, having paid each home association the princely sum for those days of £30,000, felt they could virtually re-write the laws of the game.

As I was about to climb up the ladder before the game a technician asked me who I was with. When I told him BBC Scotland he shook his head and said, 'You're there!' and pointed to the back of the stand. So, I was pigeon-holed in the very last row of the stand looking not only at the game through this aluminium web in front of me but also over the heads of the irate stand patrons. They had never experienced this before and were rising from time to time throughout the game to hurl insults at my colleagues from both BBC network and ITV, David Coleman and Brian Moore, who were sitting like monarchs of all they surveyed with a superb view of the pitch. My tiny little television monitor from which I deduced what was happening on the field of play was like a crumb from the master's table.

It was an almost impossible task. I felt like a negro in Alabama when, once upon a time, they had to sit at the rear of even an empty bus. Identification of players had been a nightmare and if you are not coping with that fluency is impossible, a feeling for the game is beyond you. It was a struggle and a failure.

There is one thought that must never pass through your mind

in broadcasting and that is, 'It can only get better.' As I travelled back from Wales that self-comforting sentiment was in mind as I mentally prepared for the Scotland–Northern Ireland game which had been switched from Belfast because of the start of the troubles there. I could not have been more wrong. On that date Glasgow was hit by a storm. It didn't stop raining for twenty-four hours, ninety minutes of which was the international match. Only 7,483 certifiable souls turned up at Hampden (the lowest international crowd on record this century) while the rest sanely remained at home taking the opportunity of watching it live on television and, perhaps less sanely, with the sound up listening to me.

In the mud of Hampden that night the game began to resemble the Eton Wall Game with clusters of shadowy players pursuing an object that was elusive not just to them but to the commentator in his position low down behind the Hampden dug-out. Within ten minutes the bedraggled players were caked in mud and their jersey numbers disappeared. Even the Scottish players looked indistinguishable from each other, so you can imagine the Pelmanistic nightmare I was having with the Irish. Eventually you could barely tell them from the Scots in the far from ideal floodlights at Hampden.

It is one of the clichés of television that as the viewers can actually see the game anyway it can speak for itself. If in doubt, shut up! This is simply not true. Viewers need a voice not just for information but also to bounce off, or agonise about, or vilify, or perhaps even be amused by. The American attempts at cutting out the ball by ball commentaries ended in failure. The much-hated commentators suddenly found new friends. The public wanted them back. It was like the Boston Strangler being suddenly perceived as the kindly neighbourhood traffic warden.

The fear of rebuke for talking too much must never predominate or you become utterly stifled. At the same time, the ability to slip into a silence is certainly one of the prime assets in a television commentator's make-up. But that is utterly different from abdicating responsibility by hiding behind the silence and 'shutting up', which is what I did that night. The game was crying out for excess and damn the consequences, simply because it was making no pattern to the viewer. Wit and a bit of wisdom would have helped but as the rain dripped off the end of my nose I froze and lapsed into incommunicable silence. The game didn't speak for itself, it mumbled incoherently. I was panned for it. I spied a solitary spectator on the East Terracing of Hampden without umbrella, shivering and bedraggled. It summed up the misery of a damp desolate stadium. I chose to use one word to describe this. 'Drookit'. It was thrown back at me by a correspondent of a newspaper who thought it aptly described my commentary.

Peter Thomson at the time was supportive and told me that he had had his disasters, but I was inconsolable. I travelled to Wembley at the end of that same week, for my first-ever broadcast there, having sleepless nights about it. A famous commentator took me to a club in Soho where the nipples were bigger than the guns of Navarone. For a fleeting moment or two sitting in this seedy setting, disillusioned by the cultural choice of this man whom I had assumed was going to show me round the Tate, I forgot about the morrow. I thought realising my ambition to commentate at Wembley would be an experience of such transcendental significance that I would be floating in nirvana. As England clinically demolished us, the whole experience was as uplifting as being stranded at Crewe Junction overnight. If you bring the news of a Scottish disaster to the public you are too often associated with it, almost as if you were an accessory after the fact. If only I could have sounded uplifting, like Thomson himself when he described that great 3−1 win in 1949. If only I could have sent inspirational sounds throughout the land I might well have benefited from it personally as a by-product. But there is nothing you can do about a 4−1 defeat by the Auld Enemy. Two decades later, I was asked during a broadcast to cheer the nation up when Scotland were playing miserably in Genoa. I had the good sense to recognise the basic phoniness of such a request and refused. There and then as a novice I might just have succumbed to such pressure and sounded even more idiotic than I had in the previous two games. The commentary in itself, I think, had been adequate but linked with the result and combined with the previous two efforts that week I was hardly regarded by the public as an infant prodigy in the business.

That is why retreating from football occasionally acted as good therapy. The Commonwealth Games in Edinburgh in 1970 was a case in point. There, I reported on a wide range of sports on radio and came into contact with, amongst others, a curmudgeonly old soul called Harold Abrahams. He had good cause to recall Edinburgh with mixed memories and at the end of his broadcasting career with radio he seemed keener to involve people in arguments about the tea being cold in the office, or where his pen had gone and how the Edinburgh weather was foul. At least some of his sentiments were not wildly inaccurate. But when I asked him if he would record some recollections of Eric Liddell for Radio Scotland he simply waved me away like a star denying a boy an autograph.

It was Lachie Stewart who made that diversion into another area eminently worth while by demonstrating the durability of what we thought was a fast vanishing breed, the true amateur, by winning the 10,000 metres on a dreich Edinburgh Saturday afternoon. This little dental mechanic who made model boats for bottles in his spare time had destroyed one of the world's first 'shamateurs', Ron Clarke. The lean and lanky Australian always ran brilliantly against the clock and broke record after record at middle distance but he had never won a gold medal at the top level. He couldn't run in a high class competitive race, apparently, but as this was to be his last ever effort and as his times were way in front of everybody else, he was not only expected to win but world athletic sentiment outside of Scotland was also clearly on his side. He lost.

At the crowded press conference afterwards most people had forgotten that it was little Lachie who was wearing the gold medal round his neck. All the questions were directed towards Clarke. To one concerning his retiral and his reasons for taking up athletics in the first place he gave vent to a philosophical explanation about how he felt life itself to be challenging, about how his sport extended his horizons and opened up his mind to the greater realities of living, and so on. Then suddenly somebody remembered that it was Lachie who had actually won the race and asked him similarly why he had taken up athletics. He looked up and replied, 'Because I got fed up going to the pictures.' The sentence came as a sudden gush of spring water in a parched field. Surrounded, as we often were, by the cynicism of professional football, and in the immediate vicinity of the pomposity of an athlete taking his running shoes a little too seriously, Stewart became an instant hero to those of us who battled daily with the spurious in search of a true original.

His breed became slowly extinct during the Seventies, though. There was little chance of him being an inspirational model to others, not when George Best was in vogue, linking his genius on the field to the rewards offered by the Marbella Club and an endless succession of blondes. Continuing after his triumph to make dentures by day and mini-*Cutty Sarks*, squeezed by leger-demain into small bottles by night, did not seem an adequate reward for the enormous effort which Lachie put into his triumph. Sport, increasingly, was being seen as a vehicle for improving life-style. It was an adjunct to the list of other social aids which the upwardly mobile sought after.

Ryder Cup golfer Harry Bannerman could certainly have moved on to higher education. His ex-headmaster, walking round the course with him, once asked Harry why he hadn't gone for his degree. Harry said, 'Wait a minute,' took out a three iron and smote the ball over two hundred yards to within a couple of feet of the hole. 'I see,' said the old teacher and changed the topic of conversation.

The footballer, never myopic when currency is on the horizon, had turned predator. In 1974 the World Cup Squad had taken their breakfast knives to rip off the distinctive stripes from their boots before a training session to be filmed by us because the sponsor Adidas had refused to pay money to everybody in the squad and only to those who actually played in the games. When Hibs won the Drybrough Cup Final against Celtic in 1972 I hauled Eddie Turnbull, the Hibs manager, out of a rejoicing dressing room, still flushed with triumph, still rabbiting on about how splen-did a victory it had been. We wired him up, got a voice level from him, got a countdown on the tape about to run to a recording when suddenly it dawned on him that he was about to be on television. 'How much am I getting for this?' he asked. 'I really have no idea,' I said. 'Well, you can stuff it up your arse then,' he replied, ripping off the mike and storming off up the tunnel.

Agents began to appear even then. Nothing wrong with the principle of having an agent. I have one myself. Except that some of the ones I met had as much money sense and deftness of touch as slaughterers at an abattoir. When we approached the possibility of qualifying for Argentina in the late Seventies that breed moved into top gear. A trend was being set. The backhander was now passé. It was all up front and it was into the outstretched palm.

It is not that Lachie Stewart was a better person than those in, or even distantly connected with, professional sport who were about to plunder the market. It is just that those nine words of explanation of why he took up athletics – 'Because I got fed up going to the pictures' – registered with me as a voice from some less complicated age, a reflection of an antique virtue that was doomed to be an anachronism. Whatever else I was to hear and see in the Seventies, the sound of those words remained with me, as if I wanted to cling on to some personal link with a past that had little contemporary meaning, just as I could never forget, even if I wanted to, the sound of a peerie being whipped in a Glasgow street.

9

Politics in Play

Sanctuary was hard to find in the late Seventies. However hard they tried, it was difficult for people in sport to elude the political tentacles which drew them into messes of other people's making. It was inevitable that the world's great controversies would impinge on sport but many of its administrators continued to believe it had a special immunity, that it could opt out of reality as it wished. This sterile philosophy was easy to justify so long as you kept your eyes selectively shut. Some of us found it difficult.

We had gone to Czechoslovakia in 1976. There, sport was supposed to be a means of demonstrating the purity of the communist system to the rest of the world. As Scotland were to play a crucial World Cup qualifying game against them, we decided to make a documentary about their whole sporting organisation, which regularly produced outstanding performers in a wide range of activities. The idea was to travel there a couple of months before the game, film what we wanted and transmit the programme the night before the match. At that time Czechoslovakia was one of the hard-line communist countries and also, because of its car, glass and beer industries, one of the most prosperous. After the usual rigmarole with their embassy about visas and documentation to film around Prague, which frustrated us no end, we flew into the city. With a relative smoothness which surprised us we made contact with our film unit and our marvellous interpreter, Yarka, who probably spoke English better than any of us. She assured us that we would be permitted to go anywhere and look at anything we wanted. We politely smiled our gratitude at that, although after the experience of our first night in the Alkron Hotel, just off Wenceslas Square, we felt that they might think us easily duped.

There were three of us: Malcolm Kellard, the sports editor, Bill Malcolm, the producer, and myself. Although the hotel was empty they had put us into a suite which housed only one single and one double bed. If the hotel had been crammed we would have put up with that but repeated requests for a switch of rooms were met by that characteristically implacable eastern European look of helplessness. We were to get used to this. Squeezed as we were into that tiny space in this huge empty hotel, we quite naturally reached the conclusion that an arrangement had been made to 'bug' the room and that we could not possibly be moved. It seemed the only explanation. Now, *Three Men and a Bug* has a sort of Jerome K. Jerome ring to it but we could not think of any other explanation. After all we were here to make a film and perhaps they might think we were less interested in muscles than we were in munitions. This country being blessed with marvellous glass, our suspicions centred on the magnificent crystal chandelier suspended from the centre of the suite. It might, in retrospect, have seemed a trifle obvious but it was to that object that we directed our remarks in loud, theatrical voices. At first painfully artificial (try to think of yourself being bugged!) we then resorted to jokes of such unambiguous filth that whoever had the earphones on in the basement was actually going to get enough material to establish himself as a stand-up comedian in the Workers Commune Club in Bratislava. Alternatively, in a fit of communist puritanism, he would wrench the headset off and slope back home. One way or the other they were going to find out they were wasting their time. Later Yarka was to admit to me that we had been listened to, although, by the contrite and apologetic look on her face, the 'listeners' had obviously not told her any of the jokes.

This early frustration was matched by the fact that we could not get the proper film stock. We almost gave up and went home but I argued that we were dealing with a system that went its own ponderous way and we must have patience. But we were blessed with great technicians. The Czech film industry is world-renowned and we ended up with a cameraman and a sound man who had both worked with Milos Forman before he had gone into exile to Hollywood to make such works as *One Flew Over the Cuckoo's Nest*, which has itself been seen as an allegory on the communist system and the durability of the human spirit. They both spoke creditable English. The cameraman was distinctly Russian orientated and kept reprimanding the sound man for criticising Russian films. The little sound man would say, 'I hate Russky films. All psycholgie. Nothing but psycholgie and war!' The tall gaunt cameraman would, in English, so that we would be aware of his inclination, cajole him and talk about the 'war when twenty million Russian lives were lost to save the world'. I was to hear that stark and truthful remark trotted out on innumerable occasions behind the Iron Curtain by people at functions who would suddenly pop up to tell you how marvellous the system was. We worked together well, except that we had no clapper board to put the film into synchronisation and Bill Malcolm had to stand in front of camera and clap his hands and shout out the number of the takes before every shot or else the editor back in Scotland would have been lost. Bill was probably the first man in film-making history to suffer bruising of the hands on a job. Then, one day, the first touch of the sinister.

We had gone to the vast Spartakiad Stadium to reflect the kernel of the entire system. Every four years the nation's gymnasts, from village and city, would take part in mass exercises in one of the most gigantic displays anywhere in world sport. To stand in the middle of its sandy surface was like being in a desert. When we had finished our exterior shots we went inside to watch some of the young gymnasts being put through their paces by an instructress whom I recognised immediately. The Golden Girl of the Mexico Olympics of 1968, Vera Caslavska, the winner of four gold medals. She had got married in Mexico City during the Games. I asked Yarka if she would arrange an interview with her. She went down into the gym and talked to this beautiful and still lithe blonde who, during the conversation with our interpreter, looked up and smiled shyly at us as if in assent to the request. Yarka returned and said it had been arranged for two days' time, a Saturday morning. When we duly showed up with our cameras she wasn't there. In her place was another, rather statuesque lady who had won a gold at a previous Olympics. When I asked where Vera had gone, Yarka apologised and told me that, unfortunately, the Gymnastic Association had requested her to hold some tests for children in another part of the city. They passed on a message from Vera saying she was very apologetic but that she was sure we would understand that her job came first. Of course we did. Until that same evening.

We were in the hotel restaurant. We had ordered a meal from a menu the size of the *Daily Record* and been told, as usual, that of the twenty thousand dishes on display only the pork was available, but that it did come four different ways. We were entertaining Yarka both for her brilliant translations during interviews and for her charm and general serenity during those periods of filming when the affable can give way so easily to the irascible. But she got slightly tiddly on the excellent and very reasonably priced Russian champagne. She suddenly went quiet for a spell and then, late into the evening, turned and whispered to me, 'I am ashamed! Very ashamed of myself!' Then she fell quiet again.

'Why?' I asked.

'I told you a lie,' she said quietly. 'About Vera Caslavska. She was not allowed to meet you. She is, what you say, persona non grata. She is in disgrace. When she came back from the Mexico Olympics she showed her support for Dubcek and the political changes he was trying to establish by presenting him with her four gold medals. That was not forgotten when the changes took place and there was the clamp down. She is in permanent disgrace now and is not allowed to speak to anybody from the western media. She would have liked to so much. Please do not breathe a word to anybody about this. I could not have forgiven myself if I had allowed you to leave without telling you the truth about that.'

I felt a slight chill running up the spine. A great athlete gives the leader of a country her Olympic medals and is now considered to be a villain? It did not seem credible but then the Prague Spring which offered so much hope for change in Czechoslovakia and was ruthlessly suppressed seemed far off. This beautiful city was now dour, dull and resigned to it all. The budding of hope that came with Dubcek belonged to another and forgotten age. Yarka was deeply upset about this.

'I am very ashamed for myself and my country,' she went on. 'There is so much of this.'

The genuine pity that I felt for her was compounded two days later when we went to film the famous Rude Pravo Road Race which was run annually through the streets of Prague and won on this occasion by the Finn Lasse Viren, the man who went in for the Dracula-like blood transfusions before each Olympics to notable effect. But it was not this running skeleton who haunted me afterwards but another figure.

'Do you recognise that face?' Yarka asked me as we filmed the dignitaries' stand near the crowded finishing line. There he was, walking slowly and almost painfully amongst the top brass of the party and army shaking hands like a fawning beggar, smiling like a clockwork doll. It was Emil Zatopek, the great Czech middle distance runner of the early Fifties, the man with the head-bobbing, pained running expression who had great clashes on the British tracks with the likes of Chris Chataway. He would always be regarded as one of the finest runners of all time.

'He is another one,' Yarka said.

'Another what?'

'In disgrace. He did the same as Vera. He showed his support for Dubcek. One day he was a Master of Sport, a distinguished man in our sports system. The next he was a clerk licking stamps and tying string. That is what he now does in a small office. You see he is with these men trying to get back into favour. But it's no use. There is no way back for him.'

Zatopek shook his last hand on the platform then, bald head gleaming in the sharp autumn sun, shuffled down the stairs out of sight. I was beginning to dislike Czechoslovakia a great deal. We had come mentally prepared to be fighting to disentangle ourselves from a miasmic bureaucracy but were ill-equipped to respond to this malevolence. We did in fact portray Zatopek as the disgraced hero and expressed, in the context of a pointedly non-political film, a diversionary comment on his plight.

Our hands were not completely free. We had been offered the co-operation of the Czech television service on the condition that when we returned for the coverage of the international match we would show them the finished documentary. This would not have affected our ultimate transmission but, as they had apparently given us the help upon which we were totally dependent, to make a film about sport we wanted to play fair with them. I was worried though about bringing back the completed version for them to view because in the delicate situation we found ourselves you could never ensure their complete acceptance.

We completed our film. We reflected on the importance they attached to developing sport and how much that meant in an international arena. We looked at how they nurtured their young talent and showed the work at a special football school in the city. We even recorded recreational activities for the general population, having been taken by one of the party apparatchiks to a 'trim' park where people could exercise freely.

We wanted to film an interview with a young family we saw walking through the park; a mother, father and daughter of about six. But we desisted when they asked for money. We had obviously bumped into a capitalist 'cell'. Yarka transcribed all the interviews painstakingly into English so that we would have no misinterpretations in our scripting back in Glasgow. However, to be as meticulous as we possibly could, I approached Glasgow University to find out if someone could check the language for us. Down to the studios came a professor who had been born and brought up in Prague. His name was Dr Emil Soukoup.

Silver-haired, urbane, mild-mannered Dr Soukoup sat in front of the viewing screen in the editing room listening to the interviews and watching the panorama of his native city unfold. His expressions varied from extreme sadness to chuckling hilarity, especially as he checked the speech with the written translations Yarka had provided. Having looked through every foot of film he turned to me.

'Oh, dear!' he cried. 'They make it sound so simple don't they? All they told you was what they wanted you to hear, nothing more. And I think we could beef up the translations a little more. Oh, dear! What a sad place!'

He had a beautifully modulated, 'mittel-European' accent which made me think he would be ideal as the voice speaking in English on the film over the Czech voices. When I suggested this to him he resisted, saying he could not possibly, he of all people, no of course not! But in truth it did not take all that much arm twisting to get him to change his mind because I think he was emotionally pulled into the documentary, as if it was providing a vicarious trip back to his beloved city. We had not asked him too much about himself since we were simply interested in translation and it was his ability in linguistics that impressed us.

'I have never been back since I left some years ago,' he explained to us. 'I am a refugee who was lucky enough to get a job in languages. I have been very fortunate. But I would not go back. I hate and despise what they have done to my country.'

So, he put his voice on the film for us and, the job completed, we set out to return to Prague. We took with us a video recording of our programme but some instinct of mine was at work. I advised my producer to hold on to the tape until we were leaving the country again, as our stay was only three days. Each day Yarka came to the hotel or phoned us to ask for the tape and for three days we played a cat and mouse game with her. It is difficult to know now how we managed to elude these requests but we did one way or the other, feigning forgetfulness or saying that one or other of us had had it in mind to come to the television station but that something had cropped up. She wasn't exactly the dumbest girl in the world and must have known that something was afoot, although, having developed a genuine friendship with us, I think she did not want to push this too much. It was not as if we had pilloried their country or their political system but, on Dr Soukoup's advice, we had altered certain translations and I had certainly changed my script in accordance with his interpretations of some of the things said to us. It queried rather than criticised and in that sense was, in my view, only mildly admonitory. And yet I felt uneasy about it.

We commentated on Czechoslovakia beating Scotland 2–0, retired despondently to our hotel, where we sought succour in the plum brandy, and generally made ourselves scarce until the following morning, just half-an-hour before the bus left for the airport, when we met Yarka and presented her with the tape. We said our farewells and my producer and I admitted to each other that there was a sense of relief at having got this off our hands. We were eager to get home, out of this frigid country. We did not reckon on the weather though. SFA Secretary, Ernie Walker marched into the lounge of the hotel just ten minutes after Yarka had left to announce that there was fog at the airport and that we could be delayed up to four or five hours. Bill Malcolm and I could scarcely believe this.

'Are you thinking what I'm thinking?' Bill asked me.

Yes, I had been. They would have plenty of time to look at the video and we still would be in the country. We thought of making ourselves scarce, going for a walk. The trouble about walking in the old town of Prague, in the twisting maze of streets, is that even with the keenest sense of direction you could so easily get lost. We considered it but, then, I had had enough. Perhaps we were being over-sensitive about this whole episode anyway. We were not.

About an hour-and-a-half later we saw two, black top-grade Skoda limousines swinging into the square beside the hotel. Out of the first stepped Yarka. She was followed by three men who did not actually come into the hotel but stood outside the swing-doors. I rose to meet her. I put out my hand but unsmilingly she suddenly broke into that chilling formalese which was so uncharacteristic of her, but so typical of the robotic communist attempts at communication by ordinance.

'I would like to thank you for coming to my country, Mr Macpherson,' she clipped. It was as if they had given her some injection so that she could talk to us in the manner befitting a female of the party, like Ninotchka. 'But we are very unhappy with the film. The English is not good. Some of the things said are distorted. We are very unhappy. Who was the man who voiced the translation?'

This didn't seem to be Yarka but some clone. At the same time a little voice in my head told me to act dumb.

'Oh, it was an actor we picked up,' I replied. 'He put on a fake sort of accent for us to make it sound middle-European. He was good at it.'

She was not taken in but did not try to contradict me.

'I think we know the voice, you know,' she said softly. 'He said things which did not please us. Certain inflections of meaning in the translation. We are unhappy with the English. Is there no more light you can shed on this?'

'No,' I lied, feeling both remorse and anger that this delightful lady had apparently been lobotomised to party conformity.

'Good-bye,' she said suddenly, turned and walked to the door.

I followed trying to think of some apology but felt quite defeated by the circumstances. At the door she stopped and merely said, 'They were very angry but I spoke up for you. You know it could have been worse. But I think it will be difficult for you to come back to my country. They will not trust you.'

And off she went in her black car leaving me distraught. I felt as if I had cheated her personally and was also disturbed by her sudden change of personality. Certainly the men had been watching her from the door. Yet I wasn't sure that accounted for it. It was difficult to grasp why this relatively innocuous filming exercise was concluding like one of John Le Carré's bleak endings.

It was possible that, after all, she was a party hack stringing us along all the time. I wanted to doubt that but I would never know for sure, which was the unkindest cut of all.

When we returned to Glasgow, after sweating for a time in Prague airport, and suspicious of even the lavatory attendants, I made straight for Dr Soukoup. I took him to lunch.

'Who are you?' I asked bluntly.

I told him what had happened.

'I am sorry,' he apologised. 'I did not want to say too much. And you did not ask too much. I was in politics in Czechoslovakia. I was political secretary to the Foreign Minister Jan Masaryk. As you probably know he was in the last government to be democratically elected before the communists took over in 1948. You know of course that Jan died in Wenceslas Square. He fell from a balcony. Many people claim he was pushed. Not physically he wasn't. Perhaps the pressure of events had overcome him and in that sense he was pushed. He knew a communist coup was on hand and there seemed nothing that could be done to save democracy. I was the first to reach the body in the square.

'If he had been pushed he would have resisted and his body would have landed in a contorted mess on the street. But as it was, there were clear signs that he had fallen like a man in some kind of trance. His thigh bones went clean through his shoulder blades. A classic suicide, you would say. I knew I was then in serious danger myself. So I did as much as I could with his body, went home, gathered my belongings, got into my car and drove over the border and I have never been back. Now I teach and occasionally I broadcast from a station in Rome into Czechoslovakia, telling the truth. I think they would really like to get their hands on me.'

He told this with a certain reluctance, as if it ought to have been confined within a strictly familial conversation. Perhaps he is now back in Prague teaching at the university. Perhaps Yarka is working for a West German branch of a multi-national company now taking executives round the city. I saw them both as victims of a brutal political system and myself innocently drawn into the convoluted mess of their lives. All because I wanted to know what made a Czechoslovakian athlete tick. In truth, whilst their national football team did enjoy a certain moderate success it gradually began to resemble a mechanical toy needing regular winding up by a toy-maker reluctant to do so. It reflected the dehydrated spirit of a country which had essentially lost its self-esteem.

But the 'free' world offered its major problems as well as we discovered when, in preparation for a possible qualification for the finals in Argentina, the SFA decided to take on a South American tour consisting of games in Chile, Argentina and Brazil. Although it was the second leg of the trip I cannot think of South American football or what the people were then suffering without first recal-ling our entry into Argentina.

The welcome party in Buenos Aires consisted largely of grim-faced men with pistols, machine-guns, rifles, and armoured cars. Cheery sorts who looked as if a body a day kept the blues away. We knew that there had been a reputation of animosity from time to time between the SFA and the media but we did not think it had reached the ears of the Argentinians. Yet, arriving, as we were, at the International Airport just outside the capital city, we assumed they thought hostilities were about to break out in the arrival lounge, thus necessitating the presence of a peace force. As we shuffled from the terminal I sought out somebody who could speak English and discovered a large man who kept sweeping his eyes round the curious crowds gazing at the Scottish party. I asked him why there was a show of force.

'The Montoneros,' he said heavily, without looking at me. 'They threaten violence.'

Anybody who could have contemplated threatening violence against this gorilla would have been deranged. He kept his right hand in his jacket, Napoleon-like; not, I supposed, to assist in philosophical meditation. There were many others like him around. The airport looked as if it were under siege and yet here we were in the year of our Lord 1977, simply coming to a country to play football. It didn't seem that the month of May was a merry one in Argentina.

'Montoneros?' I asked.

'Bad. Verr, verr bad,' he replied moving off. Our interpreters told us later that they were the guerrilla group fighting the military dictatorship in Argentina and that they had promised to disrupt the World Cup the following year, bringing hand-grenades rather than ricketies to provide background noise. It wasn't as if we had flown into this tense South American country totally naive about the political situation. It is just that such a dimension seemed to lie outwith our own interest. Reading about it didn't quite prepare us for looking down the barrel of a gun or seeing the military hardware surrounding us. There were two buses for the group from the airport, as is normal. But the separation of media from players and officials followed a different order.

'Yours is the first bus,' a suave gentleman told us. 'You will lead the way in the convoy.'

Convoy? Sure enough there was an armoured car just in front of the leading bus and, beside it and between the two buses, large cars and behind that again another armoured car. But the media bus travelling first to the hotel seemed an outrageous breach of the normal protocol, although Ernie Walker did not seem to be objecting all that much. I learned from the loose-tongued interpreter the reason for this.

'Well, you see,' he said. 'If the Montoneros were to attack they would perhaps bomb the first bus in the convoy, thinking it was the team and officials. That is why they are putting the press up front.'

Was there a smile on Ernie's face? Were we to be decoys? It might just have been occurring to the SFA that the Montoneros could once and for all rid them of a company of men who hung round their necks like lead weights at times. We had never been decoys before and we took to it with that jocular fortitude that the Scot shows in time of great stress, although we stopped short of gaily putting our names in a hat and having a sweep on when the first strike would be. Our journey into the city though left us no time to reflect on this bizarre scenario for we did not simply leave the airport, we were catapulted from it.

We took off from the airport and onto the frenetic roads of Buenos Aires at ninety miles an hour. Sirens wailing, we stopped for nothing. Just in front of us the plain-clothed state thugs were leaning out of their windows, waving revolvers at passers-by and shouting to warn them from crossing our paths. Cars sped out of our way up onto pavements, brakes screeching, horns blasting as the convoy seemed to leap at Buenos Aires' jugular. So far this was working a treat, sobering up those who had been a bit heavy on the Chilean vino on the trip over the Andes, and putting a bomb-throwing Montonero shouting, 'Libre Argentina' right out of our heads. Then out of the window up ahead I saw an old man crossing the road, hobbling slightly and leaning on a walking stick. The gangsters in the car in front were screaming at him. I swear I detected a little touch of defiance in him as he just about got out of the way but did not leave the road and stared stolidly at us as we approached.

As the car got to him I saw the policeman leaning further out of the window and swiping at him with the barrel of the revolver. The old man dropped like a stone as the bus sped by. It all happened in a blur, almost as if it had been a mirage, but from our side of the bus we could look back and see him lying in the road behind us.

We had barely recovered from that when the assault troops in front started to hammer on the roofs of cars with their bare fists to get them out of the way as we neared the city centre, leaving big dents, in some cases, on the bodywork. As we swung through the traffic into the bewildering maze of streets the police continued to lash out at cars and people until we eventually swept into the hotel forecourt screeching and coming to rest like a runaway train halted inches from the buffers. I felt drained. What kind of country was this we had come to? What kind of animals were these men purportedly lending us protection? I sensed we had come to an evil place. The incident with the old man had been one thing but what kind of tyranny was this when police molested cars as if they were people? Was not even that potent icon of Buenos Aires sacred?

This was Argentina and to a great extent the journey from the airport summarised much of what South America was in the Seventies. We were in a large military camp which was unable to comprehend the changes that had taken place in the mother countries of Spain and Portugal. It was generally governed by the men in silly uniforms with decorative braid as subtle as neon lighting. Playing football and holding a World Cup would be one of the ways of anaesthetising the population against rebellious, rousing ideas. It could even endear them to the rest of the world. In the long run it didn't work but for a while sport was used as a temporary buttress supporting a wall with little foundation.

When this tour, with its first stop in Chile, had been originally mooted, it provoked outrage, particularly amongst the political left and trade unions. In 1973, Salvador Allende, the first-ever democratically elected Marxist president in the western world, had been killed in a coup brought about by the Chilean generals led by Pinochet. Those opponents of the new regime were herded into the national football stadium and many were taken from this temporary concentration camp to be slaughtered. Chile was now a ruthless dictatorship. This did not deter the SFA from electing to arrange an international match against them some four years later.

Soon after the coup, in 1973, the Soviet Union had refused to play a World Cup decider qualifying match in that very stadium. They had sent a message to FIFA declaring that 'Soviet sportsmen cannot at present play at a stadium stained with the blood of Chilean patriots'. FIFA asked Chile if the game could be held in another ground. This was rebuffed and as the Soviet Union would not budge they were eliminated from the World Cup.

One is not sure how many telexes of protest about blood spillage and unjust internment were sent to the Gulags in Siberia from the Soviet FA. Perhaps they never got round to it. It was also suggested that since the game between the sides in Moscow had ended in a 0–0 draw the Soviets had little stomach to travel all that way for almost certain elimination.

However, to be totally fair, they had offered to play in any other venue than the notorious National Stadium. So, even though their stance smacked of hypocrisy, they had at least decided that sport was not possible in absolutely any context. That in itself seemed to me to be indisputable. The SFA though pushed ahead with their arrangements despite the Labour government's strong disapproval or, perhaps, even because of it, for there is nobody more obdurate than a sports official scorned by a politician. The trip was settled and agreed. The unions were incensed and threatened to withdraw any labour associated with departure from airports.

I had made my own position clear departmentally within the BBC. I did not think the SFA should have arranged this match but when it became clear that they would go ahead, my employers made it equally clear to me that they would like me to report and commentate on the trip, although they would not take me to task if I refused to go. There was no chance of my refusing. I wanted, at first hand, to see this country and Argentina. Journalistically, it would have been madness to have spurned the opportunity. I did want to see this stadium and I did want to talk to people. That, at least, is what I told myself over and over again.

We arrived there debauched by jet-lag having travelled all the way for something like twenty-six hours in a plane that seemed to have been designed for flights round Arran. After those cramped confines, with our knees practically up to our chins, there was little of the bounding investigative zeal left in anybody by the time we found our beds in the hotel. I surveyed the tranquil scene out of my bedroom on that first morning mentally composing a telephone report which I was due to give within the hour back to Scotland.

The Andes loomed up above us like they were about to topple in at any moment. The mountain range would come and go like a reluctant apparition as the mist flirted with them. The city itself was overhung with smog very much like Los Angeles but the physical stillness of this large bowl, scooped out of the foothills, was unsettling given the turbulent political background we had heard so much about. Imbued with passion on the subject, I was not to be taken in by this idyllic scene. So, when the call came, I launched into my two-way chat with the studio presenter by examining the political soul of this country, discussing what we might see in this stadium of shame and talking of how we would try to identify the true suffering of this nation and asserting that the eyes of the world would be on this tour. Back came the retort, 'Yes, but will Scotland be playing 4–2–4 or 4–3–3?' There was no answer to that.

That same morning, as the players and others lounged around the swimming pool, resting after the ordeal of the long flight, a silver-haired gentleman turned up and casually wandered amongst the group, sounding impeccably English. He looked like a retired colonel or a British textile manufacturer of whom there were many all down that side of the South American continent. I did not pay much attention to him until he wandered near a group of players which included Kenny Dalglish.

I then heard him pontificating about life in Chile, of how marvellous it was for everybody and of how it would be important for the players to go back home and tell the people the truth about the situation and of how everybody had distorted the facts and that in reality the people were settled and happy. I have no way of knowing if Kenny has subsequently studied political philosophy. At that stage in his career though, he was merely interested in penalty box play and not the downfall of a Marxist in Chile and the CIA's involvement in such. But Kenny has always had, and will never lose, his Glasgow street instinct for spotting a phoney when he sees one. He immediately did so here.

'You're talking a load of crap!' he told the dignified figure posturing near the sun-lounger. 'We'll make up our own minds about what we see here. We don't need you to tell us.'

The man seemed to crumple under that blast, as others have since at some of Kenny's subsequent press conferences as a manager, and sidled away in the same manner he had insinuated himself. He had obviously been sent with a message for all of us. He looked and sounded sinisterly simplistic and his demolition by Kenny was quite the most marvellous come-uppance I have ever seen anybody getting, considering he thought he had come into the midst of a bunch of simpletons.

The head of the Chilean FA, General Gordon, also happened to be head of the local police and the following day he invited the entire Scottish group to a barbecue in the Prince of Wales Country Club. This was a middle-class enclave guarded by men with guns and comprising a magnificent golf course and a whole variety of sporting and leisure facilities in a stunning setting with the Andes monstrously big above us and the streams and trees of the complex giving the impression of utter tranquillity.

The people there were at pains to tell us that if Allende had stayed in power all of what we could see would have been at risk. They did not go so far as to say that they supported his killing, or that they admired General Pinochet, but they made it clear the economy would have been ruined and anarchy would have ensued. My attempts to try and broaden the argument to the lack of support Allende got from the international community, especially the United States, whose complicity in the downfall of the President had been strongly indicated, were met with polite scorn. We didn't really know the true facts. It was all very well for us to criticise, and so on.

I pointed out that travelling through Santiago we were besieged by people begging in the streets, women and children, obviously starving. We were told that that sort of thing was quite common throughout South America and we would simply get used to it. It is certainly true I have seen it now throughout that continent. But I have never got used to it. I felt that this crowd of well-heeled British expatriates with their Chilean middle-class counterparts enjoyed not just a major recreational facility in this place but asylum as well. Outside there was a threatening world held at bay by a ruthless and convenient dictator. If the suppression was out of sight, then it didn't really matter.

But we saw the other side. Later that night a little man with a broad Scottish accent presented himself at the hotel. He was wearing a rather crumpled jacket over an open-necked shirt and was tieless. It looked as if he had walked all the way from home seeking autographs. He was in fact from Shotts and he was a Catholic priest. His name was Father Jimmy Small. This man had been in a mission in Santiago for years and was part of the worker-priest movement which was flourishing in South America. He invited us the following day to the mission for lunch which, he warned us in advance, would be very simple in nature. He took us down just before midday and outside the simple hacienda-type building he pointed to the distinct marks on the yellow, plastered wall.

'These are bullet holes,' he said. 'You will see such all over Santiago.' We had in fact noticed the scooped marks in the centre of the city where, it was pointed out to us, Allende had supposedly been gunned down. 'But we regard these as a reminder of how dangerous our situation is. These were some of the bullets they fired at Dr Sheila Cassidy the night they came to capture her.'

Sheila Cassidy's experience had become a *cause célèbre* back in the UK when eventually she had been able to get away. Her testimony about the scale of torture going on in Chile did much to lend credence to the criticism of the Pinochet regime. She had in fact been in captivity, and been cruelly tortured, but that night had gained asylum in the mission.

'They killed her housekeeper though,' the priest said. 'It is a sad country. We are watched all the time. Right now they will have us under surveillance.'

We looked round almost sheepishly.

'Oh, you won't see them,' he said. 'But I can assure you they will be taking photographs of all of us. They regard us as enemies, the way they did Sheila Cassidy. All she was doing was ministering to the poor. That was her crime. Ours is in extending our mission into helping to feed the poor. There is no good serving the soul if people are dying on you needlessly because of starvation.'

The meal was simple. Mince, bread and mineral water. We sat amongst a gathering of about twenty foreign priests from all over the world, all of them engaged in what became fashionably described as 'liberation theology'. This consisted of taking the view that you could not, in South America, separate the social conditions of the tragically deprived and under-nourished classes from their spiritual nourishment. A political stance had to be taken against the totalitarian or inefficient political systems. This was bound to cause tensions within those societies as well as within the church. But these men had seen too much of the horrific conditions of the people not to take a hard line against Pinochet. Nor could they bother too much at that time about what the Vatican thought.

'We are delighted to see you,' the little priest said. 'It is good that you came to Chile. But you must come to see the "poblaciones". These are our parishes. The poverty may sicken you.'

It did. The conditions were so appalling that the priests working there could not possibly wear their normal vestments. Rickets was the main disease of children, malnutrition was rife, sanitation well nigh non-existent and at that moment whether Scotland played 4–2–4 or 4–3–3 the following night seemed of colossal irrelevance. But that after all is why we were here. In a sense I was grateful for the SFA's impassivity on the matter. This little segment of the visit to Chile had certainly made an enormous impact on me but it also reinforced my view that turning one's back on a political system because one didn't approve could simply lead to ignorance.

The National Stadium sent a chill through the bones not only because of the reverberating echoes of all that had happened there but because, on the night of the game, a mist had enveloped it. A match of stunning insignificance became a guessing game of identity and, as hardly anybody had turned up to watch, it seemed less an international and more an inter-departmental works competition. The mist got so bad that from the commentary position we could not see that Scotland had substituted their goalkeeper at half-time.

But they won 4–2, easily, and the thin, miserable Chilean crowd seemed like party hacks drummed up for the occasion. The whole affair was, after all, quite squalid. The natural plumage of this part of the world ought to have been gloriously multi-coloured but we were now seeing it like Whitechapel on one of the nights Jack the Ripper loved. It was appropriate. We had visited a political cess-pit and although I tried to record the fact in my reports it has to be said that back in Scotland nobody was all that much interested. They wanted me to conjure up stories about the players which quite frankly didn't exist on a relatively plain-sailing tour. Politics and sport don't mix, they just shadow each other and occasionally collide like two ships in a fog. The fog of that last night in Chile clung to me long after. Call it a metaphor for the awful condition the continent was in.

The brief visit to Argentina underlined the impression. The peso kept changing in value. Beggars walked through fashionable areas in Buenos Aires like Florida, the main shopping centre. There I stopped a man to ask him the way to a hotel and it turned out, freakishly enough, that his name was McWhirter. He was of Scottish descent, several generations back, but had never actually met a European. When I questioned him about the police and social conditions he told me in his broken English that it wasn't safe to speak even in a shopping promenade about the state of the country.

This atmosphere of apprehension never changed even when we arrived at Boca Juniors Stadium for the match against Argentina and a brown paper parcel was seen just below our commentary position half-an-hour before the game. The police emptied that section of the stand and, guns flourishing again, waited until a bomb squad had arrived on the scene. The 'bomb' turned out to be a parcel of sandwiches left by one of the stadium attendants.

The only real scare that night was that we had a technical conundrum which I couldn't work out at the time. During the live transmission I apologised for the fact that there were no slow-motion replays and pointed out that the production was by Argentina television. I had been looking at my monitor for the first twenty minutes and none had appeared. Suddenly I heard the voice of my producer in Glasgow saying to me down my earpiece in the perfect communications we had with them, 'What do you mean there are no replays! We're seeing them here.'

What then followed might have appealed to those who adore *Monty Python*. For there I was in Argentina listening to my producer in Glasgow giving me his commentary on the replays all the way to Buenos Aires for me to repeat them blindly all the way back again to the unknowing Scottish viewers. After all the tensions of the trip it seemed an appropriate touch of the bizarre. Scotland drew 1–1 that night and we left the city the following day with horns blaring again, armoured escort in attendance, and the feeling that the world was in a 'state o' chassis'.

From Prague all the way over the Andes to Chile and back again to Argentina we had experienced political oppression of one sort or the other. Through it all we plied our own sporting trade with the apparent insouciance of a besieged colonial group in their compound, playing croquet as the masses batter at the gates.

10

The Argentina Experience

Strangers on a train gave me the news about Peter Thomson. I got on the subway at Hillhead and was minding my own business when I overheard them talking about the newspaper report of his death in 1977. I had forgotten just how powerful an influence his voice had on people. Indeed I had forgotten him altogether. That peculiar aroma of the Glasgow Subway used to have an aphrodisiacal tang to it after a night out along Byres Road. Now it seemed like the incense of a requiem.

It was not so much the sadness of hearing about this but of knowing that Peter had not been able to cope with leaving the BBC two years previously. Anytime I saw him after that he seemed a crushed man. He had tragically lost his wife and, in terms that he would have understood himself, was like a studio without electrical power, inert, dark, directionless. I remember, previous to this night, thinking that I could not allow myself to become so umbilically tied to the job that separation would mean some fatal wounding. I felt I had to resist that. Binding your life to the institution would be foolish. You were fixing your gaze on a date clearly and distinctly etched on a headstone. But it is still the easy option for some, and the only choice for many.

The stilling of Peter's voice broke my last tangible link with the age of 'The McFlannels', 'Aunt' Kathleen Garscadden, 'Down At the Mains', austerity, ration-books, Attlee, Crosby, Ben Hogan and playing 'wee-heedies' up a close.

We had moved off in another direction after he had left.

Malcolm Kellard, from Ireland, had taken his place, with the emphasis on more stylish presentation both on and off screen. I suppose I greeted him like someone jealously preserving his own status. I had staked my ground and no one, not even this talented import, was going to make me budge. I underrated his charm and over-rated his intention. He wanted to change things, probably took me for granted as the bearer of everything he needed to know and imbibe about the Scottish football scene, but there was nothing more sinister in it than that. He knew how to handle the BBC system much better than I could, largely because I was not wholly interested in it. I still tended to regard the work outside the building as more important to both the Corporation and myself than coping with the complexities, ambiguities and subtleties of 'getting on' within the institution. Not that this attitude of mine was much appreciated at the time.

It was not, however, a great period of upheaval within either my own area or throughout the BBC. The problems which arose were mostly about facilities and local expense. Alasdair Milne once took time off from discussing really weighty matters to ask me why, in the name of heaven, we could not get a new camera position at Tynecastle, where the pillars got in the way and drove him to distraction. As we tailed off that conversation he added, 'By the way, I get letters in saying you are biased in your commentaries. Don't worry about that. We pay you to express your views. I wouldn't expect anything else.' He was sharp, direct and stimulating.

We knew of course that the criticism was not just about what was said but how we projected ourselves. Throughout the Seventies we were castigated by the public for our poor camera work. Letters would appear in the press and comments would be made to me personally about how the English were better at it than we were. I felt sorry for our cameramen who, ironically enough, were mostly English. It was not shoddy camera work. It was lack of equipment. Whereas we normally covered a game with two cameras, network had the luxury of double or treble the number. They could place cameras behind the goal and at pitch level whilst we were lucky to hoist a couple on to a central platform on the halfway-line. We were two-dimensional by comparison and it showed painfully.

One night at Hampden Park in 1975 we lost a goal altogether because of this. Romania scored against Scotland from a long midfield pass into the penalty area that our minimal number of cameras could not quite lock-on to. The technique of commentary involves you in keeping an eye on the game and the other on the television monitor beside you so that you are reporting on what the viewer will see at home eventually. It stands to reason, doesn't it? Except that reason does not always prevail in this business. Sometimes you merely have to watch the play itself to ensure proper identification especially when danger threatens a defence in the penalty area. So I took my eye off the monitor momentarily to describe this quite brilliant goal. I did so with enthusiasm.

In those days we did not have immediate replays available to us. We had to visualise the goal immediately after and repeat the commentary in the hope that the words would fit the picture which would be not so much an instant replay, more a second edit 'pasted' on later. So when I looked back down at the monitor all I saw were men hugging each other in celebration. I thought nothing of that and continued. I left the stadium that night not realising anything was amiss because the producer had not the heart to tell me that he had missed the goal altogether.

I went back with some friends to a favourite hostelry in the East End and we set ourselves up to watch the recorded highlights of the game in the bar. Eventually we reached the point where I was lyrically describing a goal that simply was not coming up on the screen. All we saw was a Romanian in midfield admiring his own telling pass, then a quick cut to consenting adults embracing in the penalty area. If you have never been in an East-End bar in Glasgow when silence suddenly falls and about forty pairs of eyes turn towards you, glasses suspended just below the lips, then you will not know what icy terror really means. I left hurriedly without explanation.

Mishaps like that put our credibility continually on the line and unfortunately tended to detract from excellent productions on other occasions. The public by and large do not write or phone in to praise but to criticise or condemn. We were noticed for our gaffes. Competence is synonymous with anonymity. On the other hand we felt that being the BBC we were held under greater scrutiny than our rivals. This might seem unbearably arrogant but nevertheless there was an element of truth in it.

However, criticisms were never in my experience taken lightly. But they were mostly transient. We had not yet encountered the new 'philosophers' of the right and the attacks on the whole concept of a licence-based system. In defence of its uncommercial integrity we faced up to nothing more daunting than the threat of football going off the screens because of the advent of shirt advertising. The 'Long-Room' Colonel Blimp fundamentalists in our ranks believed such a thing would never be allowed. My own view was that it ought to happen and that the sole criterion should be aesthetic. When all this came to pass I could not bring myself to remind people of their faith in the BBC not budging on the issue. Instead I respected the Corporation for the way it showed it could adapt without throwing overboard its main principles.

We duly paid attention to our competitors, STV, but perhaps rather complacently assumed that in a straight contest with them we would always come out with three times the audience. This seemed to be borne out by the viewing figures for the Scottish Cup Final when we were in straight opposition. We enjoyed this in-built Establishment 'special occasion' advantage, without always meriting it. STV, in their own way, projected the Cup final just as well as we did and, I know, felt sorely aggrieved at not commanding bigger audiences. So when the World Cup of 1978 came round we felt confident that in a head-on clash with commercial television the BBC would hold its normal advantage. Indeed, on the night Scotland played Wales at Anfield in the deciding game we drew the biggest ever audience for live football up till then. Not a man, woman or child in Scotland seemed to miss that match. It was not simply the importance of the occasion which proved compulsive but also the way in which a national state-of-the-art passion had been designed by one man, Ally MacLeod.

My first sighting of Ally MacLeod was in one of his first games for Third Lanark at Cathkin. Being a left winger he was, for half the match, near the enclosure where we used to stand and looked the kind of pimply boy who might still be delivering the papers or the milk. His schoolboyish enthusiasm was the very feature which made him so noticeable. He rushed at defences with an apparently unco-ordinated whirl of legs and arms that seemed part combine harvester on the move, part irate man escaping from a swarm of bees. It was the football of impetuous youth which quickly endeared him to people. Not much changed through the years. The fountain of youth danced away behind even some of his darker moments when he led the crusade to Argentina. But, of course, it is with that period of his life he will be irrevocably associated.

But I can never think of Argentina or Ally without firstly recalling the occupation of Liverpool on the evening of 12 October, 1977. That night saw the full flourishing of the dubious emotion I had recognised at Glasgow Airport three years earlier on our return from Germany. It had seemed then that it could turn into unjustified and uncontrollable frenzy. The Welsh had relinquished the right to play this game on their own soil and, selling their birthright to Mammon, decided that Anfield would swell the coffers more. Knowing the pride the Welsh engender normally in their sport, particularly on the rugby field, where toughened veterans can be reduced to tears by the singing of the national anthem even before somebody has kicked them in a loose maul, this transplantation into England was not just tatty but lent the whole affair a spurious quality. For me, it spoiled the eventual triumph to a great extent.

The area around Anfield resembled a kind of medieval fair with pickpockets plundering the great and the mighty just outside the main entrance, people shouting and bartering for tickets, and others making arrangements about how they were going to travel to Argentina. Everywhere there was singing, drinking, and waving of banners. The final congestion just inside the main gates was claustrophobic. It was the carousal of confidence. It was the kind I have never enjoyed hearing from Scottish people. It was blatant and aggressive and intimidatory.

'I hope to God we win,' Jock Stein said to me on the television platform as we tried to settle down just before kick-off. 'If we don't I think they'll take Liverpool apart.'

He didn't need to coax me towards that conclusion. The platform at Anfield affords you a sweeping and high view of the stadium and looking round it you could see the Welsh had been confined to a small enclave on the stand side of the Kop. Everywhere else was a mass of Scottish banners and tumultuous bragging of inevitable supremacy. It was not healthy. They were not there to support possible success, they were demanding it. I am convinced that on that very night in Liverpool Stein crystallised his views on how vulnerable Scottish players are on these occasions when the gauntlet is thrown down not just by the opposition but by their own supporters.

He could see the potential for the hysteria spreading on to the pitch, quite indiscriminate in its effect. It did as much harm to ourselves as to the opposition. He was to be plagued by that image throughout his own subsequent management of the national team. Certainly the previous May at Wembley, when Scotland had won 2–1 on Ally MacLeod's managerial debut, the atmosphere had been like a grand family party which had gone slightly over the top.

One's official face had to engage in formal 'tut-tutting' over the damage to property, the pitch being stripped of some of its assets and the goalposts being divested of their cross-bar. Once MacLeod had managed to persuade the security people that he was after all the Scottish team manager and they had allowed him to walk down the tunnel, he arrived in the dressing room to discover five supporters who had dodged the strict security which Ally himself had just experienced. They were, fully clothed, swimming around in the large bath with the Scottish players.

But it wasn't a case of the Visigoths taking it out on Rome. This was a mass of men out to enjoy themselves and, having been given little opportunity for delirium in the past, not quite able to handle it in a way that would suit the text book. It was the sense of decorum which was offended then. It wasn't an intimation of the imminent demise of civilisation. But that was the turning point. From that date onwards the whole nature of the outing to London changed.

It had always been a rather jolly middle-aged or family outing, with more damage being done by the wives in the shops of Oxford Street than the men in the pubs of north London, and the banners and flags were emblematic decorations and nothing more. Now, the style changed. More people got their hands on tickets. The average age of the bulk of the support seemed to drop dramatically until you could see masses of teenagers, apparently drugged on some crude idea of nationalism, marauding their way through London and turning Trafalgar Square and Piccadilly Circus, before they were inevitably barricaded, into large-scale latrines.

You could tell that some perfectly decent Londoners were concluding that nothing much had changed since the Roman legions had tried to colonise the northern parts. Along with this new arrogant swagger emerged a bitter anti-English trend which to me, at any rate, had a fascistic ring to it.

There was a recrudescence of the Bannockburn image, a battle which certainly played its part in making me proud of our heritage but which considerably lessened in impact the more you saw its meaning hijacked by people who wouldn't have known a skean dhu from a declaration of independence. To be in central London on the Wembley of 1979, the year after Argentina, was like being present when an invading army ransacked a city.

I saw large plate shop windows smashed in recklessly, cars turned over on their sides and a sizeable element displaying gratuitous hatred in a manner that seemed to denote nothing more than the malevolent side of a massive inferiority complex. Had the English, as they certainly were to achieve in other places in Europe, embarked on the same ploys north of the border the Scottish nation would have arisen and driven them into the sea. We could hardly complain, then, when this conduct provoked such outrage in London. Neither can we ignore the fact that, although behaviour was to improve dramatically with the demise of the Wembley weekend, in the excursions from 1977 to 1981 some of our kith and kin established the procedure for converting the football supporter into urban terrorist.

Ally MacLeod had been confident about Anfield of course. But then there was nothing in his make-up, certainly then, which suggested he could think in any other way. His disposition was almost inevitably sunny, his attitude genial, his tongue and body-language irrepressibly ebullient. All this ideally suited the current mood of a swelling support which did not want a diet of realism but rather the heady words of the super-optimist, who stoked their fantasies like a parent spoon-feeding the family. He knew exactly when to reach towards the open mouths.

Immediately after the game, for example, when we did some interviews, he indulged in some whimsical remarks about the English and their inability to qualify for the finals. Perfect timing, I thought. It had nothing to do with the performance of the night nor with our own chances in Argentina but it was like cocking a snook at the bigger nation and we all laughed with him.

The study of the happenings in and around Argentina is not solely about considering a man propelled by delusions of grandeur, as some people might have interpreted it. We all fitted perfectly into the grand scheme of things and contributed, all of us, to a monumental downfall, and then looked innocently around for someone to blame.

Ally was in perpetual over-drive, the supporters were a charging army which verged sometimes more towards Nuremberg than Mount Florida, and the media latched on, euphoric and largely quiescent.

The writing was, in fact, on the wall that very night. Of course, we could not see that at the time. We were fortunate to beat Wales. The Scottish players looked as if their very bone marrow had been sucked out of them by the cacophony which continued unabated and which was proving to be counter-productive. It was the Welsh who were inspired by all of this and had not Alan Rough, always looking edgy throughout the game, made a superb save from John Toshack in the second half history would have told a different story. A penalty eased the pressure and little did I realise at the time that the handling offence would be shown like a piece of evidence in a national court case, seeking somebody's forensic footballing skills to solve the matter.

There was never any doubt between Jock Stein and myself on the platform at the time that there had been a handling offence. Watch it as I have over and over again, with the intensity of a Nessie hunter looking at some deep-water evidence, I have never really deduced whose hand it actually was. That goal did it and when Kenny scored that magnificent header for the second my voice and emotions united to sweep my larynx skywards, right over the top. I heard the replay during that year's Sports Review of the Year in London and hid under the seat in embarrassment at the thrust of my voice, which sounded like someone in the throes of the agony/ecstasy of premature ejaculation. I have deliberately avoided it ever since; the recording that is.

The sound I emitted came from an almost hysterical relief. Relief that Liverpool would be left intact by supporters whose jingoism had always sounded threatening but who could now sublimate their aggression by thinking of how they might cross the Atlantic. Our thoughts turned to the commercial potential. Ally and I were signed up by a brewery firm to travel around the country to meet the fans and to have open-ended discussion about footballing matters. Over a couple of months we criss-crossed Scotland, meeting 'Ally's Army' face to face. It was a formidable experience.

Ally himself was like a bounding gazelle, leaping from venue to venue with an inexhaustible vigour which seemed to be tapped into the true energy source, the adulation of the fans. They would quite literally be standing on table tops chanting his name. And that was just at the start of the night. It would be easy in hindsight to admit to being worried by all of this. It wasn't as strong a feeling as that. However, I felt uneasy about the uncritical enthusiasm which, perhaps rightly, he had no wish to dampen. But more than that, his weakness, in truth, was that he encouraged it.

One night, in a hotel packed to the doors with almost hysterical people doting on his every word, I ventured the opinion, as the chairman, that perhaps a few of his players might have peaked too soon before Argentina. Moreover, I said, some of them, like Bruce Rioch and Don Masson, were no chickens and we might not get the best out of them in the summer. I stopped short of actually saying what I really meant, which is that they might be over the hill ever so slightly. I was howled down. Ally criticised that view, but pleasantly. However, he did nothing to prevent me getting a roasting from supporters who thought I had been floored by him.

My view stemmed not from some unique perspicacity. This was a perfectly straightforward observation which simply was not being aired at the time and it centred on what was to be one of the most telling factors in the World Cup. But, as I sat there taking considerable stick, it did pass through my mind, and I admitted as much to colleagues shortly after, that if Ally were to fall in Argentina he would fall with a helluva clatter and that some of the very people treating him like a demi-god might not wish to pick up the bits.

Against the background of this rising hysteria we made plans to try to show the public something of Scotland's opponents. We learned that Argentina were to play Peru, Scotland's group opponents, in a friendly in Lima. This seemed an ideal opportunity to combine a look at the host nation in action along with an inspection of largely unknown Peruvian players. To this day I will never understand why Ally did not travel to see this game. He had been relying on observation of tapes of Peru in action and whilst that can provide much information it is never as satisfactory as seeing them in the flesh, if only to cover the tracks politically, in case accusations are made that the homework wasn't good enough. I suspect he regretted not doing so in the light of subsequent events.

We were not prepared for what we found in Peru. We encountered poverty at its most extreme in the faces of the Indians who seemed to portray the notion that living was merely a process of slowly dying. All over the city you would see what appeared to be bundles of rags awaiting collection for a gigantic jumble-sale. But what you were looking at were people, whole families huddled together sleeping on the pavements and, when they awoke, simply begging. One very rich Peruvian I talked to admitted that he didn't even notice the Indians any longer. To him they had become invisible, which perhaps was the only antidote to perpetually agonising over them, I suppose.

The poor played football. Out of their shanty towns they would come to the long dusty pitches which ran for mile after mile stretching out from the outskirts of the city for as far as the eye could see. It was certainly much less romantic than Copacabana's beach games but it had something of the natural quality of that as the youngsters performed miracles of control on hard, powdery surfaces. The sun rose and set on these games which suggested to me that they were helping to stave off the effects of a life constricted by horrendous poverty.

We were surprised to be greeted by a battery of cameras at the airport. Unknown to my producer and myself the air company who had flown us to Lima had told the press for promotional purposes that we were coming to 'spy' on Peru for Ally MacLeod. After this had been explained to me I hammed it up to the full. Such celebrity status in a foreign country, I felt, could only help. I was not wrong. They took us to a television studio where, with the help of an interpreter, I solemnly told the Peruvian nation that I would be scrutinising every detail of their side and would duly report back to my mentor Mr MacLeod.

Our only problem was the cameraman and the camera. For reasons of economy we thought we would hire a film crew in Lima, which, admittedly, is not as well endowed with such as, say, downtown Burbank. We did not expect a lot and not a lot is what we got. The cameraman looked like Leo Carrillo, who used to play the 'Cisco Kid', but he certainly wasn't as proficient as the Kid. He had a camera which I imagine must have dated back to the D. W. Griffith period or thereabouts. It had to be plugged into a wall for most of the time which as you might surmise did not make life easy. We faced the nightmarish problem of coming all this way, spending all that money to produce duff film.

By the time we came to film the Peru–Argentina game we had given up in despair. We knew even as they were out there playing in a rather lacklustre friendly that to take anything usable back would be miraculous. We suffered and watched and interviewed the managers, including Menotti the Argentinian, quite the gloomiest man I have ever met, assessed the Peruvians who looked slick, fast and skilful without holding any special menace, and at the same time tried to recover from the destructive effect of a drink called pisco sour which is like taking milk but does to your inside what eating raw cactus would do. We left the cameraman to his own devices and hoped for the best. As we were the only crew there any film was going to be much sought after when we returned to the UK.

However, our cameraman lived up to our expectations of him. He could not have filmed a flower growing with the camera bolted to the spot. All we could salvage on our return were little fragments that added up to virtually nothing. It had been an almost total waste of time. 'El Espion' had produced, as we say in the trade, a 'turkey'. I have to say that it had passed through our minds to play up the 'El Espion' angle for viewer consumption and imply criticism of Ally for not availing himself of the opportunity to see both sides. After watching the shreds we had brought back we kept our mouths tightly shut. That, of course, was a disaster on a minor scale compared to what was to follow. As we moved into the last phase of our preparation for the Finals we thought we had prepared for everything.

Cordoba was to be our base in Argentina. We arrived there in late May, which was their autumn, and immediately were struck by how hospitable the people were. They seemed to exist in a compartment within the military dictatorship whose intrusion was, probably at different levels, both insidious and brutal. Restaurants were always busy, the food and wine were cheap, theatres and cinemas normally packed. The population willingly opened their doors to us. Still you could not totally hide the military presence. There was one day when we visited the stadium for the first time and saw a line of about twenty men in the frisking position, with their hands flat against a wall and the legs straddled with a solitary soldier guarding them with a gun. They were still there in that same position two hours later. We never discovered why they were being treated that way but, as I was told they were the groundsmen, it did lead me to think that the penalties for not cutting the grass properly were rather severe in this country.

An hour away from Cordoba, deeper into the hills, was the little town of Alta Gracia which was to house the Scottish party. We went there to record their arrival, for which the entire town turned out. The welcome was a mix of genuine delight and curiosity. They hardly ever saw Europeans there and certainly not those fair-skinned types from the north of Europe so the rapturous acclaim as the team left their bus gave way to the more lasting habit of gawping. The hotel was a rambling building of Spanish colonial style but which carried a certain resemblance to a kind of run-down Gleneagles. The bull-necked, wide-girthed guards at the gate gave us a taste of security the likes of which made the German system for the World Cup seem like open-house. The fears were that it was not an accreditation pass we would need to gain access but a flame-thrower.

One wrong step and they might have blown your head off. Which is what made the first news story of the stay so juicy; players strolling off for a walk, going towards the casino, climbing back over the fence under the possibility of attack by the very trigger-happy guards there to defend them against the Montoneros. Great stuff. News Editors back home abed could think themselves accursed they were not there and eventually gobbled this story up with the greatest of relish. It splashed and the echoes were heard in Alta Gracia amongst the Scottish officials who looked upon the incident as a possible, but not outrageous, breach of discipline. The manner in which the story was handled in Scotland puzzled some of us but it indicated that any honeymoon between the official party and the media was now over.

There was an underlying vexation to all of this. The journey between the hotel and Cordoba was taking two hours out of the day and whilst this was not the greatest hardship we have ever had to face it still seemed a burden when you were travelling all that way for pre-ordained conferences from which not all that much emerged. It created an unnecessary tension. There were these early hints that the course of events was not running as smoothly as we had anticipated.

Ally got tenser than I had ever seen him, which was of course not at all surprising, but the alfresco interviews added nothing to the advancement of knowledge in the world. Film-wise we did try to indicate that the distant Andes lent enchantment, etc, etc. In short the pre-tournament anodyne guff was typical. But Ally was changing. He was snappier and more suspicious than normal, although still perfectly accessible. There was distinctly less bombast though.

The stadium in Cordoba was probably the worst kind for football, both for those spectating and those reporting or commentating. It was one of those pestilential all-purpose grounds which are fine for the social welfare of a community wishing to encourage and develop a wide range of sporting talents but wretched for creating the right kind of atmosphere for a football match. The players were so distant from those of us at the back of the stand that they looked like Subbuteo pieces on a table. We calculated that the television platform was about forty yards away from the touchline and very high indeed. It was going to be a nightmare of identification. In fact it was not. The nightmare took a different form.

I have to confess that Peru's victory over Scotland is now something of a void in my mind, not because I was traumatised by the result but because I suppose I have blotted it out deliberately to avoid the pain of the broadcasting disaster I suffered. From our little 'goldfish bowl' commentating position we reckoned that things were not going to be easy. The players were too far away and behind the glass all contact with the atmosphere of the stadium would be cut off. If that happens to a commentator it is like the loss of an oxygen supply to a space-walker. A commentator has to be a party of the first part, that is wholly engaged and absorbed in wilful participation. From behind almost sound-proof glass he might as well be in his own living room.

But we were poised and ready. After all we had been preparing for this for almost a year, had we not? I lifted the mike to my lips as the teams came out to warm up, so that I could make initial contact with our studio people back in Glasgow, who were primed up for the occasion just as much as we were. But there was nothing. No contact. The line remained silent.

As I had experienced this sort of thing before from abroad I refused to panic. I left my colleagues to do that for me. But when the whistle blew for the start of the game and there was still no contact made with Glasgow I suffered the first of a series of pangs of acute anguish. After about twenty minutes we gave up because our network colleagues informed us that there was no line back to Scotland for the simple reason it had not been booked in advance!

This simple explanation fell on me like an axe on the nape of the neck. The crass incompetence left me almost too weak for anger. As the viewers had probably been handed a bonus in receiving David Coleman instead of me I felt quite humiliated. I watched the rest of the game through a red mist. I knew others had had their problems before from abroad but I nevertheless felt almost emasculated. After all it had been brought about through lack of proper planning. So I did not absorb the full agony of that game, although I think I can still recall Cubillas' magnificent outside of right-foot free-kick strike that effectively sank Scotland.

I did not wait to say much after the game, lest utterances would have led to more serious infractions. I simply went back to the hotel, dumped my notes which now looked as useful as last week's newspapers, and went out to wander through Cordoba on my own. There were many twisting alleyways in that lovely old faded city and I definitely had it in mind to drop into one of the many splendid little bars and stay there until I had drunk my way into oblivion. Except as fate would have it I heard the sound of accordion tango music and much as Tam O'Shanter on his wild dark night was lured to Kirk Alloway I followed the strains of the music until I found myself in a brightly lit tango hall.

I was wearing a special casual Scottish World Cup jacket and when I was recognised as a Scot the people there greeted me like a hero. They knew nothing about my own problem but they did realise what had happened to Scotland that day and they clearly possessed that finest of humanitarian instincts, knowing how to console a depressed football man. It was a marvellously therapeutic night. I was away from the constant talk of football, from Scotland's disaster, from my own indignity and I didn't have to get stupidly drunk. These warm-hearted people sobered me up in fact and gave me a sense of perspective on what had occurred that afternoon. The sense of futility, of wasted time and effort that had dogged me since I had left the stadium drained away.

At the height of the Falklands crisis I thought of those people and of how they had wined and dined me as an honoured guest, rather than a total stranger, and felt confident that their basic nature would be unmoved by what was portrayed to us then as national hysteria. The Argentinians when they expressed themselves as a crowd or a mob were obsessively 'pro patria' and raucously obnoxious at times. They took to the streets like that every time Argentina won during the World Cup in a way comparable to the 'Malvinas' demonstrations. But beneath that there was a more controlled, decently proud people. I discovered them that night.

But of course there was no real hiding place. We had to face up to the reality that we were on the brink of a possible disaster, for Peru had exposed our apparent lack of ability to handle the pace of such as Oblitas, Munante and Cubillas. We were therefore grateful for the breathing space of playing Iran. I travelled to watch them training two days later and thought I had seen nothing quite so slip-shod as their manner of going about things. They looked clumsy in their ball control, indisciplined in their relationship with their coach and like a rabble training for a game in the Tehran and District League. But I was fooling myself. I was looking for the wrong things.

It was not that they were hiding anything. It was just that I failed to recognise one of the increasingly important factors in world football and certainly in World Cup finals, fitness. They were tall, strong, bristling with athleticism, and had borne much less of a burden than our own players whose draining league season had allowed no time for recuperation before the World Cup. I was blind to that and in my previews I spoke with confidence.

Then came Willie Johnston. The news that he had taken a proscribed drug came not so much as a bombshell but more of a stiletto stuck in the ribs. I heard about it when my guard was lowered. We were enjoying the hospitality of some expatriate group in our hotel and wolfing the canapés when one of my colleagues took a phone call and came back to whisper softly in my ear that Willie Johnston had failed a drugs test. Coming after the unexpected Peruvian result I suppose my first thought apart from finding it difficult to believe was, 'What have we all done to deserve this?' It was nothing to how it was taken up in Alta Gracia.

Ally told me years afterwards that nobody from the SFA International Committee was in the hotel when the telegram arrived informing them of Johnston's failed test. He went straight to Dr Fitzsimmons' room to find out the medical background to the reported use of this banned substance. He walked straight in on the Celtic doctor, an extremely devout man, who was at prayer. All Ally could say was, 'You'd better say one for me, Doc. Look what I've got here!'

This engulfed the entire Scottish party in a media blitz from which they barely recovered. That formal barrier of restrained fury mixed with diplomatic niceties which the SFA put up meant that the separation of themselves from the media was even clearer.

Whilst they dealt promptly and correctly with the ignorant stupidity of Johnston by sending him packing, you got the impression that Ernie Walker and company were now preparing for a long siege. The game against Iran did not help. At least they had managed to establish a line for my commentary back to Scotland and we leapt eagerly into the fray. Allan Herron of the *Sunday Mail* was at my side. Never before have I felt the gradual encroachment of gloom so remorselessly envelop us as it did that day. The Scottish players seemed to have lost all sense of purpose and the inner voice was shrieking for mercy for them.

The 1–1 draw, with the assistance of Eskandarian's own goal, embarrassed us in a way which bit deeply. The following day we went to a press conference at the team's hotel. It was a pleasant, crisp autumnal day. A mass of people awaited the appearance of the manager who, almost sheepishly, came forward to his chair on the grass outside the reception area. As he did so, a dog appeared from somewhere. It jumped and frolicked around him as if they had been buddies for some time. Ally patted it and it nuzzled his hand. As he sat down he stroked the dog and said to the packed throng around him, 'Well, at least I've got one friend here today.' Nobody laughed.

I had never seen Ally bitter before but that day he occasionally converted that touch of whimsy that was always in him into a kind of sardonic defence of what had gone on. He was restrained, though, because apart from any consideration of his tactical approach he felt he had been badly let down. That he had been by Johnston was quite evident and I do believe that even if the Scottish manager had been a representative of the US Drug Enforcement Agency Johnston would still have unwittingly carried on swallowing the things. But ever since Argentina Ally has been haunted by one event about which he still remains deeply embittered.

He had been at pains to allow access to himself by the press on a non-exclusive basis. The *Scottish Daily Express* then offered him £25,000 for an exclusive interview. He apparently refused to give an exclusive interview, but when the interview appeared the newspaper was claiming that very exclusivity. The rest of the press corps were quite understandably incensed. Ally still insists on his innocence and is convinced the episode turned certain of the big guns in the Scottish press against him. He has always felt that he would have been spared some of the ultimate personal savaging if he had not been seen to hand out a personal favour to one newspaper.

I was a mere spectator to all of this because all I was after, apart from being involved in commentary, was the occasional interview in which, as so often, nothing much was said. The hostility crowded in on him. Of course, it is obvious that the media do not pick teams, despite what people think, nor play the actual games. They could not materially alter the course of events so it might sound like resorting to some paltry excuse to bring up matters like a single interview and what it meant to relationships. However, in the totality of a World Cup campaign whose smallest nuance of behaviour can affect people and re-route the emotions in odd directions, it certainly mattered to MacLeod and his critics.

The players had been badly affected by some wildly irresponsible reports one of which suggested that they had drunk the hotel dry and had sent out a 'drinks trolley', whatever that might have been, for more of the same. That particular report went out on television and was considered so damaging that on return to Scotland Ernie Walker perused the film with the SFA lawyers, at the BBC, with a view to possible legal action. It was considered by Ernie eventually as just not worth the trouble. He wanted to bury Argentina as quickly as he could and not stir the embers with litigation.

It is perfectly possible that some players did a bit of drinking. I personally see nothing wrong with that. The Dutch who got to the final were allowed amazing social liberties in contrast to the Scots. But I have yet to hear a shred of evidence about the bacchanalian orgies which were now widely understood to have been held in the Scottish camp. Much of this reporting originated from the local press which could not tell the difference between a drunk supporter, with their identikit Scottish gear, and a Scottish player. They duly waded in with some outrageously inaccurate reporting. So not only were Scotland and MacLeod now being put to the sword but you felt that all everybody wanted was to get out of Argentina as quickly as possible. But we had to go to Mendoza first.

This town lay in the very foothills of the Andes and seemed to me to be on the fringe of civilisation. It was at the centre of the Argentinian vineyards so there were immediate consolations. You can go off a place very quickly though. On the very first night in the grotty hotel we had been consigned to I found the hall-porter ransacking my case and trying to shove some miniatures of whisky into his pocket. As he whined his apologies on his knees (he was only about four feet two) he wished all good luck and blessings to be heaped upon me and my family and victory to Scotland against Holland the following night. What finally won me over was the promise not to be presented with a bill for any wine for the remainder of the stay. But it was still unsettling and seemed to fit the picture of the gradual disintegration of this trip.

The stadium though was quite magnificent. Built into a hill, the pitch, whether by optical illusion or not, seemed to be below ground level and was circled by trees and loomed over by the Andes. It looked the perfect setting for some sort of climax. There was a kind of demob feeling about us all. This was the end, thank God. Jock Stein was in the London studio as the pundit during my commentary, on which Allan Herron assisted. Stein once told me how he had reacted to it.

'It was an amazing transformation,' he said. 'You sounded at first as if you were at a funeral. Then you got slightly more enthusiastic. Then you sounded as if you were both at a wedding. And at the end you were almost back to your funeral again.'

Nobody could have put it better. That is how the course of the game went. Dejection, followed by promise, coming upon elation, and finally sadness. There were something like thirty commentators in a row along the front of the stand and just to my left was ITV's Hugh Johns with the cotton-wool inevitably in his ears to drown out the noise of any other commentator and with the fixed tiny binoculars to his specs to aid sightings.

When Archie Gemmill scored his famous goal I experienced something I have not seen before or since. To a man every commentator rose from his seat in a concerted explosion of delight and wonderment. It was a goal of perfect commentating symmetry with a distinct beginning, middle and end. 'Will he do it? Can he get there? Yes, he's scored.' Brief but indelibly registered as the most perfect goal I have ever had to describe. But of course it wasn't enough. A victory over Holland by 3–2 now seemed hollow. I went to a club with a London cameraman and we tried the wine.

I had had only two hours of sleep when the phone rang the

following morning. It was Buenos Aires. The editor Alan Hart was not amused. A report had just been put out that Ally MacLeod was resigning that very day. Why didn't I know anything about it and why had I allowed myself to be scooped? Of course I did not know about it and I was sure Ally wasn't quitting. I advised Alan Hart that I would stake my reputation on it. Now, staking your reputation on matters is not really a very clever idea out in the field, especially when you have been out of touch with things for even a few hours. As soon as I had said it I began to panic. Suppose Ally had had enough!

I beat a hasty retreat to the rather ramshackle hotel the Scottish team were in and joined the now bedraggled media corps waiting for the gates to open. The problem was that I had a deadline to beat for the BBC wanted a straight report to camera on this matter within the hour to be beamed back to Buenos Aires. I had come prepared. I bribed one of the thugs with the guns at the gate with a bottle of whisky to see if he could slip me in to get hold of Ally.

I was of course breaking every regulation in the book but my neck was on the line. He ushered me through and I waited in the large reception area to find out if Ally would be annoyed at suddenly being confronted by me. In fact he wasn't, for when I virtually bumped into him coming round a corner in the hotel and asked him outright about this report he uttered the sweetest word I had heard in the entire trip. 'Rubbish!' So he was sticking to his task after all. I duly made my report and then rejoined my colleagues to mull and brood over the outcome of this sad period.

To those of us close to football, Argentina was more traumatic than we cared to admit, certainly in public. We went there armed with fantasies, hooked on an inadequate appreciation of our own abilities, and unable to come to terms with a foreign field. We emerged tattered. The brutal assessment was that we were not good enough, nor were we likely to get any better. That thought bit deeply.

So it is too glib to focus the inquest purely on Ally. His fall was going to resound more loudly than most because he chose to perform on the high-wire of publicity from which there could be only one direction to go with almost any slip. Hardly anybody called for restraint during that period though. You could point to certain technical considerations, like the fact that he did not really get his homework right because he did not study the opposition as he should have. He himself admits a major mistake came in the Iran game.

'I should have played Graeme Souness in that match,' he told me long afterwards. 'If I had we could have qualified for the final stages. It was a bad mistake on my part.'

I suspect though that he had got the best out of his players long before they arrived in Argentina. They had lost their bounce. He also could have done with Masson scoring from the penalty spot when the score was 1–1 in the game with Peru. But more fascinating than these inquests is how little is said about certain reactions to all of this. The spectacle of the likes of Lou Macari and Don Masson, even before they had left the country, hawking their stories around the press did not enhance the professional footballer in anybody's eyes. Many of us in the media, and I include myself prominently in the matter, had enjoyed and, by our virtually complete silence, encouraged the circus barker's approach. The idea of winning the World Cup was sold to the Scottish punter when it never was and never will be a real possibility. So, Ally was not a one-man band. We helped make him and then poured scorn on him for our own misdemeanours in the whole affair. Not too many of us should be proud about that.

Then the public turned against him in a way which I think besmirched our reputation as a tolerant people. I will long remember the faces of hate which screamed at him as he walked from the pitch after the Iran game. If they had been able to get over the barrier in the Cordoba Stadium they would have torn him alive. They contented themselves with the more civilised aggression of spitting. These ugly faces, without one redeeming feature about them, were recorded by television and used in a sequence for one of the most damning visual comments ever used about a manager and given a certain self-indulgent spice by an English producer.

MacLeod did not warrant the continual torrent of oaths from the people who, a month previously, had sworn by him. I hope those who mouthed venom and those like the restaurateur who put up a public notice in his premises advising people that Ally MacLeod did not eat there might now feel some sense of shame.

He was not a war criminal. He was a failed football manager in a nation which produces that category with predictable regularity. I think the passing of time has shown us that clearly.

On the very last day I was in Argentina Alan Sharp, who in between being a Scottish punter writes novels and Hollywood film-scripts, growled to me from beneath his wide-brimmed hat about that paradoxical victory over Holland.

'We didn't win. We just discovered a new way of losing.'

It seemed a fair summary. Scottish initiative had landed a bridge too far.

11

The Last of Stein

'The bull stands no chance!' So Jock Stein in 1982 dismissed in a sentence the ancient and enduring Iberian obsession for the duel in the sand. 'It's no contest. That's why it's no use.' Even though he had managed a club side which had slaughtered much that had got in its way, he liked to think of sport as an engagement with the unpredictable, that there was no such thing as an absolute certainty where humans were concerned.

After all hadn't Thistle beaten them famously in the 1971 League Cup final when it was barely worth while putting a bet on Celtic? Hadn't Kai Johansen materialised like an avenging warrior, just when his team were looking like overwhelming Rangers, and put them to the sword in the 1966 Cup final replay at Hampden one night? Hadn't he made a mistake about Feyenoord? He disliked the notion of the certainty, if only because his addiction to horse-racing had shown him that it was a preposterous concept even when you gave animals their own head.

Except here in Spain where they stabbed the animal first and stuck things in its neck before a man polished it off, hiding the sword underneath a cape. As Stein himself contemptuously put it, the animal was a foregone loser. It was not a sentiment that would have found favour with Hemingway, even though I suspect Stein and Hemingway, as men of action, would have got on famously.

The Scottish manager was in Malaga looking at hotels just after the draw for the World Cup finals and he had been grabbed by an oily tourist rep extolling the virtues of the Costa Del Sol, including the bull fights. Stein, when wishing to rid himself of somebody, did not mind being undiplomatic and on this occasion the man had given him the opportunity to launch an attack on the 'corrida'.

I suppose at the back of his mind too was the thought that, amidst the initial reaction to the group draw which placed us with Brazil and Russia, he was going to have to counter the most pessimistic forecasts which saw Scotland as that vulnerable bull inevitably suffering a death in the afternoon under the hot Spanish sun. The analogy wasn't hard to make. Stein had now deliberately begun to play down the pessimism. He stayed like that for most of the following months, except when another factor infiltrated his mind.

The Falklands were invaded in April of that year and it affected us all, even if only distantly. It was too soon to determine immediately if the World Cup was going to be cancelled or badly disrupted or the British teams withdrawn. But long before the start in June the South Atlantic confrontation was intruding on the best-laid plans.

I had heard that Stein was planning to go to New Zealand to see the 'dark horses' of the tournament who had surprised everybody by qualifying for the finals. When I talked to him about this he admitted that all he wanted to do was cover his political rear so that he could not be blamed for not doing his homework, as Ally MacLeod had been. When I put it to him that I could interest BBC London in making a film of his stay in New Zealand he perked up a little, realising that it would at least provide some company on the long trip. The BBC bought the idea solely on the basis of my guaranteeing that Stein was, surprisingly to them, taking the trouble to travel out there to see rather insipid opposition. They were, however, keen on the idea of Stein facing the Maori War Chant, the geysers and watching football played on sacred rugby pitches.

I did realistically think though that his travelling all the way to New Zealand by himself to see a couple of duff games was a somewhat masochistic over-reaction to the attitude of the previous manager. After about a month of planning, including establishing our film contacts in Auckland, receiving permission from the New

Zealand FA to film their two games, arranging a travel package with PanAm with the emphasis on non-transferable flights and imbued with some great ideas for using the marvellous New Zealand countryside as a contrast to Stein's industrial Lanarkshire environment, we were prepared to go. Then came the British response to the invasion of Port Stanley. The night before we were due to fly down to London for our connection to San Francisco, Stein phoned me at home.

'I don't think we should go,' he said.

My heart sank.

'This war could get nasty and they'll end up cancelling the World Cup or we'll withdraw. Something's bound to happen. I think it'll be a waste of time to go away out there now.'

After my initial shock I sensed that what he was trying to do was bounce the notion off me for my response and that frankly the war was giving him a convenient way out of a tiring journey that he all along hadn't wanted to make. I argued the point that if we didn't go, the fact would sooner or later be picked up by the press and he'd have some explaining to do. After all, at that early stage we were barely sparring with Argentina.

This of course was not the Jock Stein of his Celtic days who by and large would not have cared a toss about what might be written about him and, in any case, would deal with any journalistic insult with a wrath of biblical proportions. This was a man of more measured response to situations, tending to ration out his titanic aggression carefully and, in an astonishing way, given what we knew of him in his prime as a club manager, actually avoiding conflicts he would once have relished.

Two years previously, for instance, we had sat down to dinner in a Swiss hotel after the draw for the groups for the World Cup preliminary stage. Stein, Ernie Walker, the secretary, and some other SFA officials, including the President, Tommy Younger, myself and my producer settled down for a pleasant evening of good banter. It did not turn out that way. Towards the end, after some wine had been taken, it turned sour. To everybody's astonishment Younger, the most affable of men normally, turned on Stein.

Quietly but forcibly he tore his international record to date to shreds. Everybody was embarrassed, not least the two BBC people who should not have been privy to any of this. It was clear Younger had been stoking this up, although it seemed an odd setting to chose. No matter how much an acutely discomfited Ernie Walker tried to cap it, the well of frustration was now blowing wildly out of control from the mouth of the SFA President. At one stage Younger said, 'You have a worse record than Willie Ormond and Ally MacLeod and they both got the sack!'

As Stein sat there quietly I looked for the signs of the famous flush on the face, that journalists' early warning system interpreted unfailingly as the first sign of the retaliatory strike. But there was nothing there. At one stage he very quietly said, 'Tam, maybe we shouldn't be talking about these things in front of our guests here.' But that was all. He was taking this with barely any dissent. Certainly Younger was uttering much of the consensus view of Stein at that stage for his record then was nothing to boast about.

Stein also had a case to put. He was embarked on changing the entire approach of Scottish international football, which, up until then, could have been said to be a reflection of the spirit of the fiery cross. Stein wanted to put that light on the 'peep'. He was after a more cerebral attitude, cooler, less reliant on terracing acoustics. Whether or not it was succeeding or whether he was on the right tack, were highly debatable matters but that, at any rate, is what his philosophy was at that particular time. But there he sat saying virtually nothing. I was beginning to think his self-restraint would become one of the seven wonders of the modern world for if it had been the Stein of Parkhead the other diners in that elegant restaurant would have been entertained to a Lanarkshire 'rap' of venomous intent.

Whilst Ernie Walker silently fumed in the background Stein showed no sign of retaliation. This worried me. It was too quiescent, too much like an SFA official toeing the party line, and it was a role he didn't play well. King Lear might have suited him but certainly not the Bob Cratchit he now seemed. There is no doubt that he had been eminently qualified to take on the national team manager's job. Sometimes we avoid the obvious in these circumstances and the fact went barely without comment on his appointment that in no way were the SFA getting the same man who had endowed Celtic Park with greatness. The simple fact of the matter is that Jock Stein badly needed the SFA job.

He was in excruciating exile in England when conjecture about Ally MacLeod's future was at its peak. Ally, by this time, had been largely traumatised into a husk of his former self, bitter and anguished. His attempts to re-enact his previous ebullience had the hamminess of a rep company's worst actor. Relations with the press were strained, largely because he must have realised that most people wanted rid of him. Only a split vote in the International Committee kept him in his job in the immediate aftermath of Argentina. It was simply a matter of time. Stein, meanwhile, had left Celtic and was now with Leeds but seeking any possible way to get his hands on the Scottish job.

He had uttered genuine sympathy for Ally immediately after the World Cup, which was more humanitarian than professional, for his instinctive support for the Scottish manager could not have extinguished his notion that it was now the post for him. I simply could not see Stein bearing his situation in Leeds too long. He was not in the first flush of youth and he was instinctively a home bird. Friends who would go on holiday with him, particularly to Menorca, a favourite place of his, will tell you that he could not get home quickly enough to Glasgow nevertheless. There was little chance of Stein taking root in England and as the clamour for a change of manager for Scotland rose in intensity people started to work for him behind the scenes.

I was approached by a journalist who asked me to phone Stein one morning. I tracked him down to a hotel in the Midlands where he was staying with the Leeds team prior to an evening game. The call was put through to his room and I could visualise him lying back watching the racing on television. His voice had the sonority of a very unhappy man, deep, tired and almost mournful. There was no doubt about the point of the call. He wanted me to break cover and tout for him publicly in such a way as to indicate that he would take the job if asked. He knew that I was going on *Sportsnight*'s network programme that very night to conjecture about Scotland's future, thus confirming that he certainly had not lost all his faculties, particularly in knowing everything that was going on in the media world. He virtually wrote the script for me, advising what he thought could be said of his delicate position with Leeds and of how he had to be very careful about any of his own personal comments on the matter. He sounded in a grim and determined mood. He desperately wanted the job.

This was right up my street. I duly obliged by telling my colleagues in London what I was about to say that night about Stein so they put me right at the top of the programme. I launched into an unambiguous declaration of Stein's avowed aim to become Scottish team manager, saying that he was the right man for the job as his country needed him, that one word from the SFA would bring him back home and that it would be dereliction of duty on their part if they did not act. This is the stuff that hacks are made of, of course. But I wallowed in it. We were in a kind of no-man's land in international football at that stage anyway so that myself and others had started broadsides on a need for a change of sorts.

The following morning, lying in bed, I heard a radio interview with Stein which must have taken place well after his game the previous night and after the *Sportsnight* transmission. He was being quizzed about his future and about my report on the programme. He stated naturally that he had not seen this report but that he was not responsible for what others tried to make up and that his prime concern was the future welfare of Leeds United. 'Archie Macpherson was just flying a kite,' he concluded. Beautiful! The Machiavellian Stein was back on his best form. Anybody not knowing him might have thought they had been duped by *Sportsnight*. But in a way it was paradoxically satisfying to know that you had been drawn like others into his masterly intrigue. Even if the SFA had shown great reluctance to take him on, which was not the case anyway, we were stirring the public towards inevitable support for him. He was appointed in October 1978.

'I can adjust,' he said to me in his tiny garret-like room in that antiseptic office block of the SFA. It was like a dethroned king occupying the broom cupboard. There he sat, where once he massively filled every nook and cranny of Celtic Park, looking squashed by fate. He agreed terms with the world by fully appreciating the greatest virtue of this move. He was back home. 'People say that I won't be able to put up with not being in daily contact with a team. But it's all about adjusting. You can't look back, you've got to look ahead.'

It was perhaps not the most subtle remark he had ever made but it fitted genuinely enough to his circumstances. Like others, I thought there might have been potential for a personality clash between himself and the secretary Ernie Walker, himself of strong character, but, in fact, the two men, although of contrasting personalities, had a great deal in common. They were both intelligent to a degree greatly in excess of the job requirements, they were both West of Scotland punters whose search for the true meaning of life could not possibly exclude the influence of ninety minutes at a football match, they were both men's men who were pulled towards an admiration of strength in others. So they dovetailed in the most remarkable way, given, I suspect, that Stein resigned himself quickly to the fact that Walker set the whole tone and style of the SFA.

Four years on, Stein had gone through the most undistinguished period of his career. The results were patchy and questions about his apparent loss of touch were being aired, but discreetly, for his past club record was insulating him from the full rebuke of the media. They had long memories and needed to be told neither about his ability to handle men on a football field nor of his strength in annihilating his critics. Many people, in short, were still in awe of him. That is why Younger's broadside on him, unreciprocated, took the breath from me. I knew there had been mutterings about him and that the undistinguished way we finally clinched the point for Spain in a dour draw in Belfast did nothing to inspire great confidence. But this reaction to all of that was decidedly downbeat.

Now he didn't want to go to New Zealand and the BBC, having committed a lot of money to this enterprise, were not going to be too happy after my initial encouragement of the project. We talked for about half-an-hour on the phone before, with extreme reluctance, he agreed he would go ahead. When we eventually set out we were re-routed to Seattle because of some mechanical fault on the scheduled flight and after a wait of four hours without sleep picked up a flight to San Francisco. We arrived there feeling as if we had come by wagon-train through the Rockies. Stein was pale, drawn and obviously fed-up. I went to my room, turned on the television and flopped on the bed. Within about ten seconds the famous American anchorman Dan Rather flashed on to the screen with words which went through me like a rapier.

'Good evening. The war in the South Atlantic has taken a sinister turn with the sinking of the *SS Belgrano* and the reported loss of 99 lives.'

That message did not have much therapeutic value on my body, brutalised by jet-lag and lack of sleep. It was like trying to lull yourself into a slumber to the words of Edgar Allan Poe. A feeling of horror and revulsion swept over me. But I had no time to reflect on my own about it for within a couple of minutes I heard a loud knocking on the door and Stein appeared, shirtless, hair awry, looking almost angered.

'Did you hear that?' he asked in some amazement. 'C'mon, we're getting to hell out of here back home. Maggie'll nuke them next. I told you it could get right out of hand. Get on the phone and get us a flight back home tomorrow.'

I hadn't been expecting this and frankly I was in no mood to argue with him. There and then I made a decision just to agree with his idea and then take it up again in the morning after we had had some sleep. I wasn't caring any longer one way or the other myself. It is just that we were at a halfway house and it was probably as quick to fly back over the Pacific anyway. It wasn't easy to sleep that night. But in the morning, as it so often does, the world seemed to have taken on a different complexion.

The Californian sun was sharp and warm. The people in the hotel treated us like royalty, as they did everybody for that matter. The breakfast was huge and life-enhancing and a cheery friend of Stein's turned up. He was brimming with optimism about Scotland in the World Cup and offering to drive us round San Francisco to sight-see. The previous evening seemed light years away. I was beginning to feel that having brought him this far I would be able to manage the second half of the journey after all. He didn't mention giving up, so we toured the city then went back to our hotel to pack up before continuing our trip across the Pacific. He seemed more content. But as we were driving to the airport the taxi driver hearing our accents started to talk about the war again and then said, 'Pity about you losing a ship.'

'No, it was one of theirs,' Stein interrupted.

'I just heard you lost a ship called the *Sheffield.* Yeah, that's what you call it,' the driver went on. 'The Argies got it!'

I tried not to look at Stein who just whispered a curse. I simply strode into the airport when we were set down and made for the check-in desk. I didn't get far. The large hand pulled on my shoulder.

'I don't think I could face up to this,' he said. 'We could have a world war on our hands. People are getting killed and we're going to be fartin' about amongst the Maoris. It'll look bad, us out there making films and young men getting maimed and slaughtered. It's bad.'

He slumped down on a bench waiting for me to respond. I knew he simply wanted me to cave in but I was now at the end of my tether.

'I'm going on,' I said wearily. 'With or without you. I'll do something out there. I'll make up some kind of story.'

By this time, I suppose, my voice had the tone of Little Orphan Annie. I left him sitting there, booked in, walked into the departure lounge, had a very large whisky, slumped in a seat and waited. Ten minutes later, through he came, limping heavily, and heaved himself down beside me.

'I couldn't let you go on your own,' he said. For the first time I noticed that he was not only looking extremely tired but that his face was like an ashen mask. I have never been too happy about that, looking back. All I had needed to do was agree with him and we could have turned back. The trip to New Zealand meant precious little to him, other than protecting himself, but meant a lot more to me. I was getting him into what I thought could be an interesting film for us both and I selfishly hoped for a few plaudits for myself.

He certainly did not need that sapping, punishing journey especially as, in retrospect, I realise it took more out of him than even he thought it possibly could. The stay in New Zealand offered more than just some pretty shots of us gazing at geysers, or being bemused by the rolling eyes and tongues of the Maoris, or hearing Stein say some diplomatic things about the athletic Kiwis. It was on this trip he opened up to me in a way he never had before.

I had spent a lot of time with him in his last few years with Celtic, particularly after his car accident, when we joined forces to tour Scotland in a kind of mobile chat show sponsored by a brewery. He was brilliant at that. There was no sign of showmanship about him yet by dint of his genuine, authentic views on football he had the audiences eating out of his hand. He didn't pander to them in any way. Indeed because all had not gone as smoothly on the field for him as had been expected he was not swept along by the adulation of the people who turned up to listen to him.

Whereas Ally on the previous tour could have talked in Sanskrit and they would have chaired him round the community afterwards, Stein contented himself with lectures which at times sounded like Socratic dialogues. He argued and questioned his way logically through his philosophy of the game and defended his current policies. He interspersed this with a brilliant wit which sometimes verged on the malicious and could destroy someone who had come out on these occasions like a young gunfighter, ready to cut down the fastest draw in the business. They stood little chance against him. There was nobody he could fail to put away.

He always drove me to these outings and it has to be said, quite frankly, sometimes drove with a demoniacal urgency as if he had heard his house was on fire. He always gave the impression of being pursued by past events and hounded by thoughts of the future. Perhaps it was this which produced his constant restlessness, which he imposed on other people in the most autocratic way. If he wanted to up and go and the rest of the company wanted to stay on for a drink then we upped and went at his command. If he was the star turn then the star turn had to have his way regardless of the difficulties.

We stayed overnight once in Elgin after regaling a packed audience with thoughts on how we must put out of our minds the excesses of Argentina. Stein had agreed to this trip on the condition that the sponsor provided a private aircraft which they duly did. To his astonishment and disgust we then discovered that there were no such things as night flights out of Inverness on a Sunday night. Air-traffic controllers there went to their beds like anyone else. He had expected to be home in Glasgow that same evening. There was little overnight consolation in Elgin for Scotland's leading insomniac, who cursed his lot in life that he had taken on such a trip.

Nor was there much the following morning when I awoke to discover everything was covered in a thick hoar frost which extended to Inverness airport and the little Piper Aztec plane, which looked like a frosted favour for a giant wedding cake. When he was told the plane couldn't take off because of icing on the wings he was livid. Celtic were not playing well at the time and he was obsessed with the need to get back for Monday morning training.

He insisted the pilot try something, because he wanted to push on. No democratic vote was taken when the pilot suggested that if we were really pushed he would try a farmer's fertiliser which he thought might act as a de-icer. I certainly did not want to fly in a plane that had to be fertilised before take off. I protested and told him that not even the Wright Brothers would go up under such circumstances. 'Get the fertiliser on!' Stein shouted at the pilot.

It was as far as I know the first recorded instance of a man crop-spraying a plane. Miraculously it worked and we soared into the air only to be told by the pilot that fog had descended right across the Clyde Valley which meant we had to turn back or take a chance on landing in Edinburgh.

'No way,' Stein shouted against the din of the engine. 'Have a go at Glasgow! It's only a wee plane!'

I protested that fog took no account of the size of a plane, which could hardly be able to sneak in under its cover. The sponsor, crammed into the seat behind us, was beginning to regret he had taken on this trip in the first place. Stein looked out of the window whistling. Then the pilot thought of something.

'We could try Cumbernauld!' he shouted at us.

'Cumbernauld!' we all exclaimed as one, even Stein. But the pilot assured us that there was a landing field there for small planes and that he would contact the control there. Control? I envisaged an old woman at a phone. We swooped down towards Mother Earth, all of us suffering this communal cataract which blurred everything below. Basically I do not like flying, even though I have gone several times around the world by plane. I mistrust those who seem to make light of it, as Stein often did, and interpret that as a sign of their own unease. I therefore had to believe the big man was peeing himself like the rest of us. As we went for it, we could only see the tops of high rise flats peeking through the fluffy carpet of fog.

'Look for them signalling to us,' the pilot said peering down. 'I think I can see the strip just down there.'

We all looked. All I could see was a kind of moth-eaten veil through which there was a suggestion of ground but nothing more definite than that. I was beginning not to believe all of this. Cumbernauld? It was all going to end in Cumbernauld? I realised I had been unkind in some of the things I had said about its town centre but I was thinking I hardly deserved this.

We were about to try blind-flying without instruments just to accommodate the big man getting back in time for training? I was on the verge of screaming a protest when Stein suddenly pulled his face back from the window, tapped the pilot on the shoulder and said, 'Can you sign-write in the sky? Because if you can you spell out to them down there, "You-must-be-effing-joking!"' And he burst out laughing whilst the rest of us offered a silent prayer of thanks that Celtic Football Club were going to have to do without Mr Stein for training that morning. We landed safely, but on wobbly legs, in Edinburgh.

So, in a modest way, perhaps he did owe me one and thus agreed to New Zealand. It was there I felt I got closer to the private Stein than I ever had before. Perhaps not in the country itself, where we wandered around listlessly, trying to make up some pictorial excuse for having gone there to film, but even more so on the long hauls over the Pacific. There was the slightly droning noise of the engines in the background, the resistance to sleep we shared, which not even the normally soporific effect of the in-flight movies could dent, and the dim light of the aircraft announcing that you really should be asleep. In the midst of it sat this huge hulk, wanting to see the night through and this horrible journey eased, whispering beside you willingly about his career and his thoughts on people who had influenced his life. I knew I was beside a man trying desperately to come to terms with the fact that he was growing old.

This 'closeness' you could only use as a relative expression.

Stein encouraged few intimacies and indeed he would slam the portcullis down on anybody thinking of wantonly invading his privacy. Even some of those claiming to be his close friends found themselves bundled out of his presence with a few stark epithets on occasions. He was a complex man, carrying a mass of contradictions which seemed nevertheless to add to his substance, not subtract from it. He was gregarious, yet sullen and bitter, hostile to attention at times. He could have the company dancing to his command and turn within seconds to a man fleeing from it all as quickly as he could. He could be brilliantly philosophical in defeat and also like a man feeling persecuted. Tony Queen, perhaps his closest friend, told me that on a Saturday night after a Celtic defeat, Stein 'was the loneliest man in the world'.

Sometimes you would feel you had penetrated all his reservations and could take him on a level of your own choosing. But the next time you met him it was as if he barely knew you. He hated sycophants but occasionally used them to further himself in the most sanguine way. He liked admiration but could choke the phoniness of gush with breathtaking abruptness.

But twenty-six thousand feet above the Pacific, surprisingly, he needed somebody to talk to. He took some time to tell me about the period of returning to Scotland to play for Celtic and the effect it had on people in his old community. Of how his best pal for years came to the house to see his mother and father but would not go upstairs to speak to him even though he knew he was in, because he was now a Celtic man. He spoke of how his mother would always wish him good luck before playing against Rangers but his father never. Of how a man simply attempting to ply his trade had come back to be treated by some as a pariah.

It had bitten more deeply into him than I had ever supposed and I was surprised to hear him reveal it as such. He spoke to me sardonically of how Willie Allison, the Rangers PRO, at one stage not long after the winning of the European Cup, advised him that the 'call' would come from Ibrox for him. He had savoured that particularly but was denied the ultimate satisfaction of knocking it back in public. He talked at length about lying in the hospital after his serious car accident fighting off death, which he defined as 'like looking at a window-box of flowers. I don't know why but that's what I kept seeing.'

He kept up this introspection throughout our trip until I said to him he should get it all down on paper and that there was a great deal about him that people would want to know behind his public face.

'It's not time yet,' he said. 'Anyway they just want me to tell all I know and dig up some dirt about folk. I'm not interested in that.'

By the time, many weeks later, we all assembled in Spain I was one of the mob again, seeking as much as anybody else in the World Cup media brawl and getting no more than my fair share of news or opinions or comment from him. The portcullis was down once more.

Stein underplayed himself in Spain. He tried to be downbeat and cooler and hammered into the theme of not reliving Argentina. But I think he spent a lot of time, much more than he ought to or needed to, in combating the media. He was obsessed with outwitting them. He had not liked some of the things which had been written and said about the performances in the lead-up to the finals and whilst he had always been a brilliantly capable politician he seemed preoccupied by trying to find out what the media was thinking and saying. He would try and grill people about that. We were seeing the defensive Stein, a man holding down a job, not the man with the acute sense of mission we had known at Parkhead. The SFA knew they had hired an older man.

The Scottish squad stayed down in a golf hotel at Sotogrande, which entailed a long drive from the Torremolinos area along one of the most dangerous coast roads in the world. The SFA had allocated separate times for access to daily newspapers, Sunday press and radio and television. We all queued up and sat sedately with him or the players when our turn came. Stein spent much of his time with me criticising members of the press. He had always enjoyed a good gossip but this time he had targeted people in a way which suggested that he was thinking beyond the World Cup to when he would have to face inquests and that, inherently, he did not deep down believe that Scotland stood much chance of qualifying.

New Zealand certainly caused us some disquiet in the first

match but my abiding recollection of that night was the people of Malaga coming out on to the streets afterwards and cheering the Scottish bus through the streets. We had been expecting 6–0, we had only managed 5–2. But the Spaniards had wanted an entertaining game and they had got it.

During the Soviet Union–Brazil game I commentated on, a voice from London interrupted and told me to be quiet for a few moments while an important announcement was to be made. Then a news-reader said quite simply, 'The government have announced that the Argentinian forces in the Falklands have unconditionally surrendered.' I thought of Dan Rather and Stein and the suspense in San Francisco and I was glad at least part of the world was getting itself sorted out although not even the South Atlantic Expeditionary Force would have been of much use to Scotland in Spain, as it turned out.

There was the last game in Malaga. Scotland conceded to the USSR one of those goals which belongs in a Walt Disney 'Goofy' instructional film on how to cause the maximum embarrassment with the minimum of effort. Not even Souness's well-drilled daisy-cutter near the end could conceal the misery we all felt.

A Russian in front of me, and perhaps a journalist or someone with the official party, had been raising his arms and waving them about until he was blocking our view. Attempts at persuasion failed. In my frustration with the match I eventually punched him hard on the back, put my mike away from my mouth and bawled at him to bugger off. He stood up. He was at least seven feet tall and had the kind of build one associates with lumberjacks and Sherman tanks. He bunched his right fist into a massive piece of malevolent intent and towered above me.

Billy McNeill did all that any human being could do to help me under the circumstances by sliding under his seat in helpless laughter. Quick thinking persuaded me to put my mike to my mouth again promptly, which I did with my voice rising with great passion on the subject of another night of humiliation for us. I kept one eye on the play and another on the fist until I was convinced he was impressed with how tragic my voice was to the Scottish nation and I saw him sit down again with a massive thud.

There are times when a commentator has to do what a commentator has to do. So I spent the last few minutes of that game talking largely against a spine as big as the Urals.

Elements do intrude on a World Cup, apart from the goals, which help the recollections gel but nobody could mention Seville without thinking of Brazil and David Narey. It was not so much the scoring of the goal, about which we all enthused, as the fitting contribution it made to a night which resuscitated our belief in the compelling virtue of football as a life-enhancer. The air of fiesta never deserted the Scottish supporters as they watched Brazil's inevitable 4–1 victory engineered by the strutting Socrates and the flowing Falcao.

I knew, though, as soon as I heard Jimmy Hill, sitting in his presentation seat on top of a block of flats outside the ground watching the game on a television monitor, describe Narey's strike as a 'toe-poke' that it would not be taken lying down by our people. It was to be construed as some monstrous cultural insult, like calling the Clyde-built *Queen Elizabeth* a paddle steamer. Hill, whom I regard as an amiable and extremely sociable man, has developed the knack of arousing resentment in people more readily than other pundits.

I admire him for that. Hill, especially in his earlier days, hooked on to things that aroused you, made you think. He attacked the middle-age spread of the living rooms by provoking the armchair critic to sometimes violent reaction. Ignore him you could not. He was certainly no studio wallflower. He loved the attention of the Scottish supporters forever after. On match days that he attended or watched from the studio, that I can vouch for, no man could have been prouder of being singled out for mob abuse. The 'Jimmy Hill's a Poof' banner frequently seen amongst Scottish fans was not only singularly inaccurate but was to Jimmy simply an eccentric sign of endearment.

But after that comment the relationship between Stein and Hill was never the same. Stein, in fact, was looking for blood and became unusually anti-English, unusual in the sense that he never wished to be seen to be stupidly nationalistic and did value their football. But on this occasion he told me, that if Hill approached him he would chew him up and that had it been an English goal it would never have been interpreted in such a dismissive way. Hill himself complained of a gross over-reaction and, in truth, there was something to that. He has always insisted that 'toe-pokes' can be the product of great skill. I agree with him in the sense of his own definition and for the very fact that Dave Narey proved it. If it was one.

Seville saved us from ourselves and our World Cup morbidity. We took defeat like a unique honour. The Brazilians suited the warmth of the night, the pulse of the drums and their limbs seemed elastic and brilliant. There was nothing much we could do about it. Looking back, perhaps we witnessed the last of the great Brazilian sides, at least for many generations. Their awful country has driven their significant professionals to Europe where, in the less amenable climate, something of their spontaneous genius seems to be atrophying. We were all glad to say 'We were there!' So was Stein. He himself did not suffer much from this tournament. He had failed, certainly.

But he hadn't been put to the sword. And, unlike the bull, he was going to get another chance.

His spirit was still buoyant enough over the next three years but he was tiring perceptibly. Qualification for Mexico was draining him. I thought that he was not only involved in achieving success but in trying desperately to prove, perhaps to himself above all, that he still had the capacity to absorb all the pressure. The terrible truth was that he had not. Players in the dressing room began to notice he was forgetful of certain elements of preparation which would have been exhaustively covered in a previous era. There was no great surprise in this. He couldn't outfox nature.

The last time I spoke to him was in the Council Chambers of the SFA the week before travelling to Cardiff for the Wales match in November 1985. He had just held a press conference, after which he was speaking to people individually. Just in front of me he had taken to task a journalist for something that had been said about him years before. It made me smile. He never forgot and he never missed. But it was reprimand without sting. It seemed merely a reminder, no more. He looked drawn but nobody ever pointed these things out to him. Not in public anyway. He talked to me about his son George trying to get over from his job in

Switzerland to see this important game. There was nothing much more to it than that.

I did not see him being carried dying up the tunnel that night at Ninian Park. Neither did the SFA secretary Ernie Walker and Graeme Souness. They had both left their seats and gone down to the tea-room many minutes before the final whistle because the tension of watching Scotland hold on for their 1–1 draw had become intolerable. I knew how they both felt for I had escaped early as well, but for the added reason that I was not on official duty that night and had to speak at a corporate hospitality dinner in Cardiff Castle later. I was on the prawn cocktail when I heard he had died.

I took part in seven obituary programmes on both radio and television over the next forty-eight hours. I churned it out so mechanically eventually that I lost any of the sense of grief I had originally felt. It is the way of journalism.

Stein had grown out of the sour earth of the Old Firm patch to blossom into a patriarchical figure venerated even by those Rangers men who years before regarded him with repugnance. That notable achievement must not confuse us about the roots of his greatness, which stemmed from the impact he made as Celtic manager. I prefer to recall him as the younger man coming straight at me like a gale blowing, eyes flashing, mouth pursed ready to strike terror into the very soul. It's the warrior I remember most of all. For, as that, he was quite simply the best, in the best of all possible times.

12

The Celluloid Olympics

Lionel Richie walked to centre stage dressed in white, his voice suddenly embalming the 90,000 crowd in a respectful hush which intensified the casual cabaret tones of the singer, who was helping to bring the Olympic Games of 1984 in Los Angeles to an end. True to the nature of Tinseltown, the finale had sewn sequins onto the Olympic fabric. His rendition of *All Night Long* simpered into the velvety night as if he was entertaining late-night diners at the Coconut Grove on Wilshire Boulevard.

Beside me most of the British press corps were on their feet, standing on their cubicle desks, arms linked like the line-up from *Chorus Line*, swaying back and forward with the rest of the crowd in time to the music, although admittedly adding tiny trills of their own. It was difficult to relate this to the rather pompous and over-blown ceremonies normally associated with Olympic gatherings.

To get the British media to leave their instruments of communication for an impromptu public 'knees-up' is a rare achievement at any time and one which says much for the seductive quality of marrying the spirit of Baron de Coubertin to that of Busby Berkeley. From the opening ceremony, when fifty grand pianos strummed Gershwin and ladies who looked to be recruited straight from the Ziegfeld Follies, rather than from the 'Babe' Zaharias Memorial Club, wafted down a white staircase, these Games were to be unlike any other.

I had gone to the Olympics as part of BBC's network team with the principal assignment of capturing some of the essence of the character of the Games by filming the more 'off-beat' stories. I had missed out on Russia. BBC London invited me to the Moscow Olympics in 1980 but when Mrs Thatcher denounced the immorality of holding Games in a capital city of a nation occupying Afghanistan the BBC dutifully played ball and cut down the size of the team. I was one of the first casualties. My resulting exclusion from the team I am sure shook the Kremlin to its foundations. It certainly disappointed me.

I had good cause to go to Moscow on a personal basis for we had gone round the world in pursuit of Allan Wells to make a documentary about his preparations for these Games. We caught up with him in Melbourne and discovered a quiet, slightly dour man, monkish in the sort of contemplative way of sprinters, backed by an exuberant wife who seemed to have a Svengali-like and productive influence on him. Her vocal encouragements of him as he ran have made some of the most stimulating sports 'cut-away' shots of all time.

The documentary was of no great note in itself but it did indicate that, under Malcolm Kellard and a sympathetic management at that time, BBC Scotland's sports department was putting itself about. There had been a tendency in the past to allow ourselves to think that only our network sports colleagues in the south could attempt certain ventures. Although I did not believe Kellard was on the same wavelength as myself when it came to domestic sport, and especially football, I could not commend more the spirit of adventure that had been released by his coming.

With the arrival of James Hunter as Head of Television, Kellard's individuality seemed restricted and his trotting up and downstairs for instructions from his direct superior became a rather pathetic example of the means he had to adopt to keep his department moving. Until then, though, we flourished in imaginative ways. We did the unthinkable and travelled to Rome on the tenth anniversary of the Lisbon Lions victory, with Billy McNeill as my co-commentator, to cover the Liverpool–Borussia Moenchengladbach European Cup Final in 1977, rather than simply take the network broadcast. This piece of independent thinking in an area usually dominated by the south was greeted back in Scotland by a solemn piece in the *Glasgow Herald* asking 'Was Archie's Journey Really Necessary?' It made us despair.

My own feeling then, and it hasn't changed all that much, is that anything from the south is considered intrinsically superior by the vast bulk of the Scottish viewing public. LA was to prove that to me.

It is a city I had to get to know quickly for my basic job was to report on a widely varied basis. I had to find out where all the venues were. I started off doing that armed with the statutory local warning about impossible traffic, possible muggers and highly probable smog.

My first sight of the Colosseum in broad daylight was a disappointment. Like many other sports centres which I had only previously seen on film or in photographs it proved the camera is selective and short-sighted. What these views didn't show was that the principal stadium for the Games was surrounded by the encroaching urban decay of the town. As a general rule the more Hispanic faces you saw around you the greater the distance you were from Beverly Hills and the WASP communities in the canyons leading out of the city. The Colosseum, in that sense, might have been in Mexico.

You could see that the whole metropolitan area in fact was not so much a melting-pot but a series of apparently incompatible racial segments which defied that immediate analysis by merging in a mysteriously seamless way. I do not include the district of Watts in that description though. Barry Davies, the commentator, and I went by car to Long Beach one day to look at some of the indoor facilities there. Coming back we took a wrong turning and ended up driving through what might have been an impoverished town somewhere in the Third World. Whether or not we were influenced by our preconception of the place, we felt distinctly threatened as squads of people, perhaps of saintly intent (we were not inclined to dally to find out), gazed at us as if they wished the car would stall.

That's how it seemed as you travelled around looking for venues like needles in hay stacks. It is not until you have to move round the greater area of LA that you realise you are so easily swallowed up in this huge urban sprawl. There is all of twenty-six miles of

Sunset Boulevard for instance and to move from the athletics stadium to Anaheim for the wrestling and judo was like a whole day's journey given you could read the freeway signs correctly and if you couldn't you would end up in Pasadena whether you liked it or not.

Even more importantly there was no communal or municipal link with the Games. Normally in an Olympic city you would find expressions of sheer gratitude or pride or even bombast connected with the festival. But not in LA for the Games did not belong to the civic authorities or the people but to the sponsors. These were the first commercially self-sustaining Olympics and you really did not see any evidence of the Games being there at all until you were practically on the doorstep of the particular venues. Perhaps the apotheosis of crass subjugation to the dollar sign was seen in the fact that the American nation watching on television did not see the entry of the flame into the stadium but were on a commercial at the time.

My own professional efforts nearing the opening of the Games were distinctly stodgy. I had firstly been sent to reflect on how the Great American Breakfast was the last thing any athlete would wish to contemplate during their stay in Tinseltown and, because of a camera fault and the essential cut-away shots for editing purposes, I ate the equivalent of three breakfasts in the most famous breakfast eatery in LA, an undistinguished little café which people queued to get into. This amounted to something like six pancakes smothered in syrup, six eggs, three waffles, and hash potatoes. So far I had been in at the tail end of planning for our build-up to the start of the Games and, about three days before the opening ceremony, I hadn't really achieved all that much. I could end up as irrelevant to the action as some of the tramps who trundled around Lafayette and MacArthur Parks pushing their supermarket trolleys like women of old going to the 'steamie' with their prams. I was going to have to come up with something special.

One night I sat in my room watching the late movie. It was Bob Hope in *The Cat and the Canary*, debatably his funniest film without Crosby. The last time I had seen it was in the Palaceum Cinema just off Shettleston Road when I was still in short-trousers. I was in the middle of enjoying it when it occurred to me that I had met somebody two years previously who had claimed not just to have known Hope but to have been sponsor of his annual Desert Classic golf tournament. I had been at Gleneagles making a film about its attraction for Americans and the professional on the course, Ian Marchbanks, pointed me in the direction of a little man who came to Scotland every year on a golfing pilgrimage. He turned out to be a delightful individual of many anecdotes connected with golf, not least of which was his association with Bob Hope. His name was Jack Hennessy and although he represented the cognac people in California he was not of the original family.

But he was the organiser of the Desert Classic, so he said. After I had interviewed him on film about his liking for Scotland he gave me a warm invite to LA any time and offered me his business card. Now Americans by and large are extremely open people with a propensity for generous invitations to the bosom of the household. They seem to do it with a natural ease that might be mistaken for the rather mechanical and automatic utterance, 'Have a nice day!' Generally speaking, you do not put them to the test.

I mothballed his business card. But that night, as Bob Hope and Paulette Goddard were shrieking their way through the spooky film, I was upturning every little piece of my baggage to find that small piece of pasteboard with his name on it. I was going to put him to the test. I found it buried in a pile of brief-case flotsam and jetsam that had collected through the years and the following morning I phoned him. Within a couple of hours, he was down to take me to lunch at the Lakeside Country Club in North Hollywood in his solid white Cadillac. There was no getting away from the fact that Jack Hennessy was a man of some substance. But it wasn't just his hospitality I was after. As we drove up through Burbank and past the Universal Studios complex I was wondering if he really did know Bob Hope after all.

John Mortimer once described Hollywood as 'suburbia of the soul'. Six weeks wasn't long enough to experience that sort of seediness or to divine the misery that is hidden behind the sumptuous hoardings of sybaritic living. Perhaps I could have gone off the place quickly but as it was I lapped up the environment in the simplest way, as a tourist might do, hoping to bump into celebrities.

Naive I suppose, but if you've been brought up in cinema it seemed a natural inclination. So, with Jack Hennessy in the Lakeside Club, I was introduced to Hollywood.

The Club had boasted Howard Hughes as a member, which means it had more amenities than just hot and cold running water. The centrepiece was a magnificent championship golf course, for from the Thirties onwards golf had become an obsession amongst the stars, many of whom had been or were members. Crosby, Bogart, Hope, Gable, Buddy Rogers, Weismuller, and many others including hundreds of directors and producers from the studios had based themselves there.

The bar in the club was famous. It was there that Bogart, Sydney Greenstreet, Peter Lorre and Mary Astor would retire to every night during the filming of *The Maltese Falcon*. They told me Bogart, in fact, normally stayed there all night and went straight onto the lot, often without sleep, which, apart from his own abilities, partly explained that brilliantly rumpled and acerbic performance. In the bar Jack introduced me to a gentleman called simply Norm who had devised and owned *Looney Tunes* and had been the creator of Woody Woodpecker. We sometimes forget that the ability to sketch in Hollywood had created millionaires outside of Disney and Norm was one. He also happened to be pleasantly crotchety at the age of seventy. When I asked him how the ordinary members in the club reacted to the depth of celebrities around he snorted, 'Doesn't make a damn difference.' He had a huge mane of white hair and a glass of bourbon inevitably just under his chin, which drooped a lot towards the counter. 'Nobody bothers anybody here,' he said. 'We talk business amongst ourselves but golf is golf. When you're out there with your partner it doesn't matter a damn if they're queuing up to see you all over the world. Miss a putt in a foursome and you're just another asshole.

'Why, the most unpopular man in the club was Bogart. What a misfit he was! Nobody wanted to go on the course with him. People thought he cheated, kicked his ball in the rough and all that, and when he'd been on his binges he'd come down here with a hangover the size of Santa Monica pier and be the most miserable sonofabitch in the ENTIRE country. One day a guy in the industry was told he'd been drawn in a foursome with Bogey. He pulled

out! Almost unheard of! When he was asked for his official explanation he just told the committee, "If I want to play with a prick,
I'll play with my own!"'

Perhaps in that 'suburbia of the soul' Norm was the local gossip
columnist. He himself was at pains to tell everybody I was with
the BBC and one gent told me how marvellous it was to meet
somebody from the organisation which had helped the great broadcaster Ed Murrow during the war in London and how much he
respected their standards of objectivity and technical excellence.
Carried away by all of this, I offered him an invite down to the
International Television Centre where, if he so wished, he could
examine our operation. When I asked him what he did for a living
he explained that he was a producer.

'What have you produced?' I asked.

'*Butch Cassidy and the Sundance Kid*, *The Sting*, *Slaughterhouse
Five* . . . and I'm off to have a look at the rushes of something by
a guy called John Le Carré . . . Do you know him? . . . I'm doing
that with George Roy Hill. He's directing. It's called *The Little
Drummer Girl*. It's a swine of a book to film but I think George
has cracked it!'

I didn't think it was worthwhile the man coming down to see us
after all.

Eventually I broached the subject.

'Do you see Bob Hope much?' I asked Jack.

'Now and again,' he said. 'Do you want to meet him?'

Did I want to meet him! I tried as best as I possibly could to
remain very British and cool and slightly casual.

'Possible?' I asked languidly.

'Just wait and I'll see if he's in town,' Jack replied.

He went to a wall phone in the large dining room and started
to dial. I was sufficiently far enough away only to pick up fragments
of the conversation but I was getting the gist.

'Hi, where you been . . . just had lunch with a Scot . . . met
him at Gleneagles . . . yeah, he loves golf . . . Arch is his name
. . . Arch . . . with the BBC television company . . . yeah the good
old BBC company . . . over here for the Olympics . . . you wanna
talk to him?'

He beckoned me over. OK, it was just a phone call, but it wasn't all that usual, I was saying to myself. It's just Bob Hope on the other end of the line, no need to get carried away. It's not his autograph you're after.

'Hello,' I said.

'Hi, Arch!' the voice replied.

I suppose a pilgrim throwing himself on a shrine after a lifetime's struggle to reach the sacred spot would be so absorbed in the moment that he would be oblivious to those non-believers who might care to mock. That is how I suppose I would try to justify the juvenile weak-kneed feeling I had hearing that voice on the other end of the line. I had grown up with him, watching him grow older, thinking him the veritable citadel of ham, perhaps decreasingly funny, but always in my mind stuck in the Forties in canisters of black and white film and consequently indestructible. Now he was a two-worded voice on the other end of the line.

'Hi, Bob!' I said as if to an old pal.

I can't remember too much about the conversation because I was mentally preparing to ask him the most vital question of all. But we did talk about how much he liked Scotland and the difficulty of playing Carnoustie and of how he loved the Royal and Ancient and of how he was preparing for an autumn tour of the UK. Now I wanted him for interview.

What the BBC had lacked in LA up till then was some connection with showbiz or the film industry to add some glitter to the major Olympic Preview which was being prepared. There had been some talk about getting Michael Caine and having a barbecue at 'his place' in Beverly Hills but somehow it was beginning to peter out, no doubt because there was an agent involved.

Now Hollywood agents can be a cross between a vulture and a snake and are very difficult people to work with. I had once tried to secure Rod Stewart for an interview when I heard he was coming back from LA and was told that his agent would require the cost of a private plane to get him from London to Glasgow, an overnight suite in a hotel, not just for himself I hasten to add, and a hefty sum that could float a company on the Stock Exchange. Needless to say, Rod probably heard nothing at all about this for these people act as financial 'bouncers' as well. So to arrange a Hollywood celebrity interview was as easy as asking for some free real estate in Malibu. We were in fact getting nowhere.

So I had to make the plunge.

'I was wondering if you wouldn't mind giving us a few words for BBC television. I am sure the people back home would love it. Just any thoughts you have on the Olympics coming to Los Angeles. We'd all be deeply grateful.'

It was just on the right side of grovelling. There was a pause.

'When?' the voice asked.

I was taken aback. It seemed like interest. And then again I wished he hadn't asked that for I simply did not know. I gave myself all of 1.8 seconds to find a hypothetical time.

'Tomorrow afternoon, say about three o'clock?'

'Well I'm kinda busy right now. I'm getting my new Olympic suit fitted. They say I've put on a little bit behind. Slackening it off for me.'

I felt a kind of dangling disappointment.

'Could you bring a camera out to me?'

Could we bring a camera out to him! If it was the last thing I ever did.

'Of course,' I said.

'Then make it three o'clock and bring old Jack out with you. I haven't seen him for a while. See you.'

Just like that. But as soon as I put the phone down I realised I had a problem. There was simply no way of knowing whether I would get a camera unit or not. The coverage of the Olympics is a huge logistical nightmare which requires the most meticulous planning even down to the daily allocation of the three camera units we had with us in LA. The executive producer Alec Weeks ran it properly, like a general leading a battalion, with a stern attention to detail. It was entirely possible he would not release a unit if it was going to cover some mainstream athletics story, not even for a Bob Hope interview. I was gambling on the fact that it was the sort of portion of Tinseltown we badly needed.

Old Norm grunted his approval of Hope.

'Hope has his critics,' he growled. 'He's good on the course and he's not as mean as some folks say. Not in the same way as Bing.

He was the meanest of them all in my book. One night Crosby was down on the Strip, probably with some babes, and Dixie and the family were in the house when suddenly it went on fire. Fire brigade was called and they got word down to Bing. He came racing back in a cab and when he got there the flames had taken over. What does he do? Without asking about the family he dives into the house past the firemen who try to stop him but can't and comes back out a minute later with a shoe. Out of the shoe he's counting some bucks. Something like fifty bucks he had stashed away in a shoe under the bed. A man who could have bought the White House was willing to risk his life for fifty bucks. He was the meanest man in the ENTIRE country! Hey, ask Hope what he thought of *Looney Tunes*!'

I had other things in mind. I went back to our base with my fingers crossed. The International Broadcasting Centre for the Olympics was based just off Hollywood Boulevard in the old Columbia Pictures Studios, now used principally for television. I returned to this chilling, air-conditioned aircraft hangar of a building with the news I had Hope for interview. They wouldn't believe me at first. Indeed some of them casting an envious eye on what I apparently had achieved quite clearly did not want to believe me.

'How much?'

It was the question on everyone's lips when eventually it had sunk in that we did have him on offer. This found me very vulnerable again because I simply did not know.

'We can't proceed until we know how much. It could cost us an arm and a leg and the Games haven't even started yet. Get an idea of how much.'

Of course I thought this was a bad idea and tried to convince them that Hope was actually a friend of a friend.

'Nobody in Hollywood does things for a friend of a friend. Nobody does anything for free. Who's kidding who?'

I was being mauled. But I stuck it out.

'You can have my guts for garters if we're stung,' I said. 'I've got a feeling this is a favour.'

I could see they weren't buying this wholly but with a certain reservation they agreed to proceed. They allocated me Martin Mathewson, quite the best sports cameraman I have worked with, and indeed this was the beginning of a kind of partnership which would see us filming around the world together. Hope's house was in North Hollywood not far from the original Crosby home. Outside his main drive there were three large Chrysler limousines, part of his own personal fleet which he is given by the car company for personal appearances. The house had been added to through the years, from the original villa type, and was now a curious hybrid of mock-Tudor and Spanish hacienda.

Hope was still out when we got there so Jack Hennessy took us right through the house showing us the various sections that had been put on through the years and the *objets d'art* collected. Then we walked outside to the poolside and looked over his own personal golf course. It consisted of four par-four holes which he constantly practised on we were told. We set up the camera near his first tee with the pool in the background and only about ten minutes later than he had agreed, he arrived.

He came out from the French windows with a six-iron in his hand swinging it back and forward gently like a pendulum. Even before he could open his mouth our cameraman suddenly said, 'Excuse me, Mr Hope. Your shirt is white. The light will bounce off it badly and distort the picture. Could you change for us?'

He stopped in his tracks. I would not like to give the impression I was totally in awe of the man but I did freeze and expect him to tell us not to darken his doorstep ever again.

'Hey,' he said. 'I thought you were going to be regular guys. I've only got two shirts. I'll go back in and see if it's still at the laundry.'

At which point he turned, walked back inside and rejoined us ten minutes later with a multi-coloured vertical stripe shirt which I hoped would content our cameraman for the rest of his living days. But we were after all dealing with a consummate professional. To introduce the item we asked him if he would walk with me from his house to the couple of seats we had arranged for the interview. For various reasons we had to ask him to do it four times after which he did exactly the same leg cross position, swept his hat off exactly the same way and placed his golf club across his knee with the same meticulous precision. Even though it was but a humble interview the old habits of working on the set with Paramount were coming out in him.

I noticed that he was older looking than I had expected which is a bit like stating the obvious except that the young 'Lemon Drop Kid' Hope is indelibly stamped on the mind. The creases below the eyes seemed as if they had been stuck on to re-enact the ending of the *Road To Utopia*, where he appeared in the octogenerian trio of Hope, Crosby and Lamour. He was deaf in one ear so he made a blatant appeal to have me speak to his 'good' side. But he was bristling with good humour and made disparagingly jocular remarks about LA, its smog, its traffic, its muggings, the normal sort of thing; but right up our street.

He gave us exactly the brief summary of Hollywood and its interest in the Games that we wanted. When we had finished and we were sitting together as the cameraman set up some separate shots of the two of us I happened to ask him where his wife was. He pointed out to me that she was in fact in London at that very time. I had an idea. Would he like to deliver a message to his wife straight to camera and tell her she could see the full interview on *Olympic Grandstand* at a specific time? There was a little method in this madness. If he did this the BBC would have Bob Hope being used to plug one of their programmes. He jumped at the idea. Indeed he revelled in it. The assistant cameraman used his walkie-talkie back to base to ascertain what the starting time was for this special Opening Ceremony *Grandstand* and we turned the camera on Hope.

'OK,' he said. 'Roll 'em.'

We started the camera.

'Hi, Dolores,' he bubbled. 'How's London? Behaving yourself? Look at me. I'm being a good boy. I've taken out the garbage, haven't had the boys over for cards, kept out of the pool hall. I'll be behaving myself until you get back. Oh, and by the way. You can see all of this tonight on *Olympic Grandstand* starting just after twelve o'clock. Don't forget, watch *Olympic Grandstand* on BBC 1 tonight just after twelve. See you!'

Not once did he do it but twice to suit the sound man, for an aircraft had passed overhead the first time. I was now, ever so slightly, not believing this. At any moment, I thought, an agent is going to appear from behind the bunker on the green just ahead of us flourishing a contract as big as a mallet and I am going to be clobbered not just here but back at base too. Or else I was going to wake up. Was Bob Hope not only doing an interview for us but actually promoting a BBC programme? Well, yes he was! Not only that but he thanked us profusely for letting him talk to his wife and then strolled off back inside with that casual straight-backed grace that pled for someone to play in the background, 'Thanks For The Memory'.

There was no agent, no mention of money, no shocks but simply a star who had done a friend a favour which had been passed on to me. I blessed the day that I had met Jack Hennessy on the golf course at Gleneagles. All the same, it is never wise to think you are home and dry with these items until they actually hit the air and I was not to know that even though I returned to Hollywood Boulevard with the tape, guarding it like a gold ingot, there was trouble to come.

I deposited the tape with the assistant producer, who had accompanied me to Hope's house, having agreed the structure of the edit and the separation of the brief promotion. I then went off to have a look at some of the teams practising basketball at the Forum out beside Hollywood Park Racetrack and returned near midnight to view the final article. The large edit suite was virtually empty and there was only one video-tape editor left. She showed me what had been done to the Hope piece. Many of his quips had been left out and there was no sign of the plug for *Grandstand*. They had been dropped.

'Dropped!' I shouted. 'By whose instructions?'

As I went into ranting and raving mode, I could not get out of the poor girl the reason why it had been done. All that effort for a slack, unjustifiably brief edit. It struck me as the work of a very lazy man indeed, who simply wanted to get the job done and out of the way so he could get out for the night. I knew too that our main editors back in the office would not have known about that for it was late and, what made matters worse, it had been packaged and was sitting waiting there now to be transmitted on the first satellite time booked for early in the morning LA time back to London. It seemed beyond repair.

I went looking for blood but luckily, I suppose, did not find it, even though I scoured the bars near the hotel. The man in question could not be found. I had good reason to claim at least a tiny little scoop, against the rub of the green, as it were, and here it was now being thrown down the drain. I did not sleep much that night. I felt abused in a kind of way. I had gone after recognition for what I was capable of getting out there and now it was thrown almost in the trash can.

I was first up the next day in the hotel in Wilshire and waited for somebody to come downstairs, anybody, so I could tell my story. As luck would have it first down was Jim Reside, a fellow Scot who is a man for decision-making if ever there was one. He was in a senior position in charge of all production output from the television gallery in the complex.

'If I had to tell you that I have Bob Hope promoting *Grandstand* but that it's been dropped, along with other good bits from his full interview, on the package going back on the bird [*satellite*] what would you say?' I asked.

'Get in the car!' was all he replied.

Because of the time difference between LA and London, by the time we reached the studios we had only about half-an-hour to hit the afternoon *Grandstand* programme. The special Olympic Opening Ceremony edition was to start just after midnight. If we wanted Hope's message to Dolores, which was in effect a blatant plug for the later programme, to go out before the end of the afternoon edition we had somehow to get the original and unedited tape and send it out via the satellite, with precious little warning, to the editor in London. John Philips, the editor there, took it in his stride.

He was told by Reside what we were going to try to attempt and he passed on the message to Desmond Lynam, in front of camera, that a very late piece indeed might be arriving from LA. We searched and eventually found the tape as the hands of the clock began moving towards the end of the programme. Sending a piece by satellite requires precision co-ordination between the sender and receiver and everybody has to have their wits about them or else it could be a fiasco. We were not sure in sending the raw material unedited that it would not spill beyond the end of the programme and therefore be unusable.

In the UK *Grandstand*'s viewers were watching the very exciting final of the World Bowls Championships from Aberdeen. Exactly one minute from the end of the programme, the sweat pouring from me even in the air-conditioned production suite, I heard John Philips announce, 'We've got Hope! He's referring to *Olympic Grandstand*, Des. Lead us into it in about thirty seconds.'

Lynam, with only a moment's warning and barely thirty seconds remaining of the programme, picked it up beautifully. 'Well,' he said. 'I was going to mention what we had on tonight. But we bumped into somebody in Hollywood who can probably do it better than I can. I think you'll know him.'

Cut to Hope.

'Hi, Dolores . . .'

We had done it with seconds to spare.

I felt limp all day after that. The fight to get Hope on the air had seemed so unnecessary. That night in London, though, before they came live to the Olympic Stadium they transmitted the entire interview which was a dainty and appropriate morsel to set before the public prior to an event which was part-Olympic, part-Hollywood.

After that I had gained the confidence of the editorial minds in London and I found it easier to suggest items and to be given a unit to go out and create some colour. The day after the opening I went back to Lakeside where they produced a panel of Hollywood men associated with cinema who aired their views on how they thought the opening had been organised. Amongst them was Buddy Rogers, who had acted in the very first film to have won an Academy Award and who had married America's first sweetheart of the screen, Mary Pickford. He had that special attribute of many Californian men in their late seventies, he only looked twenty-six.

He represented a line stretching back to silent cinema and he gushed with pride in his country and its ability to still be the land of the free, unlike the Russians who had refused to come to LA as a reprisal for the Americans refusing to go to Moscow as a protest about the invasion of Afghanistan. On the theme of this merry-go-round of protest Jack Hennessy passed on a red, white and blue hat to me that day which Bob Hope had asked him to give me and which I still possess. It had a buttoned-down brim. When you snap it open the white lettering reads, 'F—— Russia!'

This crude political message from one of the popularisers of the American right simply suggested to me that it would not be a bad idea to record some Soviet press sentiments on these games. I tracked the Tass correspondent down to the huge press-centre in downtown LA and he graciously and in impeccable English told me how he regretted his nation hadn't come but that they could not have their safety guaranteed whilst here. Americans could not even guarantee their own safety. After all, just prior to the Games a man had walked into a McDonald's near San Diego and slaughtered over a dozen people for no apparent reason. It was difficult to reply to that. When I asked him if he was harassed he said he wasn't sure but couldn't care less and only worried about the appalling ignorance of even the American press who continually would ask him what time the curfew was in Moscow. When I took the recording back to base one English producer looked at it solemnly, then asked, 'What time is the curfew in Moscow anyway?'

I then began to mount interview after interview with sportsmen and women in a whole variety of sports although I obviously wanted to continue constructing 'colour' pieces in the sure knowledge that in the remorseless slog of the transmission of event after event, the viewer would like the relaxation of the off-beat report. Of course I would have loved to have been in the main stadium churning out athletic commentary. But the BBC just happens to have the strongest athletic commentating team in the world even though Coleman, Pickering and Storey and Foster were suffering in the immediate aftermath of the loss of the major athletics contract in the UK to ITV. At least I was being given the opportunity to lend a distinctive and personal imprint to these film reports and frankly I indulged to the utmost.

I took a Welsh weightlifter to the Universal Studios to try and re-enact a King Kong scene then placed him in the famous Gold's Gym down near Venice Beach. He had one look round the massive men pumping the iron and said in a voice of disdain from the valleys, 'Cream puffs!'

'What?' I asked.

'They're all poofs here. You can tell a mile away. I'd rather mix with King Kong, if you don't mind.'

Gay muscledom didn't look much different from any other kind of muscledom to me but I took his word for it.

We filmed on Santa Monica beach with British wrestlers and brought the LAPD down on our necks. A large crowd gathered to see us filming and the police came roaring in thinking there was a riot shaping on the sands. It turned out to be our version of the *Sands of Iwo Jima*. We went in on the quite unfashionable British hockey team to film them doing their laundry and other domestic chores, little realising they would turn out to be one of the hits of the Games.

Then I shared a bath with Terry Wogan.

In Hollywood we were always led to believe that the bizarre is merely the mundane. Isn't this the place, after all, where Groucho Marx once hired the entire Los Angeles Symphony Orchestra to come into his living room to play the 1812 Overture to annoy the neighbours upstairs because they had refused to allow him to join a quintet they had formed? That sort of thing. Nothing of such lunacy had we reflected but we wanted to. So I don't know that I can proudly proclaim that what happened with Wogan was a seminal incident in the history of broadcasting, but, to our mutual satisfaction, it was at least different.

It wasn't just your ordinary bath. It was a jacuzzi. That wasn't even ordinary either for it was in the back of a stretch-limousine. I am still unsure as to why Wogan and I actually ended up in it other than that we were easy prey to a streak of the absurd in the work we were doing.

There has been no radio broadcaster more skilled in developing the idiosyncrasies of individuals in his chat than Terry who could spin out a theme over a period of days which, because of the long periods of broadcasting he was committed to, was absolutely necessary for the programme. He had occasionally broadcast comments about me, on the times I passed the caravan he was broadcasting from, which were nippily dabbed with fun. So we decided to confront him on camera about his work and have a go ourselves. But as it was also his birthday, the radio lads had hired this extraordinary limousine with the jacuzzi for his delectation. It was too good to resist. We both went in. What I did not realise was that he was broadcasting live to the UK whilst I was filming him and the ribald comments that were being made must have spiced up a dreary night for some of the souls staying up to listen to his programme.

It was a duel of sorts. I was trying to get my words in before he could ask me questions. The bath bubbled, the crowd around us grew, photographers rushed from all parts. Was this what nymphettes did at Cannes for attention? Later that night, watching the tape with the pair of us sitting partially submerged in this foam, asking each other questions but giving no answers, I had the feeling that although we looked like a couple of cheap publicity-seeking wallies we had entered into the kindred spirit of Groucho. It was candy-floss broadcasting which all of us, perhaps reluctantly, admit we like in small doses.

We were now churning it out as the Games progressed but in truth not knowing what was hitting the screens back home and what wasn't. At first I deeply cared whether something was used or not but experience tells you simply to get it back to base and hope for the best. Although I had probably hit a jackpot getting Hope it had only been an interview after all. I needed another specially shaped item to convey something of Americana and of our reaction to it in this unique Olympic environment. As the Games went on it looked as if it would elude me. But there it was staring me in the face all this time and I couldn't see it. It was Bob Abrahams, the editor at base, who recognised it.

'Think it's about time you did something about baseball?' he asked one day.

Baseball was merely a demonstration sport but it was drawing capacity crowds to the Dodgers Stadium out near the Hollywood Bowl. The stadium is a man-made canyon with enough car-parking space to satisfy the entire human race, it would seem. The Dodgers of course used to belong to Brooklyn. Now they are on a hillside in LA. That sporting nomadism is pure distilled Americana in its own right, but I wanted to feel the popcorn culture myself and suck through a straw the mystique surrounding this American obsession.

So we took ourselves firstly to the press box where we sought an interpreter. He turned up in a rather coincidental manner. In short, he was the first man in the box I asked. I wanted him to sit with me in the crowd and simply talk me through the whole rigmarole as the cameras filmed us. As I spoke to him his features seemed familiar. I hate and detest asking anybody, particularly in LA of all places, 'Haven't I seen you somewhere before?' So I asked him, 'Haven't I seen you somewhere before?' rather than beat about the bush.

I was glad I did for he turned out to be the kind of man who just lived now for that very question to be asked. He had been the original television Mike Hammer in Mickey Spillane's detective series. I cast my mind back to flickery black and white video and visualised him perfectly beneath the brim of his hat. Now he had turned sports reporter to earn a living. From being a well-known, if B movie actor, to sports reporter could be construed as one of the worst forms of falling on hard times. He was small and had a voice that was pure Bronx, 'de boids and de bees' variety. Absolutely perfect. So off we trotted down into the crowd just behind first base.

We sat together and when they started to run the camera I acted the total innocent as he gave me the wholly incomprehensible jargon of the baseball aficionado. We took a shot of the scoreboard which was a jumble of statistics as digestible as computer hieroglyphics. It seemed to be going fine until I felt a tap on my shoulder. I turned to see a large lady wearing an Olympic stewardess's uniform standing over us.

'Excuse me, sir,' she said with emphasised politeness. 'Do you all have tickets for this PAR-TIC-ULAR area?'

As she had deliberately interrupted filming I was rather put out and showed it. I pointed to the Olympic accreditation card I was wearing which granted me access to every venue and explained to her what we were doing.

'But do you have tickets for this PAR-TIC-ULAR area? You need tickets for this PAR-TIC-ULAR area. These passes will not do here!' she repeated like an android, as I always thought many of these Olympic volunteers were anyway. Again, I tried to explain. She insisted though that we would have to move and since she was getting in the way of the camera there was nothing for it but to go. The crowd had been looking on at this stage with interest but no involvement. But we were determined to get our way. We waited until she had gone down a mid-stand tunnel and we crept back in again to the delight of some of the people around us and started up again. We were in the middle of the discourse when the voice boomed above us.

'I am sorry, sir. But I must ask you to leave!' It was her again. I pled with her. She stood her ground and by this time hundreds of people around us were now watching this scene rather than the baseball.

'If you don't go I will have to call the police!' she said.

That did it, the crowd began to respond.

'Hey, bud!' one large man behind me said. 'If you hold my popcorn I'll bop her one on the nose for you.'

I was now slightly regretting this. I didn't want a scene, but, on the other hand, I was angry about it. I was resigned to going when I saw her calling in three large policemen who started to wend their way through the crowd towards us. She said quite bluntly, 'That's them!'

It was just about then that a woman rose up a few seats from us and from the bottom of her heart gave us the founding fathers' stuff.

'What's going on here!' she shouted. 'I thought this was the land of the free not a police state. What did we fight the last war for? To watch some guys just doin' their jobs getting slung out the Dodgers Stadium?' There was a shout of assent and applause from the crowd who were now standing up in a multitude around us. The unknown lady seemed to be inspired by this response.

'These guys are our guests! They're Brits! They fought along-side us during the war! Have you bums ever heard of the London Blitz! These people suffered for our freedom and now they'll go back home thinking America's a dictatorship. You should be ashamed of yourselves, you bums!'

This brought the house down. People stood and cheered her to the echo. The police had one look at this response, took the stewardess by the elbow and just escorted her out of harm's way, then turned and saluted us with a quick snap of the elbow. The crowd responded to this too and well-wishers pushed forward to slap us on the back. Somebody stuck a baseball cap on my head and another gave me a bag of popcorn and, dressed as the All-American punter, I finished the item which we had started over an hour earlier with that piece of American pragmatic hokum 'If you can't beat 'em . . . join 'em'. The crowd rose to that sentiment and short of being given my green card there and then I had become at least a temporary American.

We took the tape back, edited it carefully to the rodeo music of Aaron Copland and the item was shown at least three times during the rest of the Games period.

I had been well down the Olympic cast. But at least I hadn't been left as a face on the cutting-room floor. LA had been good for me, which is why I looked at the *Los Angeles Herald*'s headline the morning after the final ceremony with some regret. It simply said, 'That's A Wrap!'

13

Face Value

Public identity has its mixed blessings. I tried not to take myself too seriously as a so-called television personality but it's honestly difficult to resist the temptation if, for the flimsiest of reasons, people do attribute to you some special status simply because of the electronic face popping up more regularly than the window-cleaner. The responses of course varied.

There were the threats. The first one I had on my life I took very seriously indeed. It was received with the gravity of some-one egotistical enough to imagine that people would actually waste valuable gunpowder on him. It came from a throaty gentleman with a glottal stop who sounded so convincing on the phone that it made the skin creep. 'Bomb you into f— eternity' was the most poetic of the phrases used. I had apparently offended him in criticising Rangers, against whom he thought I was plotting. A Papish plot to boot, just to give it its proper roundness.

Late on a Saturday night, answering phone calls after the pro-gramme in the loneliness of the office could make a message from the Samaritans sound like a warning from the Mafia. Sometimes in a perverse way I enjoyed these calls for at least it made you aware that somebody out there was paying attention. The routine of the programme, especially if it went smoothly, could easily make you imagine that the only people privy to the broadcast were the handful in the studio and the production gallery. A little private soirée, in fact.

Of course death threats were greeted, rightly as it so happens, with a kind of 'Ho-hum' sort of attitude by even those nearest and dearest. On one occasion at the BBC, though, I received a large brown parcel which whilst not ticking, rattled. I was swooped upon by a large ex-military man of hawkish appearance from admin who proceeded to place the parcel in an empty office and to open it with longish tongs from behind the fortress of a standard BBC filing cabinet, thus confirming the British military's outstanding capacity for improvisation. The parcel contained a free sample of beer. We promised to keep this revelation to a minimum of sensible people but before hours had elapsed the building was agog with the stories of this unnecessary act of valour and the red faces which went with it. I remember actually vowing to risk obliteration in future rather than face the indignity of anti-climax.

There was an assumption even by those in the business that being the face on the screen made you the sort of property which might fall under the control of a Public Works Department, with access available to everyone except on Boxing Days and Easter Sundays.

Whilst it would be untrue to say that I did not occasionally wallow in the glow of public recognition I was, throughout, always tentative about it. I feared let-downs. An old lady on a train between Dundee and Stonehaven once paid me such glowing tributes I almost burst into tears of gratitude. It was only when she alighted in that north-eastern town and bade me good-bye that I realised she had mistaken me for Donny B. MacLeod. It was as if the Open Championship had been wrested from your grasp because you hadn't filled in the score-card correctly. A journalist entertained me to lunch and superbly engineered the loosening of the tongue by amongst other things offering his appreciation of all my talents and a week later produced an article of finely-honed ridicule.

I could never relax my apprehension of the imminence of back-lash. This was the indiscriminate aspect of my relationship with the public but there was another which needed more consider-ation, more care. I was frequently inundated with requests from charities for some sort of recognition or presence. This was very difficult to cope with. You had to be very selective or else life would have become quite unbearable. On top of that there were the formal requests to speak to groups of one kind or another and I found this much more intriguing. It was then I realised that television was a useful passport to areas normally denied others.

I realised the appropriateness of what I had once taken to be a cravenly stupid and superior remark made to me by someone in administration when he said, 'I hope you realise that to be on the box is a privilege not to be abused.' In the sense that being on telly was something which had been worked on rather than bestowed on me as a favour, he was quite wrong. But in knowing that television can confer powers of entry that would undo the most ingenious Yale lock, he was absolutely right. I discovered the truth of it in the most telling ways.

In the mid-Seventies I was invited to visit that building which had so dominated my childhood skyline, Barlinnie Prison. The only reason given was that I was a 'well-known personality'. Intrigued, I accepted. After the numerous outer perimeter security checks I was taken through various inner-courtyard doors to what appeared to be a kind of temporary, detached structure that initially, and perhaps mistakenly, reminded me of Army barracks. A tall man in uniform with lots of keys on his person opened the door for me and closed it behind me. I was in the Special Unit.

I only knew vaguely about this Unit. I did know that it contained only murderers who were providing constant problems to the system. This was an attempt at rehabilitation. That is why I was so taken aback. I was in a bright, spacious room which had the strange impact of making me feel I was walking into a modern, open-ended primary school classroom. It had neither the trappings nor the stale stench of prison. About six men, mostly in shirts and jeans, were lounging around the room, casually engaged in reading or writing. The tension which I had felt entering the place contrasted with the rather indolent, sprawling scene in front of me. A slight figure with auburn hair approached me and gripped my hand in a firm, markedly positive handshake.

'Nice to see you. My name's Jimmy Boyle. Can I show you around?'

You cannot live in Glasgow without certain names ringing in the ears with the timbre of undiminished and constant threat. Boyle's name was once a monosyllabic obscenity. Even the police feared him. He had murdered and slashed and been seen as a hit man of classical iciness. At that very instant, grasping the hand, looking at the benign face but hearing the name, I realised the huge problem facing Boyle, his companions and the Unit. Not even an enlightened penal system can live down reputations. As one respected crime reporter said to me on my return after describing my visit, 'That man will never change. He's a beast and he always will be! He shouldn't be allowed out.' I somehow felt listening to him that he was almost disappointed in Boyle's transformation, as if the prisoner was on the verge of leaving a club to which both belonged. The apostate from the razor showed me through the cells.

I cannot imagine anybody who stumbled accidentally on Gauguin's work on his Polynesian island could have been more stunned than I was in walking into Boyle's cell. It glowed in a profusion of colour. Paintings, murals, and sculptures were cramped into the relatively tiny space like a secret hoard of art. Boyle himself explained his work to me although, in all honesty, by this time, even if Vasari had materialised through the walls to offer analysis, I could not have taken anything in. I felt quite overwhelmed by this.

No cell door was shut and the half-a-dozen inmates and the prison officers mixed communally in the central area. Eventually they sat in a semi-circle around me and I talked about broadcasting and sport. There was no doubting who was the dominant personality in this unconventional arrangement. Boyle was the paterfamilias of the entire establishment including, from where I was observing, the prison officers, who were not slow to recognise what he had to say. When he interrupted me to say it was time for a tea-break an officer upped and put the kettle on and then passed round the cups.

I wondered there and then whether the strength of this experiment was based on Boyle's own vivid personality, or whether rehabilitation entailed a kind of role reversal or whether, despite all their back-up, the officers could not forget he was the violent man with a murderous reputation the Krays would have been proud of. The fact that the Unit is still vigorously in existence would answer some of these views but in terms of its reputation at that time the Special Unit was The House That Jimmy Built.

He overshadowed even Larry Winters, who achieved post-humous fame through the film they made about him, *Silent Scream*. I remember Winters from that visit as a quiet, softish-looking man, gently asking intelligent questions about television, but only when it seemed Boyle was not wishing to hold the floor. The evening wore on until Boyle announced that it was getting close to lights out. He made a little decorous speech of thanks to me and invited me back some time. I left deeply impressed. However, when I made it clear to friends and colleagues I would do everything in my power to publicise what was going on there and give the whole concept any support I could I was met largely with cynicism.

They felt it was a bit of a showcase, a gratuitous attempt to appease those who wanted some modernisation of the penal system and that those men were beyond rehabilitation anyway. Perhaps I got a bit carried away but since they had shown a great knowledge of sport and of watching television I suggested that in the spirit of the whole experimentation we could mount some broadcast from there. This would demonstrate the Unit's usefulness by recognising what was going on in a revolutionary way. The idea was squashed very quickly. Nobody wanted anything to do with this. If Barlinnie wanted to play around with murderers and give them clay and tubes with oil-paint to toy with then let them get on with it. It had nothing to do with real life.

Wherever I could I drummed out the message of the Special Unit. I went back twice, once to talk, once to see their art exhibition which of course was dominated by Boyle. On that occasion he seemed more moody, withdrawn and slightly testy. This wasn't surprising. They were now becoming slightly freakish and being constantly gawped at as an exotic species kept in a special tank. I had, however, become a sort of unofficial spokesman for them. I ran into constant flak about this. 'You're being conned, hood-winked by them!' one ex-crime journalist asserted to me one day. He then proceeded to tell me in detail what Boyle is reputed to have done to his victims and I found myself visualising the face again and felt again the firmness of the press of flesh of his handshake.

But the grisly description did not fit the reality of the present and I would not budge. 'If he gets out, he'll do it all over again,' my colleague assured me. 'You can't cure these people.' But I continued to speak up in support of this experimentation. Boyle was released from the prison system on 1 November, 1982. I cannot claim to have directly helped in this, as other journalists close to him did, but at least I had added a new element of support which could have done no harm. The last time I talked to him was in Carnaby Street in London some five years later, when he was trawling through the shops like any other tourist. He seemed at ease although, perhaps through my own experience of meeting him inside, I felt he was a man who would forever now be constantly on guard against the world, not the other way round.

When Larry Winters died of a drugs overdose in the unit on 11 September, 1977 people rushed to tell me, 'I told you so!' All I felt was pity for the man, not disillusionment. I was constantly asked how I felt about the families of their victims. I didn't really have an answer to that. All I knew was that I hoped men would come through this experience successfully and that there could be nothing intrinsically wrong with any civilising process.

I have never been one for deliberately collecting memorabilia. Some things of course just simply cling. Others you stumble over in the course of moving house or cleaning out an old drawer. I have even infuriated my family by coming back from major events without a single photograph taken. I prefer the mind's eye. But one article I did preserve. It was a Christmas card. It was signed by five murderers. They had designed it themselves in the Unit. The script lettering of greetings was impeccable. But on the front of the large card was the delicate painting of a vase full of flowers, reaching appropriately for the sun.

I became quite obdurate about wanting to be of use to some cause even though the reasons for any celebrity I had were flimsy. In the earlier part of the year of Winters' death I welcomed an invitation which came to my office to visit the State Hospital at Carstairs, which houses some of the most vicious of murderers and the criminally insane, and to which it is said some people wished to send Jimmy Boyle in the first place. I was shown around by a large man with a gentle disposition, the Chief Male Nurse, a Mr Oswald, and one of his assistants, Neil McLelland. This hospital, it has to be said, has a permanent chill to it for an outsider, even on a gentle spring day, which it was then. You cannot avoid this feeling as a newcomer. I put it down then to prejudice and wished to rid myself of it but it was hard going. It was clear they wished to demonstrate to me that within the obvious constraints of security the place was not all that bad, indeed in many respects quite normal. That was hard going to accept also, but I was trying.

A month later a deputation came to the BBC with a proposal that I head an 'outsiders' committee to attempt to dispel the fear and dread the place instilled in society, by helping to arrange more public visitations, particularly from well-known personalities, to speak to selected patients and nurses. I felt that I might in fact be doing something useful here, proving my worth to society rather than just identifying footballers. I leaped at it enthusiastically.

To establish the scheme my wife and myself were invited to their sports day to present prizes that summer of 1977. The nurses did not seem put out too much when I asked when I arrived why there were no javelin or pole vault events. Some of the patients liked the quip too. Although there was quite clearly careful supervision, such was the informality, and the lack of official uniforming, that it was almost impossible to say who was nurse and who was patient. The sheer normality of the place was perhaps the most off-putting aspect of all. I was firstly introduced to a handsome, dark-haired lady whom I took to be a nursing-matron of sorts and who explained the day's events to me.

She had in fact killed her months-old baby by pushing it down the lavatory pan. I talked to a short gentleman called Ian Simpson who was charming and intelligent, on the assumption that he was on the psychiatric staff. I was told later he was the man who had killed a couple of foreign tourists in Loch Lomondside, buried them, travelled to England, come across a serious road accident, turned his collar round to pretend he was a priest and acted out the last rites to the victims.

I found myself playing out this game of hide and seek. Who were the patients? What had they done? They were our viewers after all. They certainly shared that with the outside world. By the end of the afternoon I had been totally sold on the current hospital philosophy which was, within reason, to allow the world into this place and to lower those unnecessary barriers.

In November of that year, on St Andrew's Day, as I was in the process of establishing names and events that might fit into a visitation calendar two inmates called Robert Moan and Thomas McCulloch, armed with axes, made an escape from Carstairs. Ian Simpson tried to stop them. They chopped off his head. Neil McLelland, the nursing officer I had befriended, got in their way and was bludgeoned to death. Outside they were challenged by a local policeman. They brutally murdered him. Carstairs in a few short hours had gone beyond the pale again.

I felt quite ill on hearing this. I had trumpeted the ways of this enlightened regime led by Oswald. Now I felt like some dilettante do-gooder made to look extremely naive. A decent, honourable attempt to bridge the gap between the abnormal and its onlookers had failed. To have uttered any justification, immediately afterwards, for what the nursing staff had tried to achieve with the likes of myself would have sounded like a bleat in a storm. However humane you wish to be you don't let the criminally insane get their hands on axes, full stop, end of argument. Perhaps, I thought at the time, I should stick to opening garden fêtes or church bazaars. Sometimes they paid you for doing such.

Thoughts of all that came chillingly back when I sat aloft, in the eyrie called the Hampden Park commentary area, in 1980 watching the battle ebbing and flowing underneath me, bottles flying through the air, and men and children being felled. I learned later of a friend and press-photographer colleague Eric Craig ending up with brain surgery in Killearn Hospital after being hit by a missile from a supporter. And all because Celtic had beaten Rangers in a Scottish Cup Final. I recalled the Carstairs killings and wondered about the precarious quality of the emotions. Why should we be so smug and secure, us, on this side of the security fence. This reflection gave my description of the clashes on the pitch a touch of bitterness and disgust.

Indeed a colleague, producer Nevin McGhee, said afterwards to me, quite fairly and accurately, that I had described the riot on the park better than the game itself. A *Scotsman* newspaper editorial picked up my words on the Monday morning, little knowing the memory which the riot had sparked off.

As time progressed I grew more cautious as to when and how I would take the 'telly' face into public view. But you could not always insulate yourself. After the heavy 5–1 defeat by England at Wembley in 1975 I was sitting with some rather affluent friends in a huge limousine in the insufferably congested car park outside the ground when some Scottish supporters spotted me. Linking me to the black, shiny car, to some cigars glowing in the interior and to a uniformed chauffeur they jumped to a rather surprising conclusion.

'It's the SFA!' someone screamed and we were immediately surrounded by as genteel a bunch as put paid to General Gordon at Khartoum. They began to rock the limousine whilst screaming for their money back, having wasted it coming all that way to watch such crap, and that us lot wouldn't be sleeping in the corridor of the train on the way back home like them and were we not ashamed of ourselves? They lifted the car up until we were spilling across the interior like the earliest upset in the *Poseidon Adventure*. I tried to tell them that Ernie Walker had already left and that my friends were English, although that might not have helped. We were rescued by the police who suddenly swooped out of nowhere. I was left with some friends vowing never to go again to a Scotland game with the man with the recognisable face. I would have disembowelled myself for anonymity there and then.

Or would I? In the darker moments this is what I would have preferred. But recognition did mean something. Very few of the human race would not want to be singled out from the mass but the television ego is sometimes hyper-active, hoping that upon your entry heads will turn. It doesn't matter all that much if it is done admiringly so long as it happens. With it comes the feeling, despite your rational self trying to deny so, that you could not possibly face the day when even your next door neighbour wouldn't know you from Adam.

At one stage in my career when I was interested in moving behind the camera into production I applied for a job on BBC staff which would have put an end to television appearances. It was only when I was about seven-eighths of the way through the process that I had one of those cold sweats that Jimmy Clark had talked about, not over the precariousness of my current role as presenter but at its total disappearance, at my own volition. I was preparing to kill myself off, I concluded.

Whilst a significant section of the population would not have been prepared to stand in my way it is something I realised inwardly I could not face up to. I didn't do it. I knew it was illogical to let this electronic alter ego be so possessive but only ten years into the business I had no fears that it could be my very own Dorian Gray. Television immortality is a very seductive notion. We are in the business to stay there and dig ourselves in, without too much difficulty, I thought at the time. And anonymity is simply over the trenches in no-man's land where you're sure to meet a sticky end. No more trying to charge out if you have any sense.

There was very little tranquil socialising indeed. Virtually always the subject of television, my own role, something I had said or opined on would be brought up by complete strangers butting into my life, sometimes viciously. At first the technique I employed was simply to take it all with a benign smile on the face, for after all this was an occupational hazard, was it not? However, tiring of having to listen at times to lengthy harangues, I decided to be more positive rather than being a passive target.

This consisted of slightly narrowing the eyes, stepping nearer the critic and in a voice something like Jack Palance's as he stood in front of the saloon in *Shane* saying menacingly, 'What was that you said?' This had a variety of effects ranging from those who could have been no more dumbfounded had I unzipped my fly in front of them, to those who simply stepped even further forward and repeated what they had said in a louder voice. But it either halted in their tracks those who wished to bombard me or at least truncated the vitriol. People generally did not like 'the face' answering back.

Whilst I had always wanted to 'switch' identity occasionally and enter into other fields of broadcasting I was finding it difficult. You are easily typecast. 'Why is a football commentator wanting to move into current affairs?', or 'You want to interview people outside sport? Really? How pretentious!' That generally was the attitude I faced. I suppose to some it seemed like the clown-wanting-to-play-Hamlet syndrome so normally any venture on my part in that kind of direction was greeted with polite bemused rejection. One producer though, David Martin, was prepared to back me in a series of celebrity interviews for a programme called *Three's Company* in which I would chat to two famous people who had something or other in common.

I found this plain sailing despite my own fears of coming a cropper on it. Two occasions stick out. The first was when Andrew Neil, the editor of the *Sunday Times*, and John Junor, then the editor of the *Sunday Express*, crossed swords. Before the programme it had become clear that Junor disliked Neil. Indeed he had told our researcher that he found Neil to be something of a young upstart. And he treated him like that, in the dressing-room area before the recording and during the programme. Neil was talking about death threats to himself on the air and Junor interjected with an acerbic, 'Who would want to kill *you*?' The undercurrents of antagonism surfaced, producing a very articulate slanging match.

I was inundated with letters congratulating me for this great piece of television. But really it was easy television. All I had done was act as a kind of referee who wanted to encourage this clash. Compared to what I had to do in my own sports area which more often than not entailed trying to draw water from stone this was like stumbling on a new oil well. Similarly, when I had poor Terry Waite and Jean Waddell, the Tehran nurse, together, all I had to do was sit admiringly as they nestled into a discussion about hostages and solitary confinement. All I did was nudge occasionally. Yet again, letters came to me expressing admiration for how sensitively I had handled this. What disappointed me about that particular interview was that I could not get the other side of Terry's character revealed. Far from being the gentle giant, he took over the company, in the Ubiquitous Chip restaurant afterwards, downed large whiskies with great finesse, hardly stopped talking about his views on life and emerged as a very tough personality indeed. This was clearly a man of great steel.

To receive anything remotely like praise for a programme was, however, something of a unique experience for me, coming from a region of controversy and ingrained footballing hatreds. I had hoped for a more permanent route into this sort of work but circumstances dictated otherwise. Television itself could also mock that rather vacuous abstraction, the 'television personality'. A producer asked me if I wouldn't mind taking part in a kind of self-deprecatory meeting with a Scottish punter which might illustrate and confirm at long last the transience of the influence of television on the average man in the street. This great sociological study was to take place in a programme called *Scotch and Wry* and the punter was to be Rikki Fulton.

Fulton is a solemn man. I swear it. At least he is when I'm around. He was even more solemn after he attempted his sketch with me. To watch him come alive at a rehearsal was like watching a body suddenly possessed by a comic genie. The lines of script were his very soul. The problem was that I very rarely worked with specific scripts on television. Much of my work was now in the outside-broadcast area, which lent itself to the spontaneity I loved. It was not that I intended to make a Feste the Clown from a short sketch but I thought I would enter into what I assumed would be the spirit of the occasion and throw in an unscripted line or two in response to Rikki's slightly inebriated man, fascinated by thinking he recognised the face from the box. He was to stumble up to me and tell me what a great fan he was of mine but, like the old lady on the train in Stonehaven, it was to be a case of mistaken identity.

'It is you, isn't it? Tell me, it is you, isn't it?' he said tottering towards me with that glazed look of punter wonderment I had seen so often come over the faces of those in awe of the person from the screen. I can't now remember my line but I managed it, with an embellishment. I added another line. You can perhaps visualise Rikki's face freezing into immobility, his jaw slightly hanging, his eyes in doleful bewilderment. No face can do it like Rikki's face. I was reminded there and then of those physiognomic sculptures when he played the Scottish version of Molière's *The Miser*, which gave the impression that Rikki's face even when asleep was a comic masterpiece. He had stopped. I thought this was part of the sketch and waited for him to continue. He just stood there gazing. The producer, Gordon Menzies, wandered in.

'Where did that line come from?' he asked politely.

'I made it up,' I replied like a schoolboy caught saying a naughty word.

'Made it up? Made it up?' When a man says a thing like that twice it spells reprimand. Rikki was still silent yet his immobile, puzzled but eloquent face was saying clearly and distinctly, 'Who is this eejit we've got here?'

'I think we should stick to the script,' Menzies said. 'Let's try it again.'

I suddenly realised I was not in a sketch with a comedian simply limbering up but with a comedy actor precisely honing his performance, however brief this interlude with me was to be. This was acting by a man who would be indulging in something like fifteen different sketches in the space of an hour, so there could be no fooling around. This was serious business. Came the night. I was more nervous than I ought to have been but then I didn't like sticking to scripts. My whole body was telling me that. I also knew I was going on to record perhaps the most popular light entertainment programme that BBC Scotland had ever produced. As Gus Macdonald of Scottish Television said of it, 'The only way we could beat *Scotch and Wry* in the ratings was if we could persuade Rangers and Celtic to play a game live against it.'

We went on in front of the studio audience. Up came the party scene with Rikki stumbling on across the floor towards me as the inebriated reveller spotting his favourite television personality.

'It is you, isn't it? Tell me, it is you, isn't it?'

It wasn't impish. It wasn't that I wanted deliberately to introduce the buggeration factor. But it just came. I did it again. I threw in an impromptu response, a one-liner that came from off the top of the head in the way I had been used to adding words with Des Lynam or Bob Wilson. In a display of superb professionalism Rikki allowed himself only a fleeting second of being thunderstruck. For one moment I thought he was going to call everything to a halt or that the producer would run on the set and change the party scene into a public mugging. But he was playing a stumbling drunk anyway which helped him to cover up the little hiatus that followed my additional words. But only he and I and the producer in the gallery would have noticed the stumble, the bewilderment. Beneath Rikki's Hogmanay mask was a professional staring contemptuously at a ham. The punch-line in the sketch of course was that he thought I was Bamber Gascoigne!

In his acceptance speech for his Award as Television Personality of the Year he gave me a tongue in the cheek scolding for my love of the impromptu. At least I think it was tongue in cheek. But for years afterwards that sketch simply would not go away. *Scotch and Wry* sold the biggest number of video recordings around the world for the BBC that year. In Toronto airport a Canadian customs officer of Scottish origin looked at me and said, 'It is you, isn't it? Tell me, it's you, isn't it?' In Sheffield a worker on a building site shouted the same after me. In London a taxi driver smiled and said 'Hi, Bamber!' On his very first meeting with me Jonathan Powell, Controller BBC 1, said, 'It is you, isn't it?' Little boys in the street were shouting it after me. I had been reduced to a catch phrase. It was as if Rikki was getting his revenge.

That little sketch I suppose summed up the recurring dilemma of the face on the box. It gives only clues to real identity and nothing much more. I had the good fortune to let that superficiality work sometimes to my advantage by simply intriguing people into opening doors for me. Sometimes it worked positively against me. They say of the fat man that there is a thin man inside fighting to get out, so with people constantly in front of the camera there is the struggle to emerge into the light three-dimensionally and not to be summed up merely as a figment of the horizontal and vertical holds. But we cannot ever escape from the figure of our own making and the tantalising notion that our existence, our very being, is wholly dependent on the living room and someone's hand on the switch.

14

Taking Risks

The eruption from Alex Ferguson came suddenly, without warning. He was in the main passageway at Easter Road when he launched into a tirade against me for something I had said about his goalkeeper. I cannot remember what it was I had said, nor did it seem important even then, for the row wandered up other alleys into quite lurid personal abuse as if we had forgotten what it was all about in the first place. However, I think I would have preferred to have been sued for every penny I owned, for whatever view I had expressed, rather than to have stood with the spittle of rage flecking our two faces. This was just before he left to go south in 1986. I had been very friendly with Ferguson, often publicly expressing my admiration for his talents. We seemed to get on well together and I remember distinctly being the first journalist to reach him on the pitch in Gothenburg where, both of us slicked with rain, we hugged. Now this.

In a sense the actual incident was less important than the warning it contained. In the business of expressing views you lay minefields of your own which remain quite uncharted. You feel as if you are striding through life comfortably, then bang!

I had staunchly defended him against some criticism which he inevitably sustained during and after the Mexico World Cup in 1986. It had been an anti-climax in all sorts of ways, not least of which was the absence of Stein. Ferguson was in a temporary position with other ambitions in mind. Ernie Walker, not surprisingly, was missing the man who had become his close friend. On the evidence of what I saw there was no gelling of the two. On one occasion Walker banned all television units from the Scottish team hotel. Ferguson got round that by simply coming outside the gates to talk to us in outright defiance of the secretary.

The Aberdeen manager had already proved he was of independent mind in his successful club role and could not take kindly to being tied to anybody's petticoats. He knew that the Scottish team manager's job was a thankless task. Stein described it once to me quite simply as 'impossible' and only took it the second time round, after his temporary flirtation with it in the Sixties, because it was a route back to Scotland. Living up to the wildly inflated expectations of the public was hard enough in its own way but when you are reliant on a chain of contacts with clubs throughout the UK you can very often dangle hopelessly with the same chain round your neck. Ferguson realised that very well. Stein had jealously guarded his own authority as manager which meant that he did not really tap the tactical genius of Jim McLean, as he should have, when he was assistant. Ferguson wanted, and achieved, more of a say. But he had no desire to take the job permanently.

Scotland's three games in the competition were stupendously ordinary and whilst there was much controversy over whether Souness should have been picked for the last one, against Uruguay, it was a simple case of many people being wise after the event in my view. For up in the steamy hot city of Queretaro against West Germany, in his last ever game for his country, Souness's legs seemed to go.

That particular afternoon contained so many of the ingredients of anti-climax to which I had now become accustomed that I remember it mostly for having to keep Pierre Littbarski, the German player, and Gordon Strachan company for a couple of hours with a camera unit after the game whilst they waited for their natural juices to gather so they could pee and present a sample for drug-testing because our editor, news-wise, hoped one of them would fail it. We had to stay there all night if necessary, until it happened. It says much for the deflated and tedious mood of the evening that the sound of one of them eventually passing urine into a flask elated us as much as if we had heard a fruit-machine ejaculating in Vegas.

The lesson though I had learned from my relationship with Ferguson was that you never take friendships too far in football for one day there might be the unexpected reckoning. Managers of course do wish to intimidate from time to time. It is as much part of their apparel as their padded sports jackets. That is why we all wondered how this entirely new man, Andy Roxburgh, would perform both as manager of a side and in the handling of his relationships with us. He proved articulate and friendly except on one occasion when obviously highly strung before a game with England at Hampden he accused me of trying to wreck a training session at Girvan because I had arrived with the English commentator Barry Davies whom Roxburgh thought would be on a spying mission for Bobby Robson. This unlikely interpretation of our presence came from a man experiencing a new form of pressure; a man employed to bring a fresh approach to the job. But the protest from him that particular morning sounded depressingly familiar.

Between the two World Cups of Mexico in 1986 and Italy in 1990 broadcasting was taking on a new look for me and life began to get stormier. We had decided to take the presentation of *Sportscene* to the actual outside broadcast itself; that is, to introduce the programme from the pitch or the commentary platform, either before the game or immediately afterwards. This meant recording it. The advantages were as obvious as the disadvantages. In the first place, an introduction with the crowd in the background and the teams coming on to the pitch gave the programme a look of immediacy and urgency, thus eliminating the need for a bland studio introduction. The very first programme we recorded this way was at Celtic Park, which happens to have one of the best commentary positions in the country, for you can swing a camera round easily to have the platform in vision itself.

Consequently it looked good especially at the start of the season in the fine light. Ibrox, where the existing commentary position is too low to allow the proper panoramic view of the pitch and does less than justice to the magnificent stadium, is nevertheless spectacular when you turn a camera on anybody presenting from the platform. Aberdeen was fine too, others were passable. The visual possibilities and the pitching of *Sportscene* into the midst of the action pushed the programme into new territory. This meant I both presented the programme, commentated and also contrived to summarise the Scottish results for one minute straight to camera for the network audience on *Grandstand* immediately after the game, and I mean immediately.

I had no knowledge of the news from the other Scottish games for obvious reasons but the system was that somebody back in the office would phone me with a summary. I would take quick notes, the camera would swing round to me and, once in position, Des Lynam would introduce me. Very often I would be told to truncate the report to either 45 seconds or even half-a-minute, on the spot. This was only about five minutes after I had stopped commentary. I would then rush down to the press conference to find out if anything useful was being said and then beat a quick retreat back to the presentation area again. The recording would then take place, but not in an untrammelled way.

We had a specific deadline of six o'clock. Given all that I had to do before it, it was often after half-past-five before I was in a position to start thinking of an impromptu script. But there were to be no concessions. It had to be done by six o'clock, or else. I am not sure precisely what 'or else' meant for although we over-ran by a few seconds on several occasions we always managed our recording, even if there were frequent slips. If there is one thing I have always loathed doing, it is recording pieces to camera. I would rather go 'live' in a howling gale, or amidst enemy fire than record. Somehow there is always what my late and dear colleague Donny MacLeod called 'that impish little voice' telling you not to worry and that if you don't get it right first time, you can always do it again. If it does talk to you then it can be fatal. Not only did it talk to me during that period it almost became a chatterbox.

Coming on top of finishing a commentary which completely absorbs the mind, rushing to get material for network information, obtaining statements or interviews from managers, receiving news to record for the late programme and then standing in front of a camera with men standing behind it looking at their watches and ready to pull the plug at six o'clock, the voice frequently told me, 'Sorry, pal! You're not going to make it tonight!'

So occasionally it was a struggle. But the disadvantages were not just personal but affected the programme as a whole as well. Firstly, if you record something at six o'clock at night and do not transmit it until about ten o'clock you may miss some very dramatic news. The worst instance of this was a Saturday in May 1985 when, on a lovely spring afternoon after a game to match, and with the season about to finish anyway, in a kind of end-of-term buoyancy I introduced the programme by saying how wonderful it was to have seen such a fine game of football and how everything was coming up roses, or words to that effect. It was bright and effervescent. That night, the national news which almost invariably came before *Sportscene*, ended its transmission with the most horrific football stadium pictures ever recorded. People rushed from the flames of the Bradford City grandstand and a solitary man passed across the scene like a walking inferno. I followed on immediately after that looking and sounding as if the world had just had one of its most tranquil days ever. We simply had had no knowledge of this disaster when we had put everything on tape at half-past-five that afternoon. There was nothing we could do about it. Not only did I look and sound extremely foolish, but grossly insensitive as well.

It might have been gratifying to think of the revamping of *Sportscene* as specifically geared to utilising my abilities in those various areas. But that of course would be quite inaccurate. It did have its intrinsic value but it was also very much a cost-cutting exercise. It eliminated the need to use a studio on late Saturday evenings and by shutting up the sports shop at six o'clock it also excluded the need to go into weekend extra payments. When an attempt at savings was perhaps the prime purpose you can hardly feel comfortable in your own mind that, in fact, it is the best thing for yourself. It clearly wasn't. Yet, I suppose doing everything in the programme appealed to the ego which, when you are so much up front, prefers great exposure to common sense. This one man band exercise had its severe drawbacks especially in our climate.

One late winter's afternoon at Tannadice my jaw simply froze. It went beyond central command. I was ceasing to function. It was difficult enough to speak at all that day let alone impart information to the public. A correspondent actually wrote to the *Glasgow Herald* asking for someone to take mercy on me as my red nose and general Worzel Gummidge appearance by late on a winter's afternoon drove him to charitable thoughts about me which normally he was reluctant to feel. I think he was suggesting some sort of mercy killing. Although the sting in the tail of his letter was to note how skimpy the Beeb were to handle their programmes that way. It was becoming clear that the occasions on which it could be said this system worked were being outnumbered by those when it clearly did not.

We were now of course well into the Thatcher days by the mid-Eighties. We were in the era of value for money studies and, as it so happens, while the BBC was being sifted through by the experts so another institution was being examined in exactly the same way and I enjoyed the unique position of being part of both of them at the one time. In 1985 I became Rector of the University of Edinburgh.

I am not sure if BBC Scotland realised that new dimension I had taken on for in the entire three years I was in office nobody there ever mentioned the fact to me. My colleagues from London certainly did and on one occasion would have liked to set me against the campus in a football story they planned with Johnny Haynes, who was then domiciled in the capital. I thought the better of it and kept the role at a distance from broadcasting.

The other candidates in the election were Margo MacDonald, the ex-SNP MP, Teddy Taylor MP, and Richard Demarco. I had also been told to prepare for student apathy on the matter of the Rectorship, so with mixed feelings I turned up for the first public meeting at Pollock Halls of Residence. It was mobbed. For one moment I thought I would be too scared to say anything at all. If Margo enjoyed my being in the contest she certainly camouflaged it well, for in the entire campaign she spoke but a few words to me and, at times, I thought her attitude came across too obviously as disdain. She certainly did not look happy even though I certainly had done her no harm as far as I could make out. One of my supporters had a theory.

'She thinks you're an amateur, you see,' he said, this lad who is probably now a leading light in industry. 'Perhaps it's beneath her to be competing against the likes of yourself.'

If that's what Margo actually did think then she was not far wrong. I was an amateur but if she only knew at the time, her uncommunicative attitude towards me actually gave me a bigger incentive to get through this thing well than probably any other factor. Indeed a local newspaper, rooting for her, deplored my presence and in advocating her qualities wrote, 'The nearest Archie Macpherson has been to academia has been in watching Hamilton Academicals.' One of my students studying law advised me that this could be libellous but having had worse things said about me in the media I thought I would try to turn the comment on its head. In my first speeches I regularly referred to the fact that a single afternoon watching Hamilton Academicals told you more about the human condition than a term studying Sigmund Freud. What were the problems of the Rat Man compared to an Accies supporter?

Moving from meeting to meeting taught me a lot too about the student condition. Some were friendly, some hostile, some inquisitorial. I turned up to speak to the Labour Group for what I thought would be a cosy evening amongst people from my own tradition, but I was grilled. A small woman, a mature student, took out a piece of paper when question time came up. Hers was: 'Can you tell me your views on the following: Abortion, possession of nuclear weapons, the armed struggle of ANC, student grants, siting of nuclear bases in Scotland and devolution?'

And she proceeded to tick off every reply as I tried to wade my way through it all as if she was giving me marks. I had the tremor of a D minus in my voice.

Then came the most dramatic interjection of the entire election. It came from a demure young lady with a tongue obviously dipped in vitriol.

'Can you tell me if you are, or have ever been, a member of the Orange Order?' she asked without blinking.

'I beg your pardon?' was all I could bring myself to reply. She repeated it. I looked round this austere room and every face groomed in conscientious socialism was now looking for an answer. They were taking this seriously. Should I?

'I cannot believe you are asking me that question seriously,' I said. 'Can't we discuss something that has some relevance rather than this fantasy!'

'Answer, yes or no!' the demure young lady insisted.

'I came into this University in the hope of taking part in serious discussions about education. Now you're making preposterous suggestions.'

'Answer, yes or no!'

I refused to be coerced by her so the meeting broke up in some disarray with the chairman, a nice lad from Glasgow, trying to thank me for my presence although I was making for the exit mentally noting not to go wooing the Labour group again. Afterwards my supporters, offering no shred of evidence by the way, suggested this was a rumour being put about by Margo's supporters. They smelled skulduggery. Whatever or whoever it was, it didn't work.

I won the election . . . and three days later I chaired the University Court.

I found that the next three years added a discipline to my life that was in stark contrast to the freelance television journalist's existence of hopping from one assignment to the other. It had come at the onset of difficult times for universities which were being assailed by government to make swingeing cuts in expenditure. The Jarratt Report, like the Peat Marwick study of broadcasting, investigated the University of Edinburgh and the entire UK university system to find out how cost effective the institutions were.

My sympathies lay with those people who perceived a university education as that which helped open the mind, exercised the imagination, encouraged value judgements and, quite simply, prepared you for living. The change of emphasis, enforced from the very top of government, to balancing the books and converting the university into something like a training college which would help you get a job with ICI or GEC or whoever, no matter how important that is, was a negation of much that Edinburgh had represented as a distinguished seat of learning. The whole nature of the humanities-based university seemed under threat. It is not that savings could not be made, but that the enforced cuts were, by necessity, quite brutal.

As I chaired the University Court, listening to the repeated gloom of the Principal Sir John Burnett reciting the harsh facts of life to the professors gathered round him, under the magisterial gaze of the Raeburn portraits surrounding the room, I could not help but think that hardly anybody outside the four walls would hear all of this. The public are noticeably deaf about education as a subject until it hits them in some direct way, and that is very seldom. Carnage was going on, blood was flowing yet the crisis repeatedly seemed to be contained in an exclusive debating chamber. Protests were made of course. I took part in demonstrations, helped out during the lecturers' strike, half-way through my period of office, spoke all over the UK and in North America to try to encourage fund-raising activities. Unless people had prior experience of the university system, however, you felt that provoking widespread concern would be as easy as encouraging the Cabinet of the day to fund the expansion of Greek as a subject.

The public of course were interested in the broadcasting licensing fee, always. It was perpetually cast up to me that the public's money was being wasted or frittered away or misused. Money is misused or wasted or frittered away at some time or other in all sorts of public and private businesses and it would be preposterous to imagine otherwise. All the same, in my own sphere of sport, we were not unduly influenced by the occasional hysterical outbursts against BBC overspending. In Seoul there was an attempt to embarrass the Corporation over the accommodation it had picked for the troops.

When you walked into our hotel you might have been led to believe that extravagance was the norm for us. It was a truly splendid establishment which I think probably led to a shortage of marble in the Korean countryside. At a reception for the media there some of the press from more modest lodgings, eyes goggling, saw a news story. They sniffed. One smoothie who, to my utter astonishment was briefly employed by the BBC a year or so later, quizzed me at some length about what sort of rooms we had, what they all cost and whether penthouses were involved. Even as you dodge and evade questions or answer them honestly you realise the story is going to be written quite independently of the truth. And so it was duly splashed back in London.

There were lurid tales about sumptuous living off the licence fee, the apotheosis of which was that Coleman had a suite to himself with butler. Leaving aside the fact that Coleman didn't need a butler, with the help he had on hand in the BBC, what they had studiously ignored was the expense of all this. The executive producer Martin Hopkins had negotiated a discount deal with the hotel right at the outset, and at a favourable exchange rate, which led to one of the most reasonable arrangements ever made for a huge broadcasting party abroad. But we were an easy and convenient target.

We knew we were now in the middle of fundamental changes in the broadcasting world. Satellite had arrived and, whilst there was a general feeling amongst my colleagues in sport that it would never succeed, many talented people in the Corporation and ITV moved off to join them. Money was being splashed around as if the tiny sphere circumnavigating the earth also minted pound notes.

Of course the one very effective way to get at the BBC, apart from allowing the gradual erosion of the real value of the licence fee, is to ensure that the competition to it is overwhelming. That, sadly, has been the trend. The Corporation has safeguarded many of its commitments to sport because of the general acceptance of the high quality of its coverage. But not always. They lost the Rugby World Cup contract to ITV without any due consideration being given to quality. With the best will in the world, commercial television has no real track record in that area and they didn't have Bill McLaren, a fact that cannot be overestimated. So, that ought to be a warning that new options have arrived.

In a truly free and untrammelled market BBC Television would struggle to maintain its presence as the major purveyor of sport. Such is its handicapped financial state. It is when major events like Wimbledon, or the Open Championship, or boxing title fights disappear from the public service screens, because of the more powerful purse of other interests, that people will wake up to the reality that the superb sports coverage by the Corporation has largely been taken for granted. It would be sorely missed but, by then, it could be too late to do anything about it. Only if government kept major events as special areas of public interest and allowed a natural involvement by the BBC could they survive, but that seems an impossibility. The Corporation is fighting a rear-guard action which will diminish the quality of sports broadcasting if they lose in the long run.

The University and the BBC therefore seemed to echo each other throughout that period. You could easily have superimposed the voices of one on the institution of the other without noticing much difference as both sets of values came under siege from similar forces.

It was during my period of office at Edinburgh that I almost brought a newspaper out on strike. Because of a dispute between the football authorities and the two television channels *Sportscene* went off the air. We went virtually the entire season without our regular work. Buffeted around by circumstances beyond my control I was beginning to think that life on a limited contract was as fruitful as driving down the M74 with one's eyes closed. Then one day in the middle of this awful period I got a phone call from Endell Laird, editor of the *Sunday Mail*, who asked me if I would report a football match for his newspaper. As a member of the National Union of Journalists I took this on in all innocence and accepted it as a perfectly legitimate task. At the same time I was asked by *Grandstand* if I could cover a game, travel back to the studio in Glasgow and report on it to camera. The problem was that I had to leave the game ten minutes before the match was over. As I attempted to do both, I simply ran into big trouble.

I took on that commitment one Saturday but the next week brought a reaction. On the Friday night I was in the University of Edinburgh at a function as Rector and was called to the phone. It was someone from the NUJ connected with the *Sunday Mail*. He was extremely affable in tone but his message was unmistakable and uncompromising. He told me that because someone was having to cover the part of the game report that I could not complete for the *Mail*, as a result of my early exit, I was in effect encroaching on the work rights of staff reporters. In truth, I had no knowledge, one way or the other, that it was causing upheaval and tried to tell him that. He was sympathetic but went on to deliver an ultimatum. I had to give a guarantee that I would report properly for the *Sunday Mail*, that is, the full game without leaving before the end to do *Grandstand*, or else face the consequences. They included the suggestion 'the paper might not reach the streets that night'.

I recall that sentence vividly enough. I was beginning to feel this was some sort of nightmare. However, I was fully to blame for both being naive and not having come to a proper arrangement balancing my two commitments. As a trade-unionist myself, and having already gone on strike action within days of joining the BBC, being considered some kind of 'scab' made my blood curdle. I simply told him that I would only do the report for the *Sunday Mail* under the normal conditions.

I put down the phone and contacted the editor of *Grandstand*, John Philips, at home and explained the position to him. I was in a quandary but as a legitimate exercise as a freelance I wanted to try to fit both reports in and told him that the union were so serious they might even stop the production of the paper. He did not believe this at first, as I hadn't. Eventually he saw the dilemma I was in and, against his nature, because he preferred me to be in vision for my reports, he agreed that it could be done by telephone with a slide photograph of myself put up on the screen. I was determined to show that I could practise my trade properly without giving the impression of tramping over anybody. I managed both reports that following day. But the residue of anger against me by some people who were quick to see this as an attempt to muscle in on a situation showed itself. I walked in to the *Daily Record* offices one day on some matter not long after that and heard a voice, largely anonymous, floating over the office towards me, 'He must be in for his blood money!'

It only saddened me. I had gone on the verge of falling out with a union of which I was a dedicated member. I had obviously angered colleagues I had known for some time, unwittingly. I'd had to push my relationship with *Grandstand* to the limit to get them to change their normal custom of reporting, just to help me out of a dilemma. The whole arrangement, purely temporary, came to a halt only a few weeks after that anyway. If any blood had been spilled in this whole episode I suspect I was minus a few pints myself.

Flexibility is the main asset of any contract and although it was clear from that episode I wasn't going to be able to wander into any area without a bit more careful thought I had to seek alternatives if only because BBC Scotland offered none. Thankfully the work came from the south. One of the most enjoyable films I was ever involved in was travelling to the Isles of Scilly one December to film their football league. They played League championship, Cup and League Cup games throughout the season, but there were only two teams on the island! The means by which they contrived all this formed the basis of a slightly tongue in cheek story about how football holds sway in even the strangest outposts.

We put this out on New Year's Day on *Grandstand* and showed how we filmed in a small four-seater aircraft to reveal the lighthouse keeper of Wolf Rock trying to get off his work to play in the important cup-tie. The flower farmer, a kind of laird, organised the two teams so that nobody would run away with titles and cups. We showed how the local bobby had to have his wife look after crime on the island whilst he was off playing. That sort of thing. Lo and behold as soon as it went out in *Grandstand* I began to hear murmurs that I was turning my back on Scotland. After all, weren't the Old Firm playing then, and shouldn't we be previewing their game? Even the stone-age people in Papua New Guinea had heard about the Old Firm and there is always a creative case to be made for avoiding sacred cows from time to time.

I didn't realise how strongly people actually felt about my continuing and increasing involvement in network broadcasting until one journalist described me as 'BBC London's pet Jock'. The thinly veiled jibe thereby implied the kind of relationship that one might see in the ghillie taking the patronising English gentry off to the shoot. What they didn't realise was that throughout my career many of the significant producers who had employed me were Scots themselves, and that the Caledonian broadcasting community in London was extremely strong, although I would obviously not call them the Scottish Mafia. They are much more powerful than that. It was a Scot who had helped me in a critical moment in Los Angeles and it was the same Scot, Jim Reside, who asked me to go to the Winter Olympics in Calgary, Canada in 1988.

This was a different venture altogether from the summer Olympics. The Winter Games have a micro-identity which makes them appear arcane to the less-experienced eye like mine. People were sliding down a hill whether on their feet, or on their backs on objects like large shovels or on elongated machines which look like scooped-out cigar-tubes and which have to be pushed into activity (then hysterically guided down an insanely steep and twisting track), or jumping into space bent like someone suffering an attack of the cramp to land on two feet on skis. It requires specialised judgement to appreciate all this properly. To that extent I was an outsider, required to bring the outsider's viewpoint to events and reports. And like all my other colleagues in the media sent there to do the same we were saved by one man, Eddie Edwards.

Every Games needs a moment in time or an individual to synthesise the profusion of feelings which their size and scope stimulate and for which they will always be identified. There was Fanny Blankers-Koen in London, Mary Rand in Tokyo, the Black Panther salute in Mexico. Moving about a Games is a bit like wandering, shopping in a bazaar with so much on offer that the senses are confused. You can be left with a strangely bloated but unfulfilled sensation. There was much to admire and be impressed by but the Calgary Games were turning out to be as bland as the city itself.

It sits in the middle of the prairie signalling itself to the Rockies with the universal stamp of progress; high rise glass and aluminium office blocks in an extravagant city centre which seemed always to be looking for people. Even in an Olympic period it appeared too vast for what it was supposed to serve. The Games were spread around the outskirts. When we arrived the temperatures were about fifteen to twenty degrees below freezing but an astonishing phenomenon occurred. The Chinook wind blew in from the Rockies. This has a sudden, thawing influence which sweeps over the mountains. By the time it hits the prairie it has the dramatic effect of a blow-torch being pointed at snow. Winter disappeared almost overnight, as in twenty-four hours the temperatures soared to ten degrees above freezing. It was like conjuring up spring by magic. The prairie turned from white to saddened brown and the environment, with the top winter athletes caged in by this freakish whim of nature, took on an air of unreality.

But you cannot make the weather the top event. It is always a non-starter in news and serves to remind people that you have nothing much else to talk about. But talk about the weather we did for there was little else to report as we skedaddled around this gushingly friendly town to find some reportorial gold. It came largely through myopia.

I am sure that Eddie the Eagle's courage stemmed partially from the fact that he could not see all that far through his thick bottle-glass spectacles. This lessened the shock of standing at the top of the ski jump looking into space. If you have never done this (standing looking down, not jumping) you cannot possibly imagine the surge of terror which goes through you from deep within the bowels. You do not think of it as a sport but more a ritual challenge devised by some primitive tribe to introduce youth to manhood. Eddie seemed fragile and in grave danger as he stood blinkingly at the top of the ramp. But when his first leap was so far behind the others and he looked like a lad who ought to have been mending the window-sash for you, carrying the crazy aspirations of all we ordinary people to achieve the impossible, the Canadians took him to their hearts. We took him to our headlines. Both the Games and the media needed something different to stimulate a particular identity for Calgary and it was coming, for the first time in Olympic history, from the example of bumbling mediocrity.

He became a hero. Ron Pickering, commentating previously on him in an event before he arrived in Canada, watched him fly through the air with the elegance of a flying hat-stand. When Edwards landed on the slope, wobbling and tottering to keep his balance, Pickering could not resist the triumphal but sardonic exclamation, 'The Eagle has landed!'

The phrase stuck. Other commentators picked it up. The world press followed as the Canadian crowds, starved of anything unusual in the Games, like the media, chanted his name and made of him the unlikeliest hero since Tom Thumb. A community crazed with the pin-swapping tendency and idiosyncratic tee-shirts purchasing suddenly became prey to the Eddie the Eagle entrepreneurs. His tee-shirt became the hottest property in town. Manufactured overnight, people queued to get it. We queued up for his interview. The Mayor paid a special visit and was photographed with him, probably for potential electioneering purposes. And the other British competitors fumed. After all, Eddie had done nothing. His definitive accomplishment was always to finish last. The refreshing by-product was to reverse the conventional North American attitude which helps mythologise only the successful. Now we had adoration of the failed. At least it was different. Then one day we were told an important announcement was to be made about his future at a hotel in town that night.

We scurried round with our film unit. So did the rest of the world. I had managed to get ahead of the mob and was directed through to back stage to meet the man who said he was going to sign Eddie up in an important business deal. This had stemmed from the fact that the American television company ABC, losing money hand over foot with their coverage of the Games, desperately flew Eddie all the way back during the Games to make an appearance on the Johnny Carson Show. This ultimate media canonisation was to open the financial floodgates for him, so it was said. The man I met was wearing a tuxedo, as they would say out there, with rings on his fingers bigger than knuckle-dusters, and smoking a large cigar. Behind him were six lissome girl dancers limbering up for a floor-show. They certainly did not look to me like amateurs.

'We are up here from Las Vegas with our little show and we're gonna make Eddie the Eagle a star,' the man told me. 'We're gonna put Eddie on the stage here tonight with these lovely ladies and he is gonna dance with them.' I felt slightly sick. Sick for Eddie and sick for having to go along with all of this. Indeed the man's partner, behind his back, looked at me and said, 'Care to vomit?'

It was exploitation that might just denude Eddie very quickly of his short-sighted charm overnight, as the Chinook pared the hills of snow and ice. We expected to be allowed in with the cameras to film this unique Olympic happening, a competing athlete taking part in cabaret. Then, as we prepared to walk in with our unit, four 'heavies' stood in our way and blocked the entrance. We did not try to use force against them. If you can visualise the men who came to that room to shoot Burt Lancaster in Hemingway's *The Killers* you will probably realise why. We waited outside the room for three hours for a little man who desisted at the last minute from getting up to dance with the girls and had merely been presented on stage. He had provoked a media circus which was now beginning to question its own sanity in pursuing this any further. However, in circumstances like these, the interest and fever are self-propagating. Although we all knew this was a con and Eddie was of no merit, either on the slopes or off, we were worried about who might steal an exclusive with the little man who had captivated the nation. So Eddie's very insignificance was indemnified by the interest of the people like ourselves who had helped create him. Nobody, in short, was going to ignore him.

He walked out to a battle. I have been in the presence of Muhammad Ali, Pele, Maradona, John McEnroe, to name but a few, as they faced the press but there was nothing like this. At least twenty different camera crews physically fought with each other to get close to him. I personally was hauled back by a large Austrian gentleman as solid as the Jungfrau but I stamped on his foot and pushed in on Eddie. A punch was thrown at me. I dug an elbow back into somebody's ribs behind me and in the confusion of mêlée and attempt at restraint we became one amoebic swirl. It became too difficult to strike out.

Eddie's minders, and yes he had them by now, pushed us back and held on to him. The little man looked pale and confused and I felt we didn't need any words from him. His look portrayed the bewildered stare of the hunted animal. It was as if, in the middle of the scrum, he had suddenly realised he had now pushed his minimal status to the limit and that it was time to retreat from the edge of this precipice. Perhaps, after all, it had been worth it to be in the middle of a chaotic pummelling just to capture the look on that face.

The entire media retreated from that squalid scene that night more than a little shame-faced. We were too embarrassed to talk about it much for it must have been the first time in the history of the Olympics that the event had been upstaged by a man who was as remote from the laurel wreath as Calgary was from genuine sophistication. It was time to worry about the Games. It was time to reflect on how the introspection of organisers and athletes can make them forget that the public and media wish for spectacle, colourful characters and touches of the extraordinary. We had to realise that even the most significant athletic achievement will not register if it does not spark the imagination. That is why later on in Seoul the world's media poured scorn and vilification on Ben Johnson but at the same time warmed to the excitement of the hunt and to the injection of controversy. The Games were now vulnerable to all of that.

So Eddie had dabbed a little colour on the Calgary Games which had been splendidly mounted, contained some fine athletic achievement but had been as flat and predictable as the prairie. 'The Eagle' had provided the third dimension.

I went back to continue my work on both sides of the border but within BBC Scotland I was now, like Eddie, looking into space without being able to see an appropriate landing spot.

15

End Game

The last commentary I broadcast for BBC Scotland was in Turin. It is not a city I have ever much cared for because it seems even more sprawling than Los Angeles, more constricted by traffic than Mexico City and more incoherently planned than the old city of Jerusalem. In short, it hasn't got much going for it as far as I'm concerned. Any misery I felt in having to commentate on such a mediocre event as the Scotland–Brazil match, which the game certainly had turned out to be, was compounded when I afterwards drove the Director General of the BBC Michael Checkland and his wife back to our hotel.

Their car had failed to arrive but their geniality was stretched, I am sure, almost beyond diplomatic endurance by the fact that I got hopelessly lost in this disjointed city. The hotel at last emerged from the damp bleakness of the night, but at least a couple of hours later than we had hoped, which left us feeling limp and hard done by.

Being by now well familiarised with the ways of World Cup self-pity I was probably more at ease with this situation than some of my companions who had never before experienced this now almost copyrighted Scottish experience of plummeting emotionally from something like the sublime to the ridiculous within the time-span of a few days. All the same, I was preoccupied with my own position in broadcasting and was ill-prepared to indulge in inquests over the Scottish squad when, at the same time, I was questioning my own future.

There were few redeeming features in the World Cup in Italy for me. Indeed when Maurice Johnston missed his chance in front of goal late on in the Brazilian game, which would have meant so much to the cause, I felt not a shred of disillusionment realising that yet again the Gods had written this to end in the normality of anti-climax. In a sense I was privately relieved that I would not now be subjected to a prolonged stay in Italy, in an atmosphere of increasing mistrust which I felt had been engendered for me within the BBC Scotland group out there. My destiny, in any case, would be determined by a man not in Italy, but back in Glasgow. From a couple of thousand miles away he had intervened in a broadcast which, apart from its overt meaning, also conveyed to me a message of confrontation. It happened in Genoa.

Genoa has not attained its present girth without some extreme physical effort and ingenious engineering. It is corseted by sea and mountain and, from the vantage point of one who would not have known how to fit Lego blocks together, the achievement of linking the city to the rest of Italy seems something of a miracle. You don't want to be a sufferer from claustrophobia though. You bore your way in and out of the city in any direction by a series of tunnels which gives the immediate effect of disorienting you but, despite that, it works. From our base in Rapallo, a holiday resort of considerable elegance, we would drive almost daily through a chain of these tunnels into Genoa which was to house two of Scotland's games in the section. The rectangular Luigi Ferraris Stadium looked as if it had been dumped down temporarily and left for someone to collect later and deposit somewhere more in keeping with its style and modernity. Amongst the rather traditional and flaking Italian tenements it was as out of place as a hotel in a necropolis. Inside, it was constructed superbly to create the feeling of intimacy for the game, not unlike the very first World Cup stadium I had visited in Dortmund in Germany. I took one long look and thought it would be absolutely perfect. But you can go off a place quickly.

I had an uneasy feeling early in the Scotland–Costa Rica meeting. Nothing more than that. If you have covered as many games as I have, particularly at that level, you get an instinctive sense for how a game might evolve. That is not to say you can predict the score but you can perceive certain trends, some of which can worry you. I occasionally like to speak to others at half-time in a game to bounce thoughts off them, for you can be isolated in a commentary position. I went down to the press area and spoke to the freelance journalist Ray Hepburn. I didn't need to ask him. He just looked at me and said, 'This is dreadful. The worst. I feel a disaster coming on!'

Back I went, feeling, if anything, that perhaps it would work out after all. Surely we couldn't have another Iran! Costa Rica scored. Scotland slumped. Their legs seemed to have gone and their heads weren't any better. As a commentator with some four World Cups already behind me the sense of déjà vu was almost overwhelming. Knowing that the Scottish public had suffered considerably in the past, and would not wish to be charitable about the possible defeat from a Third World country, it was hardly the time to interpret all this with a broad grin on one's face. Remember, we were not playing Brazil, but a nation which, at least before the World Cup, was considered probably the poorest team in the tournament. So the game was being evaluated in that particular light by me as I criticised what I was seeing, just like the rest of the Scottish nation back home.

Then came the message from Glasgow, two thousand miles away. It came directly into my headphones. The voice said, 'I'm sorry about this but I have to pass on a message to you from Jim Hunter. It's not from me remember. He says,' and there was a deliberate pause, '"Be more encouraging of Scotland. They are going through a crisis!"'

It was from the Head of Television in Scotland. I looked at my producer Mike Abbott who looked back in some considerable astonishment at me. Back in Glasgow Gordon Brown, the ex-British Lion rugby player who had been watching the game in the BBC studios, told me he almost fell off his seat in astonishment when he heard that this message had been passed on.

It is difficult to convey now the impact that that intervention had on me. Here I was being interrupted, for the first time in my career in mid-commentary, by a message from a man on the other side of Europe, completely divorced from the atmosphere in the stadium, which is an important factor in capturing the real essence of a game, telling me in which direction the commentary ought to develop. It must only have been for a few moments but at the time it seemed like an eternity. I stopped in my tracks as the game raged on.

'Encourage?' I said to Mike Abbott. Now you do not need to be a member of Mensa to realise that commentators can hardly encourage players on the field; not unless he intended me to put down the mike and start singing 'Flower of Scotland' with the punters. And, if he meant me to make more encouraging noises for the viewers back home, then you need not rack your memories to recall that we were all of us watching as pathetic a performance as we had turned in against Iran in Argentina, in other words the very nadir of Scotland's international fortunes. I couldn't alter the course of events.

Nor could I offer a very astute viewing audience some false optimism when not a shred of evidence existed that Scotland could salvage themselves. You can only kid the people for so long and the Scottish public, having had more than their fair share of World Cup disappointment, I knew, would be in no mood for any more apologetic waffle. I had often wondered, in fact, if Hunter had all along preferred the bland to the cutting edge anyway. It all seemed to be coming out now. It was almost as if, in some stupidly national-istic way, someone covering Culloden had to make it sound as if it were a ceilidh.

I thought that the instruction was inane and almost an object lesson in how to be professionally irresponsible.

I also thought that the impact was enormous, throwing the producer and me off course completely. I asked him simply to pass a message back saying I refused to adopt that tone or line, call it what you like. No self-respecting commentator can do a commentary by long-distance diktat. I could have dodged this and said nothing. But the source of the message I saw as a challenge. I preferred to be absolutely honest in my response even though I knew that honesty would be no asset in dealing with him. I feared that he would seek retribution in some way, whatever else he might have had in mind for me. Even though my judgement on the game was proved to be absolutely right, and the critical tone I had adopted was in fact praised by people, I believed that all that would be an irrelevance in the final inquest. I had offended against Holy Writ.

In conversations afterwards with experienced broadcasters we reached the view that it was probably the first time a senior BBC figure had actively encouraged a commentator to be biased. For if you step outside the field of objectivity into so-called 'encouraging' you are taking sides. The fact that it was Scotland I had to be biased for is quite irrelevant. Commentators are normally hounded by the public for being biased. There is enough of that without being pushed into it from the rear.

So we retreated to our hotel in Rapallo, a short distance down the Italian Riviera, licking our wounds, with my tongue busier at it than anybody else. I had to accept that the consequences of the interruption to commentary and my reaction to it might be considerable and it soured the rest of the World Cup for me. My colleagues in journalism were largely incredulous when I recounted the incident to them but it was difficult for me to communicate the underlying nature of that intervention. Coming from James Hunter, the Head of Television in BBC Scotland, it capped years of long-distance irritation which I could now stand no longer.

You can become easily obsessed by feuds or disputes or continual locking of horns with individuals which fall into the conveniently described category of 'personality clash'. I had my fair quota of such during my career with adversaries ranging from floor managers all the way through to such as Hunter. The only type of person I probably did not have a run-in with were make-up ladies although I did object once to a heavy-handed woman who insisted I would look infinitely better with a touch of eye shadow. My stand on that was based on the worry that I might get fond of it.

Rows can flare up on preposterously insignificant matters which in retrospect leave you feeling embarrassed. In a live situation, or trying to beat a deadline, they can proliferate in a way which can almost make them seem an indispensable part of the broadcasting ensemble. But this was not a row. I saw this as a reminder of an influence bearing down on me that would not go away – an authority flexing its muscles. I carried a feeling of resentment with me through the rest of the tournament, although the game against Sweden acted as a purgative which almost cleared me of any bile.

I was involved with a 'live' broadcast. I was prepared to inflict critical damage on the Scottish side if I felt it was appropriate, although I warned myself not to go over the top, to prove my independence of mind from the man back in Glasgow. But events were on my side. It was a marvellous game to be involved in. The mood of the Scottish side was one of defiance.

Commentators of course like to feel the audience is enjoying what they are watching. Scotland two up at one stage in that game suggested to me a nation watching in some wonderment, and in the early stages of euphoria. But there is an even better commentating situation and that is when anxiety is heaped on top of that, when grown men move out of the room for fear of events being over-turned by fluke or divine intervention and can barely stand the pressure. Ernie Walker, who is not known to flinch in some of the great disputes he has presided over as secretary of the SFA, was a well-known 'walker' at games. He would leave his seat and go into the depths of the stand because he could not bear to watch if Scotland were battling against the clock. With a few paltry minutes to go, and with Sweden having pulled back to 2–1 and Scotland hanging on grimly, I knew I had an audience bathed in emotional sweat and prepared to eat out of the commentating hand.

I finished the game feeling as if I had been present at a banquet. Never before in the World Cup had a match given me so much satisfaction to cover. I felt, foolishly as it turned out, that I had driven the Costa Rica experience into oblivion. You can never tell whether your commentary has been adequate to the occasion and it is extremely dangerous to indulge in private celebration. But, in the face of increasing doubts about the rather distant relationship with some of the BBC Scotland staff in Genoa, I enjoyed a moment or two of quiet purring. It had gone as well as could have been expected.

I did feel as relaxed as Andy Roxburgh the following day. My own particular idea of trauma during the Costa Rica game had been but a passing hot-flush compared to the agony he must have suffered. He was incapable, as most humans are, of totally concealing great pain. But he did better than most. His articulate dignity was not without its occasional snappiness but that was to be expected in the melting-pot of the World Cup. Even the angel

Gabriel could be turned into a profane loud-mouth there. Roxburgh's meticulous preparation was almost obsessive and gave rise to thoughts that it was all organisational structure without any real substance. But he had chosen the route of careful groundwork, knowing that even if he had everything calculated in advance right down to the last corn-plaster required, it would all hinge on how his players responded to another eleven men over ninety minutes. He had on board enough helpers to crew an ocean-going liner. His forward planning therefore made the other national managers who preceded him look almost amateurish in comparison but it also incurred the risk of a special kind of embarrassment if it failed.

I had watched Roxburgh at close quarters in Mexico during the World Professional Youth Finals in 1983 and had formed the impression that his excellence in that area was really going to anchor him at that level for good. It was not an unfair judgement, but simply one based on the clear benefits his coaching and educational insights bestowed on impressionable young men. He led well, he taught well. There was an air of the 'lad o'pairts' become popular dominie about him and his handling of the youngsters was both refreshing and impressive. But there was no trace of Billy the Kid about him. You could not imagine him, then and there, with the whiff of cordite in the nostrils, taking on some of the tougher hombres who populate dressing rooms in senior football.

There is little doubt that others saw it that way too and indulged in some rampant scepticism on his appointment. I do not exclude myself from that category for the appointment came unexpectedly and with the firm image of Roxburgh as youth coach ensconced in the mind. That this was intrinsically unfair and that there was an over-reaction to it is quite clear. It is also not too surprising that Roxburgh himself occasionally over-reacted both to this feeling of not fully being accepted and the new pressure on him.

At one point, I wrote a tongue-in-cheek piece in the *Sunday Mail* about how time might be against him in his efforts to qualify Scotland for the World Cup finals and received almost by return a letter of stinging rebuke from him for what I had briefly written on the subject. This was followed up by a lengthy denunciation of me from the hand of Ernie Walker who accused me almost of being a Quisling, in having let down a man who had offered nothing but friendship over the years. I had done nothing of the kind of course. I had merely fulfilled my function by writing a piece of criticism, however flippant the terms. It seemed perfectly in order.

I have always seen friendship with people in other, and sometimes conflicting, areas of football as very relevant but never a reason for suspending critical judgement. Any association which will not permit that is not worthy of being termed a bond between people. I was disturbed by this episode largely because Ernie Walker had been at pains to make it clear that the SFA, in opting for Roxburgh, were adopting a new and refreshing approach to national team management. I suspect that, in the informal chat amongst managers and media, the sifting out process of those 'for' and 'against' certain people still reaches a paranoid level at times.

Our relationship afterwards was proper and formal and my steadily increasing admiration for his staying powers, despite people like me who initially thought he could not measure up to the stature of his immediate predecessors, was amply expressed in different ways. I was pleased for him after the victory over Sweden even though I still felt that the chances of Scotland qualifying for the final phase were marginal.

The evening of the Brazil match turned out to be damp and grey. It made a stark contrast to the previous time the two countries had met in Seville on a warm sunny evening where there was an irresistible mood of fiesta. When you are huddling in doorways to avoid the monsoon, as many supporters were that evening, the samba hides as well. The stadium, too, was vast and impersonal. It may have looked impressive in an architects' magazine and indeed it was spectacular in concept. But football was as remote there as it was close in Genoa. The game was markedly different from the meeting with Sweden.

Firstly, the Brazilians were sub-standard. We had hyped them as we dutifully do at a World Cup but in reality they were as far removed from the Brazil of legendary renown as Rio is from Reykjavik. When we had gone to the delightful town of Asti, where they put the bubbles in the wine, virtually every Brazilian commentator or journalist who spoke English to us at the training camp there denounced the tactics of the manager Lazaroni. They were even more 'Europeanised' than their squad of 1974 and the home-based Brazilian media detested the fact that so many of their players were now resident in clubs around the Continent. There was unrest. So much so that at one of the press conferences I attended the Italian police had to be called to protect the manager from harassment by his own journalists.

I suspect they played against us that night without wishing to break too much sweat. The Scottish team were not good enough, even against instantly forgettable Brazilians. The following day we returned to Rapallo down the coast and there at least some of us thought that we did not want to prolong this with a route into the second phase by courtesy of games in other sections. Two days after the match in Turin we were on a flight back home. The remnants of the excellently-behaved Scottish support were not in any great state of anguish or anger. Most of them were sullenly resigned to it all. They had proved resilient. The 'spitters' of Argentina were now a defunct species.

The route for me though was back to London not Glasgow. Even though I knew I would have to face up to the consequences of the long-distance confrontation during the Costa Rica game my first priority was to return to my contract work for network sport at Television Centre. I had gone to London seeking not fame and fortune, but enough cash to pay the mortgage. No matter how much I tried, I could not obtain any more work in Scotland other than a Saturday afternoon commentary. Fortunately, and perhaps surprisingly, my colleagues in the south were actually delighted with this state of affairs. They gave me an entirely new broadcasting platform but simply could not understand why I needed to be in this peripatetic role, criss-crossing the border every week. Sometimes I dashed by taxi from Glasgow Airport on a Saturday afternoon to get into the commentary position in time for the three o'clock kick-off. It was exhausting, frightening and far from ideal.

One Saturday, in a taxi, we could see a terrible traffic-jam on the motorway leading to Ibrox for the game I had to cover. We went off it and then got snarled up in trying to take a circuitous route to avoid the jam, now congealed around us somewhere in the new Gorbals area. I had vowed, because of the professional circumstances I had found myself in, not to allow anything to prevent me adhering to the contractual obligations, other than illness. I knew I was now on the verge of missing the start of the game for the first time in my life.

I got out, after having paid the man, and ran. I got through the worst of the heavy traffic but the breath was giving out. Suddenly I heard a ribald comment about my appearance. I was leaning against traffic lights and a man sitting at the front of a Rangers supporters bus contrived mock concern about my health. What then followed was the reaching out of arms and I was hauled on to the bus. With some easing of traffic ahead, it took off for Ibrox at speed.

'Gie us the Sash, Archie!' was the first cry from the interior as I slumped back wondering if the lungs had gone on vacation. I could not have given them 'Three Blind Mice'. I always am glad to join in the spirit of occasions but it is better not to commit oneself, even idly and innocently, to identification with any of the predominant colours in the city. That is why I declined the request, just as, on the television platform at Celtic Park, I have not yet succumbed to the chant, 'Archie, Archie, cross yersel!'

They took me almost all of the rest of the way and with gratitude I sped from the bus, ran down Edmiston Drive, swept through the enclosure door, climbed the iron steps, crashed down on the seat on the platform, put on the headphones and feeling like Pheidippides at the end of his run, shattered but slightly triumphant, just as the teams were running out, heard the director's voice say rather sarcastically in my ear, 'Glad you could make it!'

This was no way to prepare for a commentary, but there was nothing I could do about it and before long I saw that London had obvious blessings. The immediate and very personal one was that, at the very least, in London I was enjoying something of a renaissance. On Breakfast Television I had built up a useful rapport with Jeremy Paxman who, if he wasn't eating up politicians for breakfast, was quite willing to indulge in sardonic skirmishes with me as the nation munched its cornflakes. I relished this and with the inevitable challenge of trying to make sports reporting more generally accessible to a wider audience than merely the enthusiast

I felt as much in top gear as I ever had. I hadn't looked forward to getting up at five o'clock every morning to do all of this but once I had got into the habit it came easily. The reward was to be able to drive easily through London at that time of the morning, on the wrong side of the road if you so desired, because of the astonishing emptiness. It was like seeing a city under strict curfew. Earth hath nothing more fair to show than Shepherd's Bush Green without a single vehicle in sight.

Although I had worked on network television for years this new role took me to areas I had never touched before. I was asked to unravel the mysteries of croquet at the Hurlingham Club, almost wept with emotion after having done a film at Cheltenham and stood in the sleet watching Desert Orchid win in that famous finish in the Gold Cup in 1989, sat in the Long Room at Lord's discussing the fortunes of English cricket with Mike Gatting, chattered away on the gin-palaces at Cowes, previewed rugby-league Cup finals, linked the programme live from Wimbledon, and, one famous morning, shared a unique Scottish ensemble in studio with Kirsty Wark, Sally Magnusson and weatherman Francis Wilson.

Looking back to Scotland I simply could not understand what was happening there. Faces in sport came and went. We had a season of lunch-time inserts into *Grandstand* but that series disappeared out of sight eventually. So too did Bob Patience. He had established 'Saint and Greavsie' in the south and, having returned to set up as an independent producer, he had been asked to organise the new afternoon series. He would have been an ideal choice to take over the whole of sports output but the snag was that he would have been determined, quite rightly, to have his own way. Judging by what I saw as a lack of real departmental autonomy, since the inception of Hunter as Head of Television, he would not have been allowed such professional leeway.

I was told that Hunter desired changes then but the most curious of all concerned Dougie Donnelly. An approach was made to Gordon Hewitt who, as it so happens, is a mutual friend of Dougie and myself to find out if he would be available to present either the new lunch-time programme or Saturday evening *Sportscene*. Many years previous to this I had brought Gordon into broadcasting and encouraged Peter Thomson to use him because I felt he had screen presence of considerable value. He had by now become a very successful economist, running his own consultancy business and constantly travelling the world. The first reason for refusing was that his business life would have made it impossible. But even had he been in a position to do so he made it clear that he would not have taken this further if it meant affecting Dougie's position. Being, in any case, a man of considerable honour he telephoned Dougie personally to let him know that he had been approached by the BBC but on no account would he take on anything that would affect Dougie's standing. He would not let any offer of a job get in the way of their friendship. Gordon turned the offer down. He later told me that he could not fathom why they would have thought of possibly replacing Dougie on the main programme. It is no wonder that this information almost shattered Dougie Donnelly. It simply made no sense. There was certainly nothing wrong with considering Gordon Hewitt but as Dougie had established himself professionally, built up a following, and was hardly a geriatric, why this?

I tried to discern a rationale behind it all. It is too simplistic to believe that television has simply to ring the changes from time to time. Somehow or other, and admittedly it is not easy, managers in television must go by instinct in shaping television presentation. They do use quality assessment polls which give popularity ratings for programmes or individuals. These are undoubtedly useful but can hardly be anything other than guides. It depends on what we mean by 'good' or 'average' or 'poor'. For example, Sir Robin Day, whose acerbic manner served the public interest by puncturing political egos but at the same time made him appear to be a television bruiser, was disliked by many people. That, in itself, might have affected any rating. Hugh McIlvanney once brilliantly summed him up to me by saying, 'He seemed to have a thousand things wrong about him and yet he added up to exactly the right person for that sort of role.' The opposite would be blandness but it would not be Sir Robin Day. The selection of people to sit in front of a camera requires not just census returns but an instinct for assessing impact on the public. Swapping one face for another just for the sake of it is actually opting out of accountability to the public, falling back on that laziest of all television dictums: 'Time for a change!'

It is introducing the philosophy of Max Factor to television and indulging purely in whim, juggling with people whilst the public remain untouched, unconsulted and mystified in the background. You need only look at the longevity of people in network sport – Coleman, Maskell, Wilson, Carpenter, Walker – to see the value of rooting personalities stably in the minds of the viewing public and allowing their authority to mature. The possible replacing of Dougie Donnelly by Gordon Hewitt would have been nothing other than a cosmetic exercise which, without the slightest criticism of Gordon, would have meant no seminal change of policy in sports presentation. It did reflect to me this unpredictable current which ran through a sports department dominated by Hunter.

I knew I was dealing with a man who had disliked my attempts to retain independence of view. You have to take this as a matter of course in our business, except that I knew after the World Cup the relationship with Hunter had reached its climax.

I went to see him for the last time. I noticed when I walked into his office a tape marked 'Scotland v Costa Rica' was lying on a desk. I expected him to be poring over the match for I had asked him by letter if we could talk about what had happened in Genoa. Within about a couple of sentences or so he told me he had an unpleasant task to perform and that was to tell me that he would not be renewing my contract when it expired in a few months' time. It did not come as a shock and I sensed surprise growing in him. He actually offered the view that I must be stunned. I am not sure whether he was expecting me to be prostrate with grief and was therefore hugely disappointed. This turn of events left me with a curiously contrasting and euphoric feeling that soon I would be rid of him, whatever other regrets I would have.

He told me that this was a decision made by the sports department and that he had nothing to do with it. I challenged that but he pleaded innocence and said they had only sent him to tell me the news because I was a 'heavyweight'. I simply could not accept that, having previously believed that during all these years each decision of any importance made about me was either inspired or endorsed by him.

Attitude came up. I had not attended the World Cup Press Conference prior to the tournament, which was held at Hampden Park. I had to point out to him that I had a contract to work in London and was doing precisely that when the conference was being held and had actually negotiated with the BBC press office to get back later that day after filming. He admitted that what he had quoted was probably not a good example of the wrong attitude. I cannot remember him getting round to telling me what he really had meant. 'Difficult person to work with sometimes,' came up. I ventured that if that were a criterion to be used universally in the BBC the institution could be depopulated overnight. I found it a patchy litany and wondered whether, even if he had made up his mind about what he was going to do, he was still almost seeking to justify himself. Then came a curious switch.

'What are you going to say about this in public?' he asked me.

'The truth!' I replied.

'Couldn't we be economical with the truth?' he suddenly said.

I thought I hadn't heard properly. But no, he had said it. 'Economical with the truth'. I pondered that many weeks after. Was it because he thought it was such an insignificant matter that he felt free to say virtually anything he wanted? Or was it because he was genuinely disturbed about something? Or was I making too much of that in my own mind because of the circumstances, for after all those words had become the rather modish catch-phrase of moral sleaze, a kind of wine-bar note of decadence that one ought not to take too seriously. I would not have thought it would represent some consensus BBC modus operandi. I certainly hope not. I was even more shocked when he quickly added, 'You see I got into the front page of the *Glasgow Herald* twice recently in such matters and I want to avoid that again if I can!'

I remember thinking that I had not up till then considered an appearance on the front page of the *Herald* as being synonymous with public ignominy. Before I left his office he expressed the hope that my departure could be handled with dignity. I was left to wonder how one squared 'economy with the truth' with dignity. On balance I thought it better not even to try.

At a time like that you imagine fancifully it would be right to make a fuss, that it would be productive to throw yourself on the mercy of the public after having been so much the public animal for so long. It is hard to cage the ego. Of course no such court of justice exists. It is also doubtful what the verdict would be even if it did. However, you do feel you want to be heard somehow or other. But there seemed such an imperturbable certainty and determination to what Hunter was doing that I doubt if pleading even the most emotional case would have made a difference.

I believed it was right to say nothing and hold my silence until such time as I thought something sensible and more meaningful could be said, outside the context of mudslinging. I resisted the temptations dangled in front of me by various newspapers to 'come clean'. The news did in fact make page one of the *Herald*, which noted my imminent departure alongside an exasperatingly anodyne comment of praise by Hunter, which I read the way Trotsky must have viewed sentimental overtures from Stalin. I did note with a wistful satisfaction that when Hunter left the BBC a year later his departure was also noted by the *Herald*, but only on page five.

Before I left, he had already made his contacts to get another commentator. When I phoned my lawyer who also happens to be Jock Brown, then STV's commentator, he told me, after I had explained what had happened, and much to my great surprise, that in fact they had approached him. A go-between, a mutual acquaintance of ours, had been used to sound him out and he went on to tell me that he thought the reason I was leaving BBC Scotland was to go to London to work. I thought it best under the circumstances not to wait around for the expiry of my contract but to seek release from it, even though it was going to cost me a considerable amount of money. I wanted to put this muddy situation well behind me. I kept my London contract, which I treasured, and was released from the BBC Scotland element.

Leaving BBC Scotland after over twenty-three years was not painless. It was a bit like leaving the church which you've been in since the cradle and which nurtured you carefully. It might even have been too protective at times. You can begin to be deluded by that rather atheistic notion that there is no such thing as life after the BBC. Ultimately, I suppose, when anyone puts his name to a contract he must realise he becomes, by that very act, a terminal case. Nobody in that category is exempt, not even through longevity. That is the brutal and quite uneconomical truth.

16

Keeping up with Souness

Not time yet to roll the closing credits. The game's still on and you're still a player. I offered myself that little piece of gimcrack philosophy walking away from Queen Margaret Drive. When the offers came in from Caledonian Television, Scottish Television and Radio Clyde I knew that at least some others shared my own sentiments. These contacts meant I could remain in Scottish sports broadcasting rather than end up in rather uncomfortable exile in London. To accept the offers though I had to give up my Television Centre-based contract. Although I tried hard to hold on to it, the powers-that-be thought there would be a clash of interests involved. To renounce such a contract is the equivalent, in our profession, of committing infanticide. I felt the work there had given me a new dimension in the profession but I was also aware that you cannot, at that stage in life, walk easily away from your own identity. For better or for worse my voice was my living and it would not have sounded the same without football.

I had missed the Glasgow football voice penetrating the ear anyway. Sometimes you would wish to run screaming from it. But that feeling was a bit like getting away from the family for a while in the knowledge that you are going back again. The thought of not ever working again in Glasgow actually appalled me. Getting into the scene again properly as opposed to being a sort of weekend guest gave me an opportunity to look closer at one of the most interesting phenomena in European football, the rise of Rangers under Graeme Souness.

He was indisputably the most significant figure I have met in football since Stein. They both commanded attention by their sheer physical presence. When they spoke you found it hard to disregard the substance. But they were not the same kind of men in other equally important aspects. Stein belonged in Scotland. Souness did not. Stein understood the West of Scotland psyche. Souness did not. Stein succeeded in conquering the media, Souness did not. Stein won a European Cup with local lads. Souness did not. But Souness helped prevent Scottish football from sliding into a kind of League of Ireland mediocrity. In England they couldn't believe all that was happening under him. It annoyed me to know of English visitors who would mount the marble staircase at Ibrox, pay sycophantic lip-service to his achievements, and then belittle them on the way down again. Unlike Stein, Souness did not appear to have a real working knowledge of what Hemingway charmingly called 'the shit detector'.

I had known Souness as a player many years before he became Rangers' manager. But of all the conversations I had with him the one which stands out is the first he had with me in his new position. It was not in Glasgow though. It was in a setting which made it difficult to apply all of his thinking to that segment of Scottish society who massed in Govan every other week and who felt they had now acquired a new Messiah.

The Pueblo Indians of Santa Fé, New Mexico barter their goods in one of the arcaded passageways of the pink-adobe style central square of the town with a panache that owes more to the spirit of Woolworths than that of The Great Manitou. They were probably unaware that the new manager of Glasgow Rangers was in their midst. It did not seem likely that the beads and bracelets, the rings and leather pouches on display on the pavements would hold much attraction for the matt-tanned man who was with the Scottish football squad in town for altitude preparation before the World Cup in Mexico in 1986. Indian artefacts would hardly be to Graeme Souness's taste.

After all, he had just come from the country of Gucci where a successful footballer, as he still was, could rightly achieve rewards that would make the Elysian Fields appear to be on this side of eternity. As Sante Fé seemed to have attracted a reasonably mixed bag of the human race – artists seeking space and light, settlers from New York who thought you needed a passport to get into New Mexico in the first place, gays with sweet pinkish little restaurants, architects who designed houses out in the brush that looked like landlocked lighthouses, and bland-looking nuclear scientists from Los Alamos just up the trail a bit – it seemed perfectly in order for this place to try and rid itself of the cow-town image once and for all. It had the chance to accept a man with a cosmopolitanised Scottish accent in a blue tracksuit who vowed out there in the Wild West that he would sign a Catholic footballer for a famous and staunchly Protestant club.

It was there in the hotel on the hill looking across to where one supposes the cattle-herders used to bring in prime stock that Graeme Souness talked to me for the first time of his recent appointment and of the path in front of him. He knew it would make the Santa Fé trail seem like a stroll along Princes Street. He wasn't detailing anything but he was eager to talk about Glasgow, about the Rangers–Celtic thing, about the obsession with religious identity in the city. It was the tone of the rather removed exile who must have known something of the environment from his childhood but who, having come from Edinburgh and never having played senior football in Scotland before acquiring credentials that were now impeccably European, was having to brush up on the patois of the Glasgow rivalry. The contrast with his predecessor could not have been more stark.

Jock Wallace, who had been sacked from Ibrox the previous month, was essentially a man of the people and without that umbilical connection with the hearts of the loyalists he might not have lasted as long as he did. He was a good big man with a much softer and more sensitive side to him than he cared to project to the masses. They preferred to see him as the jungle-fighter and a leader of the Walk. He thrived on this but he also created staunch friends across the religious divide because paradoxically he was one of the least bitter men in a city where bitterness has more varieties than Alpine flora.

Some of the most insufferable bigots I have met are more suited to the dark corner and the sibilant whisper. Wallace's trumpetings of his Protestantism had, to me at any rate, a theatricality to them that suggested he had to be heard by his patrons at the back of the hall. He would be wiping off the grease-paint once the performance was over. He was desperate to get back to Rangers and in his final days at Motherwell, in 1983, he phoned me and asked if I could contact the Rangers chairman John Paton to tell him that he was ready, willing and able to take the call. Sadly, what I could not tell him was that Rangers were not interested. I knew that with John Greig reaching the terminal stages of his period as manager at Ibrox the club were far more interested in the man in the granite city than anybody else.

Alex Ferguson was never offered the job by Rangers in the official sense but he was most certainly 'tapped'. He sat with me one day in the little cubby hole at Pittodrie, opposite the dressing rooms, agonising over the prospect, however distant, of going back to Govan. He did not really like the idea. The son of a Celtic-supporting father, he used to go to Ibrox without parental approval. As a supporter and player he became as obsessed with the club as Jock Wallace ever had been. He would have been the perfect choice for the job. But he had changed.

'How could I go back and not sign Catholics,' he told me. 'What would I tell my friends who are Catholics? "You lot aren't good enough for us." I just couldn't do it.'

One night just after that the phone rang late at home. When I picked it up I heard singing. At first I couldn't recognise the voice, but the song was 'The Sash My Father Wore'. At the end of the well-known refrain, the singing stopped and the voice simply said, 'I got it, son!' It was Jock Wallace's way of letting me know the Ibrox job was his. Much as I liked the man I could not help but feel that the Rangers board were playing to the crowd and thinking with their hearts not their heads. This was confirmation that the Protestant ascendancy would remain. And who in the rest of European football would give a tuppenny-toss about that?

More locally, and in no way less significantly, I am extremely doubtful if anybody at Celtic Park lost any sleep over that appointment. But there is little doubt that some insomnia was experienced there after that morning Souness made his first appearance in front of the media in the Blue Room in a slightly ill-fitting Rangers blazer. For the Wallace style did not work a second time round as

Rangers manager. He lacked the steely grip of Willie Waddell round his jugular. That interplay of character was missing. He had certainly left Ibrox because of monumental rows with Waddell, some of which could be heard after matches as far away as Arran. Achievement in Wallace's second term had been minimal and the crowds disappeared. Two versions of the 'Sash' were heard; one sung and the other, the echo coming back from a half-deserted stadium. If Souness had been asked that day for a rendering of the traditional airs someone would have had to write the words out for him. Something special was happening.

In the brash New Mexico sunshine sitting by the poolside he looked brimmingly fit, ready for the task, and, as I listened to him talking, I could not help but think that the Rangers supporters, nay the entire city of Glasgow, with its preoccupation with the Old Firm, did not know what was about to hit them. Compared to what had just gone before this was Armani replacing off-the-peg. It was a wonderfully frank and refreshing conversation. Indeed I would go so far as to say it was something I had wanted to hear for years but thought I never would.

He made it clear to me that his travels had made him contemptuous of the football parochialism of a city such as Glasgow. He knew it could be a hard place with entrenched views but he had his as well. This was stirring stuff. Particularly the bits about religion. He would not recognise the conventions. He was unhurried and casual in the way he expressed himself but there was no detracting from its seriousness. There is such a structured calm about Souness at times that it is difficult to know if you are touching any of his inner feelings. There is a suggestion of great depth there without the actual seismic proof.

Certainly, at that time people were still bemused by the suddenness and audacity of his appointment. However, they had so far heard only from him the dutiful utterances of a man who had obviously gone to Ibrox for more than the promise of a free yearly ticket on the Glasgow underground. Yet his life in Italy had not been weighing him down. He had been living well in a villa only a Mercedes' gentle purr away from the importunings of the Italian Riviera. Glasgow certainly has its intrinsic charm but we can hardly say the grape flourishes on the vine there. Why go where the westerlies can still be unkind? Souness had always given the impression that life-style was as important as his profession so the move, at the same time as it shocked, also aroused a cynicism which effectively placed Souness in the 'carpet-bagging' mould.

The 'nudge-nudge, wink-wink' brigade went underground almost on the day he arrived but they surfaced again in the following years in the less subtle mode of muggers of reputation. Whatever maulings he received, and deserved, in the time he was at Ibrox I never perceived him as one who exploited his position and used it out of mere selfishness as a staging-post to further his career.

'People will have to change I'm afraid,' he said distinctly. But did he mean it? Could this man, so far removed from the actual sectarian bitterness of the West of Scotland, which is yet as tangible as the 'stour' from Dixon's Blazes used to be, actually mean this? I think my excitement at the prospect of such a confrontation led me to blind my eyes to the other possibility which was ultimately to prove correct. For all that he knew it wasn't going to be easy, for all the backing he was going to receive inside the club, for all the admiration he might engender from outside, Graeme Souness really had no idea what he was letting himself in for. Nor, ultimately, was he fully able to cope. It is one thing to talk with good intentions. It is another to live with your actions. I warmed to his sentiments at the time though. Indeed, such was my weariness at the prospect of another inevitable disappointment in the forthcoming World Cup that I regarded the conversation in Santa Fé with Souness as probably of greater significance than anything that was to occur later the following month in the land of Montezuma's revenge.

We had good relations thereafter. When he spoke to me he always opened out frankly. He never uttered a view without at first explaining in detail why he reached his conclusions. He never rubbished any of his players to me although, when he was disappointed and angry, he would talk his opinions through sensibly and realistically. I was impressed by him. It was to become decidedly unpopular to say so even amongst some of his own supporters but that impression of clarity and purpose he exuded, despite his apparent obstinacies and mistakes, is not something I am required to dismiss from mind and won't. Nobody, not even the critics who speedily flourished around him, could deny, especially in those heady early days of the revolution when anything seemed possible, that he was driven obsessively by the job to the point where he would virtually sacrifice his marriage. His first chairman, David Holmes, himself underrated just how possessed the man was even before his very first season. The proof was in the hunting of an English internationalist.

Souness wanted Terry Butcher. He wanted him badly. He told me in one of our earlier conversations in his office that when he had played in England he had early deduced that you could have the best football-playing team in the land but if you didn't have a defence you had nothing. He negotiated and, with Holmes, agreed the figure that would be offered for Butcher. Holmes went on holiday considering the deal done and since he treasured peace and quiet only his close family knew the whereabouts of the villa near Marbella.

He was only there a couple of days or so when the door-bell rang and there was his new manager outside with a taxi, engine running. He wanted to talk. Could he pay off the taxi? Holmes was astonished that he had tracked him down to where he was in the first place and sent the taxi off. After a swim in the Holmes's pool Souness opened out. He had hit a major snag over Butcher. He needed another fifty thousand pounds. If he didn't get it the deal would be off. Firstly Holmes had been impressed by the resourcefulness of the man in finding him in Spain. But he wasn't going to allow this piece of enterprise to affect his thinking on the limits applicable to even the Ibrox budget. He had set a figure and that was that, even though the outside world believed that Rangers could sign any sort of cheque. So he had to shrug his shoulders regretfully. Nothing doing. But Holmes had to admit he was bowled over by the sheer doggedness of Souness on the matter, for after persevering with his point of view on the importance of Butcher he simply said to the chairman, 'Give me the fifty thousand and I'll give you the championship.'

If that now sounds slightly stagey we can satisfy ourselves that some historic moments have been accompanied by utterances which sound either banal or preposterous including the supposed famous plea of Bosworth Field, 'A horse! A horse! My kingdom for a horse!' Suffice to say that King Richard got less out of his plea than Souness did his, for the chairman, struck by the audacity, stretched out his hand and shook away fifty thousand pounds. Souness of course delivered his part of the deal some time later.

It was a touch of swank that poses the question of just how much latitude you can permit such self-assuredness. I think arrogance, the kind which we say to ourselves we think we admire, all depends on context. Stein, in a hotel in Cadiz before a game with Spain in Seville in 1985, was quite unperturbed that the interview which I had jointly arranged with himself and his captain Souness was overdue by about an hour. Graeme had not appeared. When he did saunter into sight he took his time strolling around the tables talking to other players and journalists who immediately dropped what they were doing to listen to him. Stein, sitting patiently beside me said, 'Class. The man's got class!'

He said that with genuine admiration.

'There's no substitute for that,' Stein went on. 'On and off the park he's got it and we badly need it. You won't push that man around!'

What had seemed outrageous lack of consideration to us had appeared to his manager to be the epitome of the arrogance and self-possession he desperately required from someone to lead others, less capable, into the cauldron of the stadium in Seville. He liked the man's demeanour, his effortless disdain. But it all depended on the time and the place and the angle from which you were looking as you made up your mind. If I hadn't had the access I occasionally did to him, from some of his press conferences it would be easy to conclude that he was nothing more than an ignorant boor. No doubt many people within Ibrox, from where they stood, revelled in the way he frequently handled the aftermaths of games. But too often they were merely exercises in contemptuous brevity. You might have concluded that his understanding of the collective noun for the press was 'arseholes'. The reluctance with which he spoke to them was compounded by distaste. It was particularly difficult to miss in the 'Now-you-see-me-now-you-don't' routine.

You watched in dismay. As one who was in support of all he

was trying to do, I simply had to wonder why. Why this? His dislike for the press became intense.

It is not that other managers haven't drawn the line in the sand and come chasing after you across it. I have seen Jock Stein clear a room of media, as a cannon-shot would remove a flock of roosting pigeons. He once so harangued one of my BBC commentating colleagues, in the passageway between the dressing rooms at Hampden, that the poor man took months to recover. The argument Alex Ferguson and I had in the tunnel at Easter Road was eventually broken up by a large Leith policeman. Jim McLean has made it clear to me on occasions, in his uniquely blunt way, that I would not exactly win his commendation as Commentator of the Year. I have seen Bobby Robson treat his press conferences as if he were in a can of worms. Abrasions are a constant factor. Helluva rows far from rare.

But, no, this seemed to me to be different with Souness. This was like someone sniffing conspiracy, feeling that most people were against him, out to get the club. He gave the distinct impression anyway that he simply did not care what people thought of his attitude. Stuff everybody. That's what came across loud and clear at times. In public life there is really no value in only being privately congenial.

I tried once to give him a small piece of advice about his television interviewing technique for he had a habit of cutting across your voice before you finished the question, making you look foolish or giving the impression that he was bullish and insensitive, which he never really was on those occasions. It was simply his eagerness to get out what he wanted to say. But since it happened so frequently it came across badly. People put the wrong interpretation on it. Even when Stein was at his most truculent with us, he was a different man when the cameras rolled. He knew he had an audience, that he was up front and his personal views on the interviewer, or indeed the question, were less important than communicating with the audience. Souness was less aware of that and I am not sure that what I pointed out to him ever really registered. When he had set his mind on things I doubt if he would have listened to Saatchi and Saatchi.

He certainly would have needed them to explain away some of

the incidents on the field. On 29 August 1987 Celtic played Rangers at Parkhead and Souness was sent off for fouling Billy Stark. I looked at the tackle on the tape back at the BBC that night and could find no redeeming feature about it whatsoever. If the referee had not sent him off he ought to have been sacked. Yet I was not aware that, on the back of this refereeing decision, Souness had made his mind up to leave Rangers there and then because he felt people were out to get him. I thought it was a gross over-reaction of the worst self-pitying kind. When he had gone back to the dressing room, David Holmes had found him in a great state of distress and anger. He poured out his resentment and made it clear that he could carry on no longer in Scottish football and that he was finished with Rangers. Holmes was taken aback both by the sentiment and the power with which it was expressed. It was done in such a way that he hoped that a cooling down would occur. But later that night, in the chairman's home, Souness made it clear he wanted to go. Holmes knew that he was dealing with a strongly determined man and whilst he had, and still has, the greatest admiration for his player-manager, he decided to relent and told him that he would not stand in his way. That night David Holmes thought Rangers had lost Souness.

We have to ask ourselves now, and in light of subsequent events leading to his ultimate departure, what would have happened then and there if a job of note had been available for him somewhere else? Was it merely expedient to hang on? Was the quest to transform Rangers really and truly over long before any of us imagined? It's an intriguing thought for it was increasingly obvious now that he felt the whole rigmarole of being player-manager, working in Glasgow, and coping with some people who refused to hang on his every word and others who were sly and treacherous, was getting too much.

On Monday morning he went back to Ibrox, though. But I am sure he was an irrevocably changed man, not just because of the incident on the field, but because he felt there were insidious forces acting against him and Rangers. Of course there were. There were people who were deeply envious of how Rangers were transforming themselves. There were those who traditionally would have liked to see Rangers disappear like the Glasgow trams.

There were people who had been offended by Souness's reactions to them, ranging from the off-handed to the downright belligerent, and wanted revenge. But so what? Wasn't this exactly what men in his position have always had to face up to? Wasn't the eventually beleaguered Billy McNeill to show him how to cope with the rack upon which all Old Firm managers eventually land with considerable courage and dignity? Haven't people talked face to face with Celtic managers and then gone behind their backs to speak of their religion as if they were vermin? What have they had to put up with through the years? 'This is Glasgow, for God's sake!' you felt like screaming at him.

He was steadily misreading the environment. He had imagined initially he could rise above the inanities of the bitternesses and tribal loyalties but he couldn't. In the first year at Ibrox he sat comfortably in his large office and told me with conviction that he would not mind if Celtic beat Rangers four times in the season so long as the club ended up with the title and that people had to stop thinking that the Old Firm match was a life or death affair. Interesting new theory this. Quite admirable. But worth a stoning in Larkhall. It would also bring on a sharp dose of scepticism in those who supported the revolution at Ibrox but did not want Rangers' Lion Rampant replaced by the white flag. The Souness revolution surely was not to mean putting up with indignity as well? This almost charming innocence of his in this matter did not last of course. Exactly a year later he told me that he had made a mistake about that and that he now knew what the Old Firm meant in the city and that he wanted players who would fight for the club because he had never before experienced so much hatred as he did in Glasgow.

I would note this as the beginning of the end for him. He was not giving any conscious thought to abandoning the task in any way but the idealist I had conversed with in Santa Fé, with dreams of elevating a great club to a level that would release them from their parochial past and dignify them with a new non-sectarian future, had gone. Now he was to take the jacket off and go in there slugging with the old rivals as if to the streets of Glasgow born. It is said that at one team talk before an Old Firm game he said to the players he would not speak about football but instead showed them a photograph of the Queen and told them that's who they were playing for. Jock Wallace could not have done it better.

Paradoxically, it is in that context I have always viewed the Maurice Johnston signing. Judging from the quite stupendous over-reaction to the acquisition of Rangers' first Catholic in modern times you would have thought that Ibrox was about to evolve into a Jesuit seminary. I believe his coming to Ibrox was of much less social significance. Rangers were not setting out on the Via Dolorosa to a state of spiritual bliss. Souness was simply stuffing Celtic, taking from their very bosom one of their most talented sons. It was a piece of good business and brilliant show-manship but really did little to further the cause of ecumenism. When he stood there that day being interviewed by everybody except the *Osservatore Romano* Souness actually did mean it when he said he had simply signed a good player. There was nothing much more to it than that. Maurice himself looked as bewildered as the rest of us that morning and, as we surveyed this delightful, bubbling personality, with the harum-scarum tendencies and a taste for a good vintage we put well to the backs of our minds the thought that the first Catholic in the inner sanctum hardly had a life-style which accorded to the principles of Thomas Aquinas. He would not be going straight from the Blue Room to confession. Since we had waited all those years for it to happen, but had thought it less likely a phenomenon than the Second Coming, we laid aside certain technicalities of religious description and wallowed in an orgy of cant.

Of course it took a certain courage to bring Johnston there but it was not the courage required for the beginning of a whole new moral order. It seemed to me then, and still does now, that Rangers, having been condemned for their sectarianism, could successfully stem criticism and not be held to account by the rather finicky comment that their new signing probably attended fewer masses than the average worshipper. Rangers' critics probably would have preferred the litmus test to be the signing of an Italian player with six weans whose piety was revealed by the prominence of rosary beads. But here they were being pre-empted.

On the basis of 'Once a Catholic always a Catholic' Mo Johnston qualified. And as the odds were on Rangers continuing to be a successful team it was likely that Souness could ride out any Orange storm over a short period. It was a very shrewd and useful exercise indeed.

There was a developing view within Ibrox which I feel was hardening some of their older resolves then that there were elements at Celtic Park who would like to have seen an all-Catholic club. To hear those views expressed was like listening to the echoes of days past. It did not matter whether this was fantasy or fact, it simply indicated that you cannot lift up the tram-lines and pack away into a museum the different rickety vehicles of sectarianism as we nostalgically did with our trams. Nothing upgrades and modernises itself so much as bigotry. The continuing rivalry between these two clubs proves it.

Celtic have never articulated their position on this of course but it would be extremely surprising if it was not part of a hidden agenda to have an all-Catholic club. Those skilled in the 'Kremlinology' of the Old Firm would eagerly tell you the trend is there. Then they settle down to the old numbers game of 'Spot the Protestant'. In a sense, like Rangers, Celtic are entitled to run their own business as they so wish. Perhaps they even had the further entitlement of responding in their own particular fashion after years of being told by another institution that to be Catholic was to be inferior. As a prominent supporter said to me when talking about fund-raising for the financially struggling club in North America, 'It's Catholic money we are looking for!' There is no doubt that Celtic have enjoyed a greater community identity than any other club in the world but it would be a perversion of that unique relationship, and the final triumph for the bigots of all persuasions, if Celtic used Rangers as their role model and brought on to the market their own style of laager mentality. The adoption as manager, in June 1991, of Republic of Ireland internationalist Liam Brady, as articulate and friendly a man as you would ever wish to meet, nevertheless seemed to be confirmation in the darker recesses of the Glasgow mind that the old battalions were being assembled. I myself sensed a polarisation as extreme as there had ever been in my broadcasting involvement.

Souness certainly wearied of this background then became caught up in his own personal troubles, which compounded the normal hassles and seemed to me to demonstrate his unyielding nature. He told me he had received a reprimanding letter from Ernie Walker of the SFA about some comments of his which had appeared in the press. The rebuke seemed to Souness to be well beyond the representation made by an organisation and more that of a criticism from an individual. I could tell he was looking for blood for he told me he would answer along those very lines and put Ernie in his place. That, I knew, would not be the easiest of tasks. Nor was it wise. There is a time when you ignore confrontation, let it slip past you, and feel the better for it. Easy enough to say, particularly in retrospect, but valid nevertheless.

It seemed not to be in his nature and, whatever the protestations to the contrary, I am perfectly satisfied Souness was now a target figure. He had to take much of the blame on himself for allowing that situation to develop but his suspicions were only partly paranoiac. I was told from a very reliable source that one of the members of the SFA referees' committee, about to call Souness to attendance for one of his track-side transgressions said, 'We're going to sort him out once and for all.' Even supposing Souness deserved everything heaped upon him by his own actions, that remark did not suggest the dispassionate atmosphere in which the SFA ought to operate.

It was during the spell of publicity surrounding the departure of his seminal signing, Terry Butcher, that I wondered why Souness was tolerating the job any longer and said so distinctly during a Radio Clyde broadcast. The furore which the splitting up of manager and player caused might be said to be quite simply the dropping of a player who was decidedly out of form. It seems to me, despite what happened behind the scenes in the personal row, that the manager had been more than loyal to the man by continuing to play him when he ought to have been rested. Of course Butcher was no mere mortal. He was a folk hero of considerable proportions amongst the Rangers fraternity.

If you link this with what happened when Graham Roberts, a player of great popularity, was shown the door and the long-lasting love-hate relationship he had with another player, Ally McCoist, who is almost as popular amongst the Rangers supporters as King Billy's white horse, you can see Souness did not feel compelled to ingratiate himself with anybody. He could have played the popular card by abdicating from his own assessments of these matters but he chose not to. I admired him for that. He had come to the club in the first place to help rid it of its populist tradition and make it face up to harsh realities. He was running the club his own way. But at the same time he was losing touch with the terracings.

He was now, quite wrongly in my view, being perceived purely as an arrogant dictator. I cannot think of another example of such a successful manager held in such contempt by so many of his own supporters. This ingratitude I believe stemmed from their long held suspicion that this 'openness' he promised for the club would take away their birthright, their long held identity, their pride, their reason to hate. Many of them could not abide the Mo Johnston signing although the player's quality has stifled criticism. This was the street philosophy which I believe Souness felt, eventually, he could not defeat. It wasn't the specific reason why he left Ibrox but in turning matters over in his mind it could not have offered him any sort of consolation.

Perhaps he should have taken evening classes on the subject. I would have lectured him free of charge. The hostility, the bitterness and suspicion of the football scene I have worked in over the years distinguishes this part of the world from any other. Trust is a notable casualty of our environment. Very few take you at your face value and mostly actions and words are interpreted through the sieve of someone's fundamental perception of you. The nature of the judgement can be summarised, rather more poetically, in the phrase, 'Which foot does he kick with?' The criticism has therefore ranged far and wide, from a globular spittle from a Rangers supporter landing on my black raincoat like a crushed tarantula, to a pompous letter from a Celtic director telling me that, by his count, I was using the first names of Rangers players more than of the Celtic players and warning of dire consequences if I didn't mend my ways.

There were the crank calls threatening violence, the letters of sinister quality, including one from a group calling themselves the Bridgeton Loyalists, advising me that my time on this earth would be limited if I did not desist from impugning the Sons of William. There were the frequent snubs by both Rangers and Celtic players, managers, and directors, spiced with occasions when they displayed great courtesy. But from certain individuals there was always suspicion, bitterness having its subtle manifestations.

I had looked on this divisive scene from a special angle years before, when I was the headmaster of a primary school in Lanarkshire. I admit that I had by then developed a distaste for organised religion of any sort, although acknowledging the right of parents to have religious education in the curriculum of state schools as part of the Christian tradition we all emerged from. There was a falling roll in our school and we had empty classes. The nearby Catholic school was over-flowing and out of common sense, and not untouched by the feeling of contempt for the stupidity of all of this, I suggested informally to a local councillor that some children could be transferred to the empty rooms in our school. It would be an example. Oh, no it wouldn't! I had simply opened up a hornet's nest. Some of our parents thought I had suggested housing sex-criminals. The other side treated it with haughty disdain. The classrooms remained empty. That was me told off in no uncertain manner.

Leave it alone! Leave it be! Leaving it alone produces much of what we disapprove of in the Old Firm phenomenon. For whatever the compelling reasons for church schools one of the prices we pay for the segregation is the children's continuing ignorance of one another. The school experience is, or ought to be, about a sharing of lives. Community separation simply solidifies the battalions. The more they are separated the harder they'll hate. It is a complicated situation which forbids an easy solution. But whilst it is there, those who pour ridicule on the crass bigotries ought to recognise one of its strongest sources.

There seems no way round this. A prominent Celtic supporter and friend of several directors of the club sadly concluded to me in discussion of the status of the Old Firm game in a European football context, 'All we have left is bigotry. That's what makes us all turn up and watch this match. Nothing much more.' The remark seemed chillingly irreproachable judging by the standard on show and the disproportionate interest aroused. It is as if we who could not do without the Old Firm match grudgingly have to accept something of value coming from sectarianism.

Supposing the hatred vanished, the bitterness disappeared? Could we contemplate a city lobotomised, its passion lost, the gain a twee encounter of the nature of Liverpool v Everton? Those of us brought up on prime Aberdeen Angus cannot easily change to a soya substitute. What a terrible price to pay, I hear my ancient voice saying, for becoming civilised.

Rangers had Englishmen, one acknowledged Catholic, another prominent one whom the club wished to keep secret, cups and leagues, triumphs, the occasional disasters and a manager who had not finally won his fans over. As he himself was later to admit he had all of the Celtic support hating him and half of his own people. Although that sounds as if there was no way but out, he did turn down the Liverpool job immediately after Kenny Dalglish resigned and made it clear he was staying at Rangers. But then came a row with a tea-lady at Perth which produced some undignified scenes and apologies exchanged afterwards between the respective chairmen. Then a disagreement with Rangers' strong-minded owner David Murray about the nature of a transfer deal for the Hibernian goalkeeper Andy Goram. That was enough. He was off.

On the last day, at the press conference strongly chaired by Murray, Souness was calm but slightly tense. When he made his brief statement about leaving because circumstances made it impossible for him to do the job in the way he would like, he was looking straight at Murray. Pronounced mention was made of the fact that he was still on good terms with the chairman and that the pair would be dining together on the following Saturday evening. They never did and the truth of the matter is that Murray felt badly hurt by what happened. The relationship was at breaking point. Souness left the room almost at a trot. His eagerness to get out of the stadium as soon as possible was underlined by the fact that he had agreed to be interviewed for a possible documentary on him. When we went downstairs to the camera crew, he had gone.

So, too, I think had the notion that he had been a success. The statistics will certainly tell you he was, but in his declared aim to change the historical nature of the club he was not. He turned his back on something which had really only started. I had supported him to such an extent that, in the many arguments I had, mostly with Rangers supporters, about his objectives and methods and tactics I had become something of an apologist who had, at the same time, to be a contortionist to keep faith. No doubt his departure rather exposes as hollow much of what I believed him to be about. I was left with a sense of personal let-down after having backed the most interesting man to have entered the claustrophobic climate of Glasgow since Stein. It was finally proved he wasn't of the same mettle.

I had been carried away with the image created for me in New Mexico that day in 1986 when Souness sounded like a crusader, the harbinger of a new order. 'Bliss was it in that dawn to be alive,' sort of thing. Or perhaps, after all, with Santa Fé lying 7,000 feet above sea-level the headiness I had felt was merely due to the rarefied air.

17

Body and Seoul

It was the morning after the very long night of the sakes. Soft, velvety rice-wine sometimes makes for heavy landings, which meant that I was far from appreciative about being wakened by the telephone. It pierced and I fumbled and got it to my ear. It was the morning of Tuesday, 27 September in Seoul in 1988. The voice at the other end of the line was polite but firm.

'Ben Johnson has been tested positive for drugs. Would you go out to the village and see if you can get any pictures of him or any interviews with anybody. Yes, I know it sounds incredible but alas it is true!'

Even fully alert, which I was not, it would have been difficult to take in. At that time, and in that state, I was not into forming moral judgements but only able to reflect on how unkind life was. A major figure in the Games had not only taken drugs but was letting the news break at an ungodly hour, thus souring for me the few fleeting hours of freedom given over to licentious eating and drinking the previous night. Ben Johnson on drugs? Perhaps somebody had got it all wrong.

There had been rumours of course. I had heard them back in Los Angeles four years previously and Carl Lewis was not slow to drop hints. Did Johnson really think he could pocket the gold medal in the Blue Riband event on the back of drugs? Then, incredulity took over as I wondered if the lads had known I'd had a heavy night and just wanted to get me out of bed at the crack of dawn. There would be a message for me at reception saying, 'Nice to have you up, Arch!'

Even as I stumbled downstairs into the marbled magnificence of our hotel and then outside to the Alka Seltzer sharpness of the cool morning I was refusing to believe this. In the taxi going through the uncannily empty streets of the normally traffic-atrophied Korean capital, disbelief mixed readily with drowsiness. I reached the village and saw the crowds of journalists and reporters and television crews queuing up in the incredibly disor-ganised and infuriatingly slow bureaucratic quagmire called the security office. I knew then that something was stirring and it was not a complaint about the village catering. Indeed the place was buzzing with the Johnson story and that special irate quality of the journalistic beast on the prowl had crept into the voices of those trying to gain access to the village quickly lest stories were lost. They were being held up by the statutory smiling morons who are now an indispensable part of the Olympic scene as inspectors of credentials and purveyors of frustration.

As Olympic villages go, the one in Seoul was a city. Walking up the broad main avenue to it was like walking into Castlemilk in its infancy. The honeycomb of blocks of flats was housing the biggest-ever assembly of Olympic athletes and it was never less than stimulating to visit as the various nationalities merged together in gaudy, clamorous unity. The restaurant was always thronged as a central meeting place, although many people gave up trying to eat there as there were always queues, even early in the morning. That day, though, a pall had descended. The area seemed listless and quieter, distinctly so. The advancing tide of media were caus-ing no ripples for the place looked as if it would take an earthquake to wake it from this stupor.

People were numbed already that early Tuesday morning. I doubt if a single piece of news, with the exception of the act of terrorism in Munich, has made such an immediate impact on such a vast gathering of athletes. Johnson had cheated. He had let them all down. He had created almost immediately a new form of Olympic Games – the Games of mistrust, of doubt and suspicion, the unclean Games. Nothing could remove that stain. I got the feeling up there that morning, listening to groups of people talking about him with some aggrieved incredulity, that a deadly virus had been let loose. There is little doubt in my mind that the mood and atmosphere changed in Seoul. The Games took on a graver aspect.

But, of course, that morning there was no sign of Johnson. Philip Marlowe couldn't have found him. Indeed as we were racing round the village trying to make sense of all of this he was, as we were later to learn, being shoved through customs at Seoul Airport on his way out of the country minus his gold medal. And there was no sign of any Canadian in the village. Normally they were very demonstrative and colourful. But only a couple of hours after the breaking of the news they had taken down all the banners which were splashed along the balconies of their apartments and they were behind locked doors. The Maple Leaf had contracted Dutch Elm disease overnight.

We could extract nothing from their representatives, who refused to make any comment. So we made for the British Team Headquarters where the BBC had installed a remote control camera which was operated by technicians in the International Broadcasting Centre on the other side of Seoul. The balcony was small, the technology of global dimension. With the help of surely the nicest press-officer known to mankind, Caroline Searle of the British Olympic Association, we managed to persuade Linford Christie to get up out of bed and give us his reaction. This, as it turned out, had its ironic element.

'He's a disgrace,' Linford told me as I took him up to the small balcony where the camera was. 'The man should be hounded out of this business.'

I turned on the lighting switch, the engineer several miles away in the centre of Seoul pressed the right button, the camera jerked into life and swung round towards Linford and his brooding face was seen live back in London. His two-way interview was deeply critical of Johnson. It was also quite impressive, for his tone was of a man betrayed. He sounded as if he had appointed himself as a kind of ad hoc spokesman not just for all the Games' athletes but particularly for that esoteric clan, the sprinters. In their obsession with shortening space and time they have cultivated their own strange ethic.

Indeed, I recall the great aerobics guru Dr Kenneth Cooper who set America off jogging telling me almost dismissively of sprinters that in his cardiac lab in Texas he had tested for endurance a fifty-year-old woman and Hasely Crawford, who won the gold medal for the 100 metres in Montreal, and the woman beat him hands down. 'They have a special kind of fitness,' he said. 'They cannot really be models for the rest of us. They are a unique species. Being fit and capable for what they do does not make them necessarily fit for life as a whole.'

This enclave they create for themselves can lead to bitchiness. Stories circulated in Los Angeles about Carl Lewis's sexual preferences and there was an even more scurrilous one about his attitude to cocaine. They were put about with relish inside his own fraternity. Lewis himself had long murmured suspicions about Johnson's abilities and whether they were aided or not. So, Linford was talking of Johnson as if he had just been defrocked from a sort of priesthood of the cult of brevity. Indeed he pointedly said that people like himself would now be unfairly tarred with the same brush. It was a plea for the innocents. Those words stuck. I associate them now with the look on the face of the late Ron Pickering, the BBC athletics commentator, some two nights later when, going into his hotel room very late on, he told me grimly, 'Say nothing about this at the moment but I hear a British athlete has been tested positive!' And I remember the pause, a long one. 'I think it's Linford.'

He got out the malt whisky and we let it soften the blow. Like all big men, Pickering looked particularly devastated when he displayed shock. He sat massively on his chair, wondering over and over again what this was all about, sounding alternately pessimistic and optimistic. 'I'm sure if it is him it won't amount to anything serious.' If he said that once he said it fifty times in the space of the next couple of hours.

Pickering was a man of sharp intellect and towering passion. The lucidity of his arguments over such matters as sporting boycotts of South Africa or the cheating of drug-taking athletes was supplemented by an almost evangelistic fervour which inevitably won him both admirers and detractors. Some of his criticisms came out like biblical denunciations but, although he always gave the impression of possessing a Calvinistic regret that a code of ethics was being swamped by current political and social immoralities, he never was, as his critics tried to portray him, a pompous pontificator. I saw him essentially as a man's man. He could hold his booze with the best, converse on your terms as well as his and was one of the best dispensers of the risqué joke in the business.

Although it was still only a rumour, I knew that Ron had got information from somewhere and that he feared the imminent disintegration of the Games. 'If this is true,' he told me that night, 'I will never believe what another athlete says about drugs so long as I live. How could anybody?'

Certainly the Johnson disclosure had stunned us but what Ron had just told me about Linford seemed like confirmation that the disease was virulent. He had warned me not to mention any names but to keep on the alert for something sensational. When I got back to my room in the wee small hours I found a message informing me the word was out that an unnamed British athlete had failed a test. Everybody was now really on edge. From having come to cover a sporting festival we were now all on battle stations. But our discomfort was as nothing compared to what was happening within the British Olympic Association.

Two days after the Johnson news broke, they were hosting a party for their sponsors without whom there would have been precious little team there in the first place. The evening was going smoothly and although these poor officials needed another canapé orgy like they needed a drug scandal they were going through the diplomatic motions of keeping everybody happy. The function was obviously a jolly affair, but only for so long. Back in the almost deserted British Team headquarters an envelope was hand-delivered to the remaining official there who took receipt of it and might have pigeon-holed it until the morning. However, he had the presence of mind to act on what was stamped on the outside. 'Seoul Medical Commission. Urgent.' There is urgent and there is urgent, but during a major sports event if you have any business prompted by the medical authorities it is, given the worry about drugs, as well to act quickly. Otherwise, at the very least, rumour gets out of hand. The quicker you ascertain the truth the better for any possible defence. It also gives you the chance to keep it under wraps.

The official took the note to the party. There, it was read in a quiet corner. It told them that Linford Christie had failed his A test. Caroline Searle admits she wanted to scream. Dick Palmer, the Head of the British delegation and the soul of rectitude and diplomacy, showed the classical British skill at underplaying a crisis by proceeding with his socialising and encouraging the others to do likewise. At the same time, he wished that the ground would open up and swallow him. They were particularly devastated in view of the high moral tone of Linford's denunciation of Ben Johnson. Eventually the news seeped out and Linford was besieged by the media.

To this day, some of the British officials are convinced that a person in the laboratories, or in the Medical Commission itself, was bribed by someone in the media to disclose this finding. Linford himself was determined to get out and about. Even though he knew that he was in the centre of a controversy he chose to go down to the relay training at the practice track, where the media were awaiting. The fact that so many people were acting as if he must be guilty outraged him. He was now to be hounded, though.

He wanted to keep his head held high and not to go skulking in a dark corner out of the way. On one occasion I actually thought he was going to lash out physically at a group of hacks but he controlled himself. Linford was like a man straining to get away from his blocks but held back because the gun has yet to sound. The tension was building, the mood was grim, and Caroline Searle, representing the BOA in her first Olympics, was facing up to a constant barrage of media questions whenever she appeared in public. Her renowned equanimity held but her face was visibly paling and she looked as if she had hardly slept for days. And yet it was all so needless.

Linford had taken ginseng, which is a famous Korean product. Its name is derived from the aromatic root which, ironically enough, is called in the original Mandarin 'Jen Man', meaning it resembles human legs. This was a normal practice of his. He had been taking it for years. Ginseng is merely a root, not a substance banned by the IOC. But he had bought some which had been corrupted in some way and which contained a pseudo-Ephedrine, a stimulant which is most definitely on the proscribed list. Fifteen American athletes had tested positive for this very substance only a few months before and the medical officers of the BOA had expressly warned the sports' governing bodies of its dangers. In this instance Linford had bought ginseng which must have been 'spiked' for extra effect and it slipped under the guard.

In the post-Ben Johnson period of hysteria Linford was treated like a common criminal by some of the media. The acute embarrassment felt by the British officials, who were still looking around to see who they could blame, was less painful than that of a man whose reputation and integrity now looked gravely at risk. He knew that previous to the Johnson disclosures two British Modern Pentathletes had been found positive for taking illegal substances, but they had been cleared after their explanation was found adequate. There had been little publicity attached to that. The sprint silver-medallist, though, was to be a special case. He also accrued much more publicity than the wretched judo athlete Kerrith Brown who had taken Furosomide, a diuretic, to help with a knee swelling. It has weight-enhancing properties and is consequently a banned substance. Brown was certainly technically more culpable than Linford, in that he must have known of the dangers, and was ultimately disqualified.

There was no real elation amongst the British medical people on the eventual clearing of Linford when he appeared in front of the Medical Commission, for they knew what the future was going to hold in store for every athlete from then on. As one doctor told me, 'We'll have to ban athletes from visiting the chemist's during Games for if they want to cure the common cold they're going to be in trouble. Ephedrine is in every respectable cough mixture. There is a veritable stimulant jungle out there which we'll have to carve our way through very carefully.'

Pickering was more forthright.

'They're still cheating,' he told me later. 'There are still people out there who should be put behind bars for what they're doing, the pedlars as well as the athletes.'

In the face of this it would have to be concluded that there was something amateurish about the checks and warnings which were supposed to exist amongst the British team. Pickering knew better than anybody that the anabolic and hormone growth treatments which athletes engaged in throughout the year could be less easily detected at the Games and, Orwellian though it might sound, the problem would have to be combated throughout the world by a 'flying-squad', spot-testing for the use of these substances. Without that we would still be watching cheats rising to the Olympic rostrum.

For it was the ones who got away with it that people were eventually talking about all over Seoul. There were beanfeasts of conjecture. 'How could she have so improved her performances over six months? Look at her muscles now, anyway!' That was the favourite comment. Some of the most prominent names turned up in conversation. But, then, nobody could actually prove anything. Triumph therefore was compromised by doubt and suspicion. People simply could not be sure any longer. Ben Johnson had left not only his gold medal behind but also a considerable psychosis.

This was all some eighteen months before the World Cup in Italy but I felt that somehow Korea represented the apogee in my relationship with BBC Scotland. Yet, although I was so exotically remote, I was never able to quell the unease I felt about not sitting on a platform on a Saturday afternoon at the edge of a Scottish football pitch, regardless of weather. Whatever the attractions of broadcasting in network on an occasion such as the Olympic Games, if you go desperately seeking football results from a land six thousand miles away at the same time as you are juggling with a totally alien project, you are still rooted to your own soil. My work in Korea made me ponder more seriously than I had previously just how far I could go in balancing these elements. I had to reflect on my willingness to work in this way. I knew that some people in Scotland saw it as an inevitable drift away from my stereotyped role. Professionally it always seemed extremely odd to me that nobody in BBC Scotland ever discussed my work on my return. It was as if I had never attended the three Olympics.

It was in Korea that I began to wonder if I had reached the

outer limits of broadcasting credibility. Was I, in trying to marry the different elements, losing the absolutely essential feature, for a broadcaster, of clear-cut identity? Apart from that, the Olympic Games in Korea remain vividly in the mind because they contained so many surprises, not the least of which was the capacity of the people there to host them so spectacularly.

We had gone there querying the IOC's decision to take the Games to the divided peninsula. How could those orientals possibly follow Los Angeles anyway? What presumption, one thought! Their opening ceremony, in fact, stunned the senses and made the LA display seem like watching the death throes of American burlesque in a seedy theatre in Hoboken. It was that good. The sheer range of varying cultural displays, cemented by the underlying presence of Korean aggression and meticulous organisation, took us unawares.

Of course they would forever after be identified as the 'Drugs' Games because of the Johnson affair. But that unjustifiably constricts the achievement of these people in making the Games work splendidly. There were many people around to let us know that all this was a phoney show, that too much had been sacrificed to foot the bill. Probably. But no Olympics can be staged now without some dislocation of normality. Perhaps the people who appreciated this less than anybody, and to everybody's surprise, were the Americans. The Koreans hated them. This mood sprang initially from the growing dissatisfaction with having an American Army stationed heavily in their country. Although it was serving a defensive role against the eccentric regime in the north it was now being perceived as superfluous to requirements.

As we were later to see for ourselves, at Panmunjom, the uniformed pantomimical confrontation of eyeball-to-eyeball glowering between the Americans and the North Koreans, within a few feet of each other, made a Punch and Judy show seem as meaningful as *King Lear*. Anyway, the Russians and the Chinese together had warned the North Koreans not to indulge in any hanky-panky during the Games and the only danger to person was if you happened upon a violent student demonstration in Seoul itself. These apparently took place at times convenient to the foreign press. It was a sort of phone-a-riot phenomenon.

The Koreans were not slow to tell us they disliked the Yanks for talking their culture down. One charming woman university professor who figured prominently in the feminist movement in a strongly male-dominated society said to me, 'At the end of the day all that the Americans have introduced to us from their culture is AIDS.'

If this sounded, and probably was, harsh it nevertheless indicated that the Koreans perceived the Americans as an occupying force who could not imbibe the local ways and made their only venture into the culture by entering the shops and prostitutes of the famous downtown Seoul area, Itaewon. All this seemed to be confirmed by NBC, who nightly during the Games trivialised anything Korean, probably innocently, but quite insensitively. 'Hey, getta load of this,' one male presenter would say to the inevitable female co-host. 'I can use these chop-sticks now. Me likee!' She would reply, 'Yes and last night I went to a restaurant and do you know what I had? Kimche. You know, that pickled cabbage that tastes like old socks.' And, with a grimace, 'Well, I did try!'

Jesus wept, you would say to yourself watching this. Their insensitivity reached a climax when a Korean boxer refused to get out of the ring after a verdict went against him. He sat there unbudgeable until the shame of the whole episode was brought home to him. It was an isolated disgrace for which the Koreans sincerely apologised. But the American media in particular waded in as if the entire Korean nation was in insurrection against the ideals of the Olympic movement. I went to a special reunion held by the President of the Olympics for those who had been connected with the torch-run and he was besieged by American journalists who simply would not let this matter drop and harassed the man.

The President dealt with this brilliantly. He would occasionally emit that sloughing adenoidal noise which seems to be endemic in the Orient and in which mucus is obviously being cleared from deep in the tubes. It sounds like a personal drain being unplugged and can be very off-putting at times but I felt that here was a Korean trait being thrown back in the face of the Yankee intruders. It echoed throughout the plush Presidential Suite in the Olympic offices like a thunderstorm. Other than that, with a cool use of colloquial English and sounding as if he had graduated from Harvard Business School, he tried to explain that the boxer had not committed a crime but had indeed offended against etiquette and that, of course, he would be made aware of that. He seemed to take no great offence as the Americans totted up what they thought were the failings of the Games. A Dutch journalist beside me quietly bemoaned, 'They have a hamburger mentality. The Games are not for them, they are for everybody.'

Their arrogance was met more forcibly by the Korean people who began to give them the cold shoulder. Some of my friends in NBC television took the full brunt of the backlash because, while transmitting throughout Korea to their own troops, they had also been picked up by the locals. Having given the impression yet again that only Americans were involved in the Games, they had to stop wearing their distinctive blazers for fear of being shunned in shops and restaurants. But, like anybody else, they knew a good story when they saw one, and they joined the throng chasing after Royalty the day Mark's horse broke down.

I still think of that day I pursued Mark and Anne as some sort of watershed in my broadcasting career, almost as if I could say to myself, 'Now I've done everything.' For this took me into my Nigel Dempster mode for the first and probably last time. There was I, a student of the half-time pie and Bovril and the ululations of ranting football managers, about to assess a Royal relationship.

It was a case of drop everything and head for the hills for not only had we heard that Captain Mark Phillips' horse had gone lame but also knew that the Princess Royal was to be there to see the eventing. With the conjecture mounting by the day about the frailty of their marriage we felt, as did every other television unit in the business, that if we could only get them together somehow, showing some cordiality (a touch, a smile even) it might clear the air. After all, they hadn't been seen together for some considerable time and we knew that as soon as Mark lost interest in the Games he would head for one end of the world and she the other. Now we knew he was out. We got in a fast car and headed out of the city. Nobody was interested all that much in the event or the horses. After all, one remembers Charlton Heston from the chariot race in *Ben Hur*, not the animals.

What we got after waiting around all day for the specially desired 'togetherness' shot was the sight of them walking towards camera without so much as looking at each other as they went towards the Princess Royal's limousine for the so-called farewell scene. They barely spoke. They simply split up and went in opposite directions. Later, viewing the pictures in the editing suite, I felt as if I had just confirmed the end of a relationship. And I also paused to wonder just how easily the media snoopers on Royalty lived with themselves.

It had also taken me further out of my natural habitat than I had ever gone and whilst the feeling of being a minimalist Court reporter did not last long its contrast with other work had been stimulating. If you are reporting during Olympic Games anyway you have to be prepared for a mad whirligig of an existence, hopping from one extreme to another and prepared to grab anything. For great is the broadcasting maw during that period and it needs constant filling.

By now, we were feeling the Games were suffering from elephantiasis. We did not intend to make that a theme of any of our filming yet I hope that it came across as such in our collection. They have spread and fructified to over-ripeness. The entry of the athletes during the opening ceremony is fast becoming a re-creation of the Boers' Great Trek or Mao's Great March. It has now exceeded its boundaries of self-glorification and requires radical surgery. It is not merely a case of stopping growth but of severe pruning. Heaven only knows how that can be achieved given the self-propagating nature of the beast. The mind boggles at certain recreations/sports lining up for acceptance. Regardless of the different sort of athleticism involved it would be difficult for example to reject the claims of ballroom-dancing whilst synchronised swimming so defies objective assessment. Aesthetic equilibrium on the dance-floor is no less exacting or fairer to judge than holding your breath and smiling like Esther Williams for some seconds.

Other categories are excluded on the same fine-line basis but are beating at the door. They must be resisted and others weeded out. If they continue to expand, world championships in the different events could take over as the leaner but more meaningful competitions (as some already are) and the Games would be a sort of World Youth Festival. Their glamour will then appeal more to those who simply want to get on the stage rather than those who chase excellence. Consequently they will be diminished.

The Korean experience was sometimes emotional though, genuinely so. You can feel you are hard-boiled enough to avoid the lump in the throat and that, by and large, you can do without such a manner of feeling anyway. But it comes to all of us. It's probably better to admit it when it does. As I do now.

It was perhaps because I was sitting nearest the editor that I was asked if I would help carry the Olympic flame on one of the stages of the relay on its way up the Korean peninsula. The organisers wanted media representatives to take part in this enterprise. I was too coy to ask just how far I would have to run but if I was going to collapse in the effort, then, having helped to carry the sacred flame, the ancient Greek gods and goddesses would surely see me all right on the other side. Looking at myself in the pristine white running gear they had handed me, though, I decided Terpsichore would have rather overdosed on hemlock than have consorted with me.

Middle age does not necessarily creep up on you. It can also jump out and surprise you in one blinding leap as horrific as a Stephen King spectre coming out of the dark, the more vengeful for your impertinence in ignoring it for so long. The mirror I was staring at in the hotel reflected all those lunches and late nights and years of simply believing in nothing changing. Funny how that torch forced me to look at myself that way. And I hadn't even seen it yet, just the gear that was made for youth but which was now helping me to cut an odd figure.

When we arrived in Chongju we could find no one who spoke English. English-speakers in Korea, despite the long American presence, are like London taxis, only there when you don't really need them. Try miming, 'I am here to carry the Olympic torch on its way to Seoul.' It's not funny for one who could only ever do *Gone With the Wind* when he played charades. Eventually we found a student who had some idea of what we were about and we found the spot where the torch was to be picked up. It was near a crossroads just outside the town. They told me I was to run only one kilometre like everybody else. This seemed bearable. But I had to face up to constructing something for the camera out of the handover, the run and the finish. We agreed that I would start speaking at a certain moment and the camera, having picked up the incoming runner some distance down the road, would then reveal me waiting for him. The words would have to start at the right time and finish just as the runner reached me and above all there would only be one chance to get it right. I hate recording things but on this occasion I could hardly ask the torch officials if we could please try it again. I felt genuinely scared about messing the whole thing up.

That afternoon, looking at the river on one side of us and the low houses on the other and the deserted road along which only an occasional lorry passed there was the feel of a little town too preoccupied with its daily load to be bothered by the fleeting visit of a travelling flame. But when we arrived at the spot half-an-hour before the handover in the early evening the transformation was enormous. Tens of thousands of people were bordering the road straight in front of me leading to the edge of the town. I felt the same sort of stagefright I had experienced all those years before, setting out to broadcast for the first time. I desperately wanted to get the words of commentary right if I never did anything else again in my life. It was a sort of audition. It was to prove one's worth in handling a situation that could easily be overloaded with significance until simply cloyed. It had to breathe naturally and television, in a recorded situation, very rarely allows you to achieve that.

We saw the flame. The cameraman started to record. I awaited the signal from him and I started to speak. When you do these things you sometimes cannot hear exactly what you are saying but the sensor within the broadcaster still registers a flaw, particularly a fatal one. It is an instinctive ability to be able to think of something else whilst the mouth is on auto-pilot. The sensor detected nothing untoward in what I was saying as I stared the camera straight in the eye for the last few seconds. Then I turned to look up the road as my last words fitted the gasping entry of the incoming runner.

Thank God I got that bit right. The small ceremony of the anonymous bartering of flames took but a few seconds and off I went with the sudden realisation that the oil-filled torch seemed to weigh a ton in my right hand.

Half-way down the route, with the people greeting the flame and me as if we had relieved the town from a siege, I was glad the weight of the torch was forcing me to lower it bit by bit so that the smoke blown back by the slight breeze was getting into my eyes. They had already been affected by something more than smoke. I felt that since I was on camera the whole way and had to conclude the run with another chat to the lens I had to have an excuse for the amazing stirring of emotions I felt. I was finding self-control almost impossible as this wave of genuine warmth and appreciation of the presence of the torch surged towards me from the thousands packing the streets. It was the torch and the people who were leading me. Not the reverse. I was sharing, not appearing. It could have been Shettleston Road and that oft-conjured fantasy of the Junior Cup being borne aloft and brought home to Greenfield Park. I imagined this is how the East End community would have reacted, just like this. It made me feel as if I were coming home.

I reached the other runner, tilted the flame towards his torch, ignited the fuel and away he went. I turned to camera to make my final statement and tried to pretend that it was shortage of breath that was causing the hesitancy and not that embarrassing tightness round the throat. When I had finished, presence of mind was beginning to return and I thought that by fading away into the descending gloom I could simply take the torch into my eternal possession. However, a blazing torch is not the easiest thing to stick up your jumper and escape with. I had only walked several paces from the camera when I was seized by three very muscular men who promptly grabbed it from me. I tried to mime the fact that I thought the torch was mine to keep but they were having none of it. They waved me away impatiently and snuffed the torch out somehow. It and they then vanished.

A week later, however, I was invited to a reception where they presented me with the same torch. They had not cleaned it. It was scarred and, indeed, almost deformed in part by the inferno that it had contained. It looked aged, almost beyond repair. But I knew that with fuel and a light it would spark into life despite appearances.

Like when I lift a microphone.

INDEX

(For individual football games, Cup Finals and World Cups, *see*: Football Events)

All Chapmans books are available at your local bookshop or newsagent, or can be ordered direct from the publisher. Indicate the number of copies required and fill in the form below.

Send to: **Chapmans Publishers Ltd
141/143 Drury Lane
Covent Garden. WC2B 5TB.**

or phone: **071 379 9799 quoting title, author and
Credit Card number.**

Please enclose a remittance* to the value of the cover price plus: 60p for the first book plus 30p per copy for each additional book ordered to a maximum charge of £2.40 to cover postage and packing.

*Payment may be made in sterling by UK personal cheque, postal order, sterling draft or international money order, made payable to Chapmans Publishers Ltd.

Alternatively by Barclaycard/Access:

Card No. | | | | | | | | | | | | | | | | |

              Expiry date: _____

              Signature: _____

Applicable only in the UK and Republic of Ireland.

While every effort is made to keep prices low, it is sometimes necessary to increase prices at short notice. Chapmans Publishers reserve the right to show on covers and charge new retail prices which may differ from those advertised in the text or elsewhere.

NAME AND ADDRESS IN BLOCK LETTERS PLEASE
....

Name _____

Address _____

_____

_____

Post code _____ Tel. no. _____